Bodyslams!

Memoirs of a Wrestling Pitchman

Gary Michael Cappetta

also by
gary michael cappetta

"Fall For The Dream"
A Wrestling Based Work of Fiction

Requests for permissions should be addressed to
GMC, Inc., PO Box 83, Jackson, NJ 08752

Printed by Signature Book Printing, Inc.
Manufactured in the United States of America

The dialogue in this book has been reconstructed
from the author's personal recollection in order to
more effectively portray the personalities and the
atmosphere surrounding each anecdote.

The names in this book have not been changed.
We all are held accountable for our actions.
Mt 13:36

ISBN 0-9703991-6-2

First Edition

Little Bro', Ltd.

To the many fans who joined me on my twenty-one year journey.

Thank you for your support.

Bodyslams! is dedicated to you.

acknowledgements

What I am about to share with you started as a therapeutic exercise in 1995. Its purpose was simply to facilitate my transition to a more sedentary lifestyle, after spending my entire adult life as a public figure. But once I started writing, I never stopped. From conception to print, many people have lent encouragement both actively and passively. To acknowledge all of you would be impossible. But I feel the need to try.

Many thanks to
~the members of my family who never doubted my ability to stick with it all.
~my friends and family, Carol Cappetta, Maureen Maroney, Hugh McKenna, Frank Monaco, Pat Rooney and Alida Wainczak for your generous offers to edit this rookie's work.
~Phil Nanzetta and Tony Santeramo for lending your technical expertise in the production of this book.
~my colleague and friend, Steve Smith for your editorial assistance and for helping me to keep me *somewhat* literate.
~wrestling historian Tom Burke for helping me to keep my facts straight.
~BlackJack Brown, and Eddie Gries for generously contributing photos from your collections.
~the legal team at Davis & Davis, New York, and special appreciation of the patience and confidence of John Kelly and legal wrestling loyalist, Maureen Guerin.
~my literary agents over the past five years, Lenny Minelli and Catherine Cronin. Your faith in this work psychologically legitimized my efforts.
~the entire staff and crew who have worked selflessly on *Bodyslams!*, The Event.
~the administration, faculty and staff of CBA who have graciously tolerated my roller coaster ride of emotions throughout the process. Special acknowledgement to my students at CBA who were forever keeping me abreast of the current wrestling scene.
~ Wayne Coulter, Scott Dunlap, Bobby Eaton, Jody Hamilton, Mike Maraldo, Harley Race, Larry Sharpe and The Dean of All Wrestling Announcers and my announcing mentor, Gordon Solie, for your continuing friendship and connection to the wrestling world.
~CM Christ for your friendship, support and wacky, but effective promotional insights.
~"The Inner Circle" of Cathy Carroll, Darlene Greene, Jim Hagerman, Mitch Seinfeld and Tom Treiber for tirelessly listening to my war stories.
~ Michael Vale, the Little Bro' that I never had until now. Believing in Him is one thing. Living for Him is much more difficult. You inspire me to try. Php. 4:13
~"Hollywood" Joe Starbin. Your friendship and confidence will forever be appreciated.
~Sherry Lambert, my soul mate of twenty-eight years. Without your fateful and encouraging words in 1972, I would never have had the confidence to embark on this journey. You are about to find out more than I think you want to know!

contents

THE WWF YEARS
(1974–1985)

Contents

introduction

Y ou are about to join me on an eye-opening journey through the most significant two decades of pro wrestling's long and celebrated history. My first hand, no holds barred account of the players and the process, as I witnessed throughout my twenty-one year announcing career, is an extra ordinary adventure. You will be amazed to learn what has never before been revealed about this most controversial form of entertainment.

As we begin the new millennium, pro wrestling is enjoying a boom period, the likes of which have never before been seen. After a ten-year slump, today's phenomenal resurgence once again is capturing widespread media attention resulting in unparalleled profits. Instead of focusing on rigid good guy versus bad guy rivalries as in the past, the industry now showcases more violence and sexually explicit story lines in which good and evil are not easy to define.

The public, which has become increasingly permissive and forgiving of even the most shocking indiscretions of our prominent public figures, is living vicariously through wrestling's new breed of superstars. Strong performances by updated characters have convinced a vast television audience that the human drama presented each week more accurately reflects backstage rivalries and real life political skirmishes unlike the unsophisticated themes that were presented in the past. Not only has the *audience* been misled about what goes on behind the scenes, there have even been instances in which *wrestlers*, in cahoots with management, have duped fellow performers into believing their well-planned story lines. But while an inordinate amount of TV interview time has been used to air personal differences among the players, there remains a core of unspoken secrets that the industry will always attempt to protect.

Determining the correct answers to specific questions, simple, seemingly harmless questions, will bring you closer to the dark side of the business where industry insiders don't want you to go. *How is it decided who will be featured and who will not? ..... Does anyone really get hurt? ..... If so, what are the most common causes for the wrestlers' lapses? ..... What are the athletes really like? .....* Once you have accurately answered these questions, you will better understand how the seduction, the acquisition and the maintenance of the glory that wrestling has to offer can affect its players. The glare of the center ring spotlight can alter, and sometimes destroy performers whose sense of reality can become as blurred as the characters they portray.

Unlike when I began my career, those inside the business will now admit that pro wrestling is not a sport where individuals compete to determine who can win a match. Like other forms of episodic television, the outcome of every exhibition is predetermined. Before each wrestler makes his way to the ring, he is told who will win and how. The money that each earns has nothing to do with who is victorious.

But while acceptance of this initial premise disqualifies pro wrestling from consideration as a competitive sport, these very basic facts add many more dimensions and pose many additional questions about the operation of this multi-billion dollar worldwide enterprise. For instance, if financial success is not achieved by winning a match, what are the determining factors that decide who profits, who disappears from the scene and who never gets a chance to participate? While the question seems harmless, you may be outraged by the scandalous implications of the answer.

Since past generations and most of today's participants have attempted to protect the inner workings of the wrestling business, it is natural that many misconceptions continue to exist. Historically, those involved with pro wrestling were committed to shield the secrets of their profession from outsiders. Reminiscent of the silence that was demanded by early Mafia kingpins about the inner workings of their underworld, the traditional members of the pro wrestling fraternity are equally protective of *theirs*. While a disgruntled participant occasionally raised a vindictive voice, for the most part, the public at large was still fed misleading answers to the most often asked questions about the grunt and groan game. It is no wonder that even in today's climate, skeptics have devised explanations for the logically inexplicable illusions of wrestling which are sometimes more fanciful than the truth.

Pro wrestling is a form of entertainment that is highly satisfying to the performers and immensely entertaining for the audience when creatively conceived, carefully nurtured and properly executed. It is a scripted exaggeration of real life. At its best, it is an art form.

Introduction

Pro wrestling is also a game of deception. And all too often, it is the deceiver who falls prey to the fantasy of his own making. When the lines between make believe and reality become blurred, the results can be destructive and at times, even deadly.

I invite you to join me as we travel through my often bizarre career in order to explore the many myths of the mat game and to uncover the personal side of the most colorful cast of characters imaginable. Witness how my perspective of the art form evolved, as a young spectator at ringside to a performer positioned squarely in the eye of the tornado. The naked truth about the most outlandish of all entertainment forms will gradually become apparent to you, as it did to me.

Bodyslams! is filled with my many memorable experiences alongside the principal players of The World Wrestling Federation, World Championship Wrestling, and promotions that strive to emulate both. While I don't intend for *Bodyslams!* to provide *all* of the answers, I do guarantee that you are about to read an evenhanded and straightforward examination of the high stakes at risk for wrestling's superstars and corporate game players alike. And most uniquely, *Bodyslams!* offers insights into many questions that have remained unanswered, along with others, that until now, few ever thought to ask.

prologue

Speeding southward on the Garden State Parkway, we weaved through the vacation bound traffic. I knew the territory as well as anyone. As a child, my family lived every summer in the shore community of Seaside Park. The month that I graduated from Kearny High School in northern New Jersey, my family moved to Ocean County where my father had established a lucrative amusement business on the local boardwalk. I appreciated both prevailing mindsets of the people who populated the area each summer. I understood the local attitude toward the seasonal trade as well as the visitors' thrill of running wild in the land of sun and surf. Having just completed a day shift at the family amusement arcade, I was on my way to the Wildwood Convention Hall for an evening of pro wrestling.

Paul and Frank are two cousins who shared my fascination with the sport. During the journey to Wildwood our lively conversation centered around the wrestlers who would be performing on that evening's card. We had been looking forward to this night all week. The main event was a heavyweight title defense with Nikolai Volkoff challenging Bruno Sammartino for the coveted world title belt. Bruno had always been my hero. Always wrestled by the rules. Always tried to be an exemplary sportsman. Always faced with despicable rule breakers who more often than not paid little attention to fair play. And of course, I always rooted for Bruno. His television interviews were so filled with passion. He would look directly at me and in a most quiet, most sincere manner assured me that he could overcome the insurmountable obstacles that faced him. But he always asked for my help. Can you imagine? Bruno Sammartino,

Bruno Sammartino, my childhood sports hero.

the World Heavyweight Champion, promised to win this one for me! The least I could do was to be there for him. And that is why we were making our pilgrimage to Convention Hall. It was the least we could do.

I had been supporting Bruno for years. As a child of eleven, alone one Saturday night, bored with the usual network programs, I started scanning the local New York stations. As I flipped by one of the regional independent outlets, I saw something that I didn't understand. Something quite bizarre. Two giant, scantily clad, sweaty men were rolling around on a dimly lit platform surrounded by throngs of screaming men and women. Well, I didn't know what to think. I moved on to one of the network shows, doubting what I thought I had just seen. Certain that this peculiar event was not intended for adolescent eyes, I waited to be sure that my parents weren't within viewing range. When it was safe, I turned back to take a second look. This time, a bulky man, neatly though not stylishly dressed in a suit and tie, whom I later came to know as Bruno Sammartino, was talking to me. Speaking in a pronounced Italian accent, he was asking for my support. Well, I thought that was strange. Why would this hulk of a man, whom I didn't even know, be pleading with me to help him? (After all, he didn't look like he needed my help.) Mom walked into the room and I switched the channel.

The next week I tried it again and sure enough, a similar spectacle was taking place, except this time there were *four* men rolling around and tossing each other. Two had the blondest hair imaginable. The other two were bearded mountain men wearing overalls and carrying animal horns from a bull or maybe a goat that they drove into the blond men's foreheads. When they won the contest, they blew into their horns to make a whining animal sound as some sort of victory celebration.

Week after week I continued to eavesdrop on these unusual proceedings. And I soon discovered that this was an activity in which not only men, but *women* as well participated. And the week I spotted *four dwarf sized men*, I thought there was something wrong with the picture tube. After a few weeks I didn't care who was in the room. This was something that I couldn't see anywhere else, and I was intrigued.

After a while, watching the weekly wrestling show on television just wasn't enough. It became my mission to scrutinize this surreal spectacle up close. And besides, Bruno kept inviting me. As a sixth grader, my only hope of attending was to find someone to take me. I started to pester my parents without satisfaction. Finally I learned that one of the workers employed by my father was an avid wrestling fan. With a little arm twisting, I was allowed to accompany her to an event in Asbury Park. Although I didn't understand all that went on around me that night, I was not disappointed. The energy that filled the hall was exhilarating. And now I was hooked.

As we sped toward Wildwood, Cousin Paul and I entertained Frank with many of our shared memories of North Jersey wrestling events. Paul too, had become glued to the weekly wrestling program and together we found ways to get to local shows on a regular basis.

Since this was Saturday night of the Fourth of July weekend, Wildwood was alive with overflowing crowds. It was an hour until show time as our vehicle exited the Parkway. With traffic backed up to the highway, my Volkswagen crawled onto the main thoroughfare leading toward the ocean front Convention Hall. Continuing to chatter about the family, music and of course, wrestling, we inched toward the boardwalk with anticipation.

Usually, wrestling nights were free from worry. They became carefree getaways. That was part of their attraction. And under ordinary circumstances, I wouldn't have been concerned about the time. But tonight was different. My insides were twisted into a giant knot. It felt like Killer Kowalski had applied his painful stomach claw. And the closer we were to the arena, the tighter his grip became. Although I was able to maintain a lighthearted facade, it was the first time that I actually dreaded our arrival at the matches. Not because I had a premonition that something horrible was going to occur, but because I feared that what I hopefully *expected* to happen *wouldn't* happen. In just one hour, as my cousins settled back in their ringside seats, I expected to surprise them by becoming a very important part of the show.

Earlier that year, three months shy of graduating from Monmouth College, I began to take a look at how I could continue to attend the matches without paying. It was becoming expensive to follow The World Wide Wrestling Federation around the circuit and I needed a way to offset the cost. Far from being an athlete and finding pain unappealing, I immediately ruled out the prospect of becoming a wrestler. That wasn't for me. How about becoming a referee?

No. Nobody was ever happy with the referees' decisions. They were constantly faced with grief from both wrestlers and spectators alike. And I didn't need *that* kind of abuse. I knew nothing about the business side of wrestling. (At that point, I didn't even realize that there *was* a business side of wrestling.) Finally, I decided that the one thing, which I was qualified to do, was to write. The newsstands were always filled with wrestling magazines. Someone had to supply the publishers with fresh material. Why couldn't that someone be me? So I looked inside the front cover of the most prestigious wrestling periodical of its time, *The Ring Wrestling Magazine*. From the top of the page, next to the table of contents, I wrote down the name of the man who held the key that could allow my free entry to wrestling events: publisher and editor, Nat Loubet. His offices were located in New York City. All I needed to do was to convince him to issue me a press pass. I told myself that this was going to be easy. So the next day, more optimistic than reasonable, I hopped into my car and drove into Manhattan.

It was a freezing March morning as I stiffly found my way to an old office building at 120 West 31st Street. Filled with determination, I scaled the steep staircase. Winding through the narrow, paint chipped hallways, reading the worn stenciled lettering on the frosted windows of each office door, I experienced a brief flash of "What am I doing here?" reality. Before I could answer my own question, I reached the far end of the hall where I faced a door that announced: "The Ring Incorporated. Publication Office. *The Ring Boxing Magazine. The Ring Wrestling Magazine.* Nat Loubet, Publisher and Editor".

Taking a deep breath and without further thought, I decisively marched into the editorial offices. Sitting behind a large, cluttered, wooden desk I found a very plain, stern looking woman whom I assumed was the secretary. As I stood over her, she ignored me as if I was just another piece of useless office furniture. Finally, she looked up over her eyeglasses and stared at me for a few seconds. She then squinted, shook her head and continued to shuffle through the papers on her desk. I silently stood my ground not knowing what else to do. Moments later, she peered up over her eyeglasses once again. By this time, I was arching my eyebrows in an earnest attempt to be noticed. Eager to return to her work, she was not amused.

"Yes, may I help you?"

Prologue

Now that I had her attention, I turned on the boyish charm. "Sure. I'd like to see Mr. Loubet, please."

"Do you have an appointment?" she asked, knowing that she was safe from being surprised by my response.

But I anticipated this question and had prepared my answer while driving over from Jersey. My delivery was self-assured just as I had rehearsed in the car. "Well, no. But I think he will see me."

Her response could not have been anticipated.

"That's interesting, but *I* don't think so. Mr. Loubet is a very busy man and you just can't show up and expect to speak with him without having a confirmed appointment." That's when she smiled at me for the first time. It was clear that her smile and my smile were meant to communicate very different messages.

"Oh, uh, I understand. How about if I just wait here in the outer office and maybe he'll be able to see me a little later."

"Suit yourself," she snapped. "Just don't make any noise. I'm very busy."

I slowly backed away until I fell into an old wooden chair on the other side of the room. I tried to convince myself that my plan was working well. It was 9:45 a.m. I had nothing else to do so I sat and I waited. ... 9:55 ... 10:05 ... 10:20 ... As the time passed, I started to wiggle my defrosting feet which drew a loud, impatient sigh from my unappreciative office partner. ...10:35 ... 10:50 ... 11:05 ... Every ten minutes or so, she peeked at me from the other side of the dingy office. When I could, I timed her glances so that our eyes would meet ... 11:15 ... 11:35 ... 11:50 ... Any hope I naively had of penetrating the facade of this distempered guard dog had rapidly faded.

Finally, a rear door creaked open and a thin, balding, gentleman slowly ambled into the outer office. He appeared to be friendly and approachable even though the dark circles around his bloodshot eyes showed signs of a man pressured by deadlines. A woolen overcoat was draped over his arm as he walked toward the door. I sprang to my feet as he headed my way since surely this must be Mr. Loubet. As he passed me on his way to the exit, I opened my mouth to make my long awaited introduction, but I could not speak! The words seemed to freeze in my throat as he slowly ambled by. He reached for the doorknob, as I shot a helpless glance at his smirking secretary. He opened the door and in an instant he was gone. My heart was pounding. I sank back into the chair, defeated and embarrassed. Suddenly, the door slowly opened once again as the slight smiling man arched his head around and calmly asked, "Did you want to speak with me?"

"Yes . . . uh . . . yes sir", I sputtered. "Are you Nat Loubet?"

He quietly grinned. "That's right."

"I'm a big admirer of your magazine and I'd like to talk to you about being a correspondent." Now I was on a roll.

He took a couple of steps back in my direction. "What are your credentials?"

"Well . . . uh . . . I'm a senior at Monmouth College in West Long Branch, New Jersey majoring in Spanish and I've had a journalism class. I'm a fan of wrestling and thought that maybe you could give me an opportunity to write for *Ring Wrestling*."

"You know, there's not a lot of money in writing for the wrestling magazines".

I just stared at him. I had never considered getting paid for writing. All I wanted was to get into the matches for free. But I couldn't tell him that. When I didn't respond, he said, "Look, I'm just going to run to the deli for a sandwich and I'll talk to you when I get back. Maybe, fifteen minutes."

My ticket to the BIG times!

By the time I left his office that afternoon, I was armed with the coveted press pass and more relieved than delighted that I had accomplished what I had set out to do. As I marched victoriously past his secretary's desk, I looked over my shoulder, locked my eyes with hers and grinned. "Hope you enjoyed our time together this morning."

As we slowly made our way toward Convention Hall, the bumper-to-bumper traffic was moving at a snail's pace. I was telling my cousins about the Gorilla Monsoon interview that I had written for *Ring Wrestling*. Armed with a copy, fresh off the press, I showed them the July '74 issue which was autographed by the Gorilla himself. As they scanned the Monsoon article, I began to wonder how I might reveal my secret. While I considered forewarning them about my part in this evening's show, I feared embarrassment in the event that things didn't go the way that I had been promised. Instead, I kept the incredible news to myself.

For an entire week I had lived with my secret. The previous Saturday I had brought a good friend to Wildwood for the pre-season show. I met Sherry while working in the '72 presidential campaign and she too, became intrigued by the pro wrestling scene. It was only one week earlier when we slipped by the ticket-taker with press pass in hand, took our seats, and awaited the start of the show. Attendance was poor. Vacationers would not arrive until the holiday weekend and the locals didn't expect much of a show, knowing that this was considered somewhat of a trial run for the following week's July 4th season kick off.

When the wrestlers for the first match got into the ring, they just stood still staring at the referee. Traditionally, a ring announcer welcomes the crowd, calls for the national anthem and then introduces the opponents for the first match. As usual, there was a table set up at ringside with a microphone resting in its stand sitting next to a large battered bell that you would expect to see in an old fashioned schoolhouse. Years later I learned that many of the ring bells were, in fact, lifted from schoolrooms.

Willie acts as Vince, Sr.'s front man when Bruno wins the WWWF title from Buddy Rogers in May 1963.

The fans were becoming impatient with the delay. They anxiously began to clap in unison and then proceeded to jeer the wrestlers who were hoping that someone would soon show up to make the introductions. Finally, a frail, gray haired man, whom I knew from TV to be Willie Gilzenberg, the president of the WWWF[1], shuffled up to the announcer's table. He clumsily lifted the microphone to his mouth and mumbled a series of unintelligible sounds, which echoed throughout the near empty hall. We could only guess what he was saying. Nobody really cared because

---

[1] The World Wide Wrestling Federation (WWWF) name was shortened to The World Wrestling Federation (WWF) in 1979. Both abbreviations are used throughout this book as is appropriate to the relevant time frame.

when he finished and shuffled back into the darkness, the first match was under way. At the end of the match, when the ring announcer would usually jump back into the ring to declare a winner, the slight old man slowly wandered back up to ringside from the dim corners of the hall and mumbled into the mic once again. Watching this same routine continue for the next two matches, I started saying things to Sherry like, "I can't believe this guy's going to trudge back and forth all night." "If this guy collapses from all the shuffling around, we'll never get to see the main event." "By the time we get to the last match, we might as well get in line for next week's card."

Finally, I guess she got tired of listening to me. "Well, then why don't you go up there. Ask him if he wants you to announce. *You can do it*." These were the four words that I needed to hear. After all, if Sherry thinks I can do this, then I guess I can. She usually knew what she was talking about. So the next time I noticed Willie wearily rambling out of the darkness, I slid from my ringside seat and met him at the microphone.

"Excuse me, sir. If you'd like, I'd be happy to make the ring announcements for you."

He unsteadily shifted his feet in my direction until we were facing each other. Straining to focus his eyes, he carefully inspected my tee shirt and jeans. "Okay, kid. But you sit here at the table. Don't go into the ring. Announce from right here."

I obediently took my place as he wandered away. Looking over my shoulder, I triumphantly nodded at Sherry and went on to announce the rest of the show. Not a difficult task, having heard all of the ring introductions from my years of observing the pros. It was fun. It was like playing.

At the end of the night, the house lights came on and I noticed Willie making his way up to the ring. But this time, with a little more purpose to his shuffle.

"Hey kid, that wasn't too bad. Do you have any experience doing that?"

"Oh, sure I do." Thank the Lord he didn't ask for a resumé.

"Well if you're interested, come back next week. Wear a tie and you can announce from inside the ring. Next week's the big July 4th show, you know."

"All right. I can do that," I confidently assured him in an attempt to disguise my disbelief.

Prologue

I wasn't too sure whether or not he intended to keep his promise. Did we have a deal or was this his insurance in case the real announcer didn't show up again? That was the question over which I agonized during the week leading up to this night. Sitting in the holiday traffic, we inched closer and closer to the answer.

At last, with Convention Hall in sight, I pulled into the first available parking space. As soon as we found our seats, I left my cousins without a word as to where I was going. When I found Willie, he was not pleased.

"Hey, kid, where the hell have you been? Do you know what time it is?"

"The traffic, Mr. Gilzenberg. The traffic was awful."

"We've got a big show tonight. And your clothes... I told you to wear a jacket and tie."

"They're in my car. I have clothes in the trunk of my car."

"Well, go get them and meet me at the dressing room door."

When I raced back, carrying a suit draped over my arm, he ushered me over to the opposite side of the packed arena to a small holding area reserved for the emergency medical personnel. I was instructed to change clothes and wait for him to return. (With time I learned that acceptance into the private sanctuary of the wrestlers' dressing room only came after earning their trust. But more on that later.)

"Don't go anywhere. If you move from here, you'll get into trouble. And I don't need any more headaches tonight."

In all of my excitement, I never had an opportunity to let Paul and Frank in on what I was up to. It wasn't until I nervously made my way down the aisle that my cousins realized that I had surely lost my mind.

I clumsily climbed up the three short steps onto the ring apron and stopped. It was the first challenge of what promised to be a very long night. I couldn't figure out how to get through the ring ropes. I had seen the wrestlers accomplish what I thought was a simple feat hundreds of times. Do I duck under the bottom rope? Squat between the ropes? Leaping over the top wasn't even a consideration. Some of the fans immediately picked up on my dilemma. I hadn't even uttered a sound, and they knew that I was lost. When people started to hurl insults and a few other things, I somehow pushed my way through the ropes and spun off-balance to the center of the dimly lit ring. As

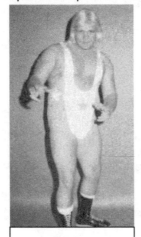

Larry's first match was mine too. Our pro careers began at the same second!

if dizzied by the erratic motion of The Giant Twister on the amusement pier outside, the capacity crowd began to whirl around me. I staggered forward, bracing myself on the ring ropes and looked down toward the floor to gain my balance where I noticed a man frantically shouting over the noisy, impatient fans as he tugged away on my pants leg. He flung a scrap of paper at me shouting, "This is for my son. Get it right!" It was the ring introduction for Pretty Boy Larry Sharpe who sneered at me from the opposite side of the ring. It was his pro wrestling debut too and his father was determined that I wasn't going to ruin his magic moment. Then he pointed to the nervous, but proud "Sharpe" family, who were all sitting in the front row, taunting me with a "you'd better not mess this up" kind of look. What pressure. What abuse. What a mess I had gotten myself into!

As the night progressed, more and more of the fans picked up on my constant struggle. The more I fumbled, the louder I was jeered. But the more they mocked me, the more determined I was to pretend that I was in control. I tripped over the mic cord, looked out at the taunting people and sheepishly grinned. I stumbled up the ring steps and blushingly waved to acknowledge the crowd's delight in my misfortune. Although the people continued to mimic and mock me, I provided additional entertainment between the matches and they loved it.

Somehow, I got through the night. Curiously, Willie asked me back for the following week and every Saturday through the rest of the summer. While I questioned his judgment, I didn't say so. I figured that regardless of how graceless my ring debut had been there must be something about me that he liked. And anyway, until this Saturday night in the summer of 1974, to be the one to officially proclaim my hero victorious could only have happened in a dream. Yes, once again, Bruno Sammartino had successfully defended his World Heavyweight Championship!

Part One

THE WWF YEARS

1974 – 1985

Chapter One
"The Preliminary Event"

I don't want realism. I want magic! Yes, yes, magic! . . . I try to give that to people. . . . I misrepresent things to them. . .I don't tell truth. . . . I tell what ought to be truth. . . . And if that is sinful, then let me be damned for it!

Tennessee Williams, "A Streetcar Named Desire"

Salt Lake City, Utah - October 14, 1994

And now, Ladies and Gentlemen (a dramatic pause)*, it is time for the match to determine the WCW World Heavyweight Championship!*

Upon hearing my proclamation, the scattered attention of the crowd, temporarily diverted by matters more mundane, becomes focused on center ring. Like kids rushing to class when the school bell rings, the masses stampede toward the security railings that surround the brightly lit platform. As adults try to balance tottering infants upon their shoulders, awestruck youngsters are crushed against the metal barricades. All hoping for a closer look, maybe one fleeting touch of their wrestling idols.

A casual nod to my sound tech brings forth the rising blare of trumpets and the dramatic pounding of drums. The anticipation of the crowd is heightened as I purposefully spin to face the entrance where tonight's main eventers wait in the shadows for their grand entrances.

"Presenting first, the challenger . . . He's from Charlotte, North Carolina . . . he weighs 243 pounds . . . and he is ten time former World Heavyweight Champion . . . 'Nature Boy' . . . Riiiiic Flaaaair!"

The overture from *2001 Space Odyssey* pulsates through the hearts of the assemblage. The regally robed Ric Flair strides into view. Falsetto shrieks of "Whooo", Flair's signature expression of rapture erupts from the smiling mob. A striking figure, the veteran's fashionably styled bleached blonde locks offer a stunning contrast to the dark leather-tanned tint of his skin. Strutting down the carpeted aisle, he barely escapes the callused hands extended by his pawing admirers.

Upon reaching the ring, Flair carefully mounts the steps. With nonchalant certainty he motions for the referee to pry apart the ring ropes, facilitating his gliding entry onto the canvas covered stage. It is a courtesy extended only to The Nature Boy.

There is no better showman than "The Nature Boy".

Once inside, Flair acknowledges the crowd's adulation with hands elevated overhead. Reminiscent of the Pope greeting his faithful followers from high atop his Holiness' exalted balcony, the princely presence of this cunning craftsman captivates the intoxicated crowd. The purple sequins of his long flowing robe shimmer in the spotlights. Violet colored feathers free fall through the air from his plume fringed outfit. With a majestic strut, Flair flaunts his fame and fortune before the faceless rank and file.

In stark contrast, my sober, tuxedoed figure stands steady in center ring, as The Nature Boy twirls around me in all of his glory. He menacingly brushes closely against my fixed frame, coming within inches of causing a collision. As if stunned, I spontaneously sidestep his intrusive advances with an offended expression, as Flair shoots a devilish grin my way.

The fans respond to our comedic pantomime with a deafening roar of approval. My spine tingles with excitement. I am overcome with a sense of accomplishment.

Through deliberate movements and carefully selected words, pitched to fit the message, the power that comes from manipulating the emotions of thousands live, and millions via television, best explains the allure that performing in the ring holds for me. It took years of self-training through trial and error, in smoky arenas and tiny community centers, before I stepped into the spotlight of the Skydomes, the Superdomes and the Royal Albert Halls of the world. Mastering the art of ring announcing is the difference between being in awe and being in control.

During the summer of 1974, I unwittingly took my first unsteady steps along a career path that ultimately placed me beside pro wrestling's most noted performers. With a pressed sports coat draped over my arm and a bow tie carefully tucked in its pocket, I reported to the

Wildwood Convention Hall every Saturday. Since childhood, my interest in pro wrestling had grown while my money to support the habit had dwindled. It was therefore natural, that by becoming part of the show, my wrestling appetite would be satisfied at a price that I could afford.

Throughout New Jersey's summer season of weekly wrestling events, many of the WWWF regulars reserved their preferred ringside seats well in advance for the entire season. They showed a devotion to pro wrestling only equaled by their unwavering allegiance to church bingo and the Friday night bowling league.

While the fans freely allowed themselves to be suckered in by the antics of their wrestling heroes, they were just as quick to denounce an incompetent player whose work fell short of a believable performance. Pro wrestling drained a sizable sum from their weekly paychecks, earned by the sweat of their brow, and in return for their entertainment dollar, they demanded the same exhaustive effort from the performers. It was clear that anything less was unacceptable. When disappointed, their harassing heckles carried the same stinging sensation as a Stan "The Man" Stasiak heart punch.

It was therefore inexplicable that the tightly knit community of wrestling buffs took an immediate liking to me when I began popping up as the master of ceremonies of their favorite night out. Perhaps my enthusiasm compensated for my incompetence. Maybe the novelty of a twenty-one year old kid, serious in his attempt to emulate the smooth pros who had come before him, was ridiculous enough to be entertaining. Nevertheless, something clicked between my demanding audience and me. It wasn't that they excused my embarrassing blunders. It was that they looked forward to my humiliating predicaments from the start. It became part of their fun. And on nights when the wrestling didn't live up to the pre-match hype, they created embarrassing situations for me to sweat over. Early on, the fans had me pegged as an entertaining sideshow when a particularly dull card was in need of a boost. If the promoters weren't going to deliver an exciting night of wrestling, the ever-resourceful fans were intent on providing their own entertainment.

Just a few weeks after arriving on the scene, the unruly rabble-rousers decided to put me on trial. It was during the announcements for a finale featuring two lackluster old timers who had no chance of living up to their advance publicity. I began my over-exaggerated introductions, listing their past accomplishments as my only hope of exciting the crowd. As they eyed the first of two veterans, who sadly hobbled to the ring, my words rang hollow. Doubting every overused superlative that I spouted in my attempt to sell this as a main event, the insulted crowd muttered its disbelief. A core of insulted fans began to rush toward the ring. They were not upset with the promoters for signing such a clinker. They could hold no resentment for the performers whose uninspired effort would surely be a retread of the only match left in their repertoire. Their anger was directed at me. They were offended by my blatant misrepresentation of what everyone knew was going to be an insufferable ten-minute snoozer. And they were not about to let me get away with it.

Oblivious to the bad blood that had begun to simmer in the arena, I slyly, but foolishly stretched out the ring introductions, expanding each syllable of my long-winded eulogy. And, of course, my ineffective attempt to stall for the extra time necessary for these lifeless legends to amble down the aisle served only to raise the tepid temperature in the building to a boil.

As I began the second introduction, I was blind-sided by a flying object that slapped across my forehead. Reeling backward, I suddenly lost the sight of my right eye. In a desperate bid to regain my balance, I took a few frantic steps forward. In doing so, I squished a slippery substance under foot, which propelled me across the mat. Too startled to stop, I slid across to the opposite side of the ring. Too proud to lose my composure, I stoically forged ahead with my announcements. When the fans saw that I refused to miss a beat of the rousing introduction, they burst into uncontrollable laughter. As taunting catcalls echoed from the far reaches of the hall, I stumbled out of the ring in a daze without knowing what had hit me.

The laughter of the crowd outlasted the dreaded special event. The night had concluded on an upbeat note due to a frustrated fan from Philadelphia. It was this offended watchdog who appointed himself protector of the crowd's sensibilities. My shameless attempt to shove a bunch of bull down his throat, was more than he could stomach. So with one well-placed pitch, he rid himself of the two things that caused his indigestion.

He was the fellow who flipped the mustard-covered hot dog from ringside. The same hot dog that smacked me in the forehead and wedged between my brow and eyeglasses. As my emotion-filled introduction continued, my vengeful jury relished at the sight of the frankfurter sliding down my cheek as it smeared mustard across the inside of my eyeglass lens, causing the temporary loss of vision. They rolled in the aisles as it rolled down my chest, perfectly positioned to propel me unflinchingly forward. Here I was, the bow tie clad representative of the World Wide Wrestling Federation, the organization's conservative alternative to its bizarre wrestlers, enthusiastically delivering my announcements while gliding across the mat, courtesy of the wiener that had dangled freely from my face.

The trial was over. The verdict was in. The punishment was immediate. The fans found me guilty of the most contemptuous crime of all . . .the crime of condescension. They paid to be entertained, not to be offended. For each of my deceitful sentences, they delivered a sentence of their own. It was a merciful judgment, if not for the humiliation, then for its swiftness.

It took just one direct hit by a self-styled major leaguer to turn the promotion's straight-laced pitchman into the buffoon of the night.

For years to come, I'd think back to the humiliating price that I paid by underestimating the intelligence of my audience. It was the first of many valuable lessons that I learned from listening to the fans.

But as each week passed, I became more comfortable with my new role. I began to take note of the weight that my ring introductions could carry. A rousing delivery excited. A solemn tone soothed. Logic became the key to the delivery of my every word and movement in the ring.

My early role models were men whose work was distinctive, yet diverse. I admired the professionalism of Philadelphia ring announcer Buddy Wagner and the stylized excitement created by Jimmy Lennon, Sr., the Los Angeles announcer of movie fame. "Friendly" Bob Freed, from Washington, DC, was another favorite. He was a large, clumsy oaf of a man who constantly sported a moronic grin. I liked him. He was real. He was approachable. From the early days of my career, I began to strive for a style combining the professionalism, excitement and approachability of my three predecessors.

Although I gradually befriended an interesting assortment of characters during my early exposure to the wrestling subculture, many years passed before being fully accepted by the wrestling fraternity. Even though today's professional wrestling community remains very closed to the uninitiated, it was nearly impenetrable in the 1970's. Outsiders were distrusted. Breaking into the business was often a hopeless undertaking for starry-eyed athletes and eager announcers who were driven away out of utter frustration.

WWWF president Willie Gilzenberg kept me separated from the wrestlers for my first summer in Wildwood by declaring the dressing rooms off limits. But I didn't feel slighted. I was just grateful to be asked back each week. However, his repeated and forceful warnings to stay away from the wrestlers' private sanctuary, piqued my curiosity. Since I had never expressed a desire to enter, I wondered why he was so insistent. It brought me back to my early school days when one dare not invade the privacy of the faculty lounge. After numerous threats, I was even afraid to go near the teachers' room. And that fear came with the knowledge that my favorite teacher, Miss Callahan always answered the door. In Wildwood, Gorilla Monsoon was the door monitor! Willie just didn't realize that I would never have barged into the wrestlers' locker area. Not a chance. Especially since I was in awe of half of the wrestlers and terrified of the rest.

As I have seen through the years, trespassing in the wrestlers' private quarters can be dangerous. It's amazing how many intruders try. Several have been roughed up. The wise guys are senselessly bloodied. Many through the years have been bounced past me as I readied myself for show time. I've always wondered what they expect to discover. Believe me, there is little to be learned in the wrestlers' locker room. Half of what is said is exaggerated bravado and the rest is relatively uninteresting. On a typical night you might find the boys bragging about their latest escapades with the local women, the veterans reminiscing about the good old days, a few guys mapping out the best route to the next town on the tour, someone reading a newspaper in one corner and maybe a quiet card game in progress in the opposite corner. Typical of the old time mentality, Willie simply didn't want me to catch a glimpse of the baby faces and the heels playing a friendly game of gin rummy.

To those who hunger for the latest news about everything and everyone in pro wrestling, forget about invading the backstage areas. And if you're looking for honest answers about the game, don't even think about publicly cornering the performers. In the best of moods, they'll concoct any fanciful answer to get rid of you. And by all means, don't believe what management tells you. Wrestling talent as well as office personnel spend much of their time convincing each other that they alone have the formula for a successful promotion. If they concentrated on promoting wrestling, instead of promoting themselves, the industry would be much better off. Both wrestlers and wrestling executives begin to believe their own exaggerated self-publicity, resulting in a distorted view of the truth.

If you're interested in learning what really goes on in wrestling, my advice is simple. Befriend an informed, impartial bystander. Ask a roadie.

The road crew, transporting the ring from town to town, views the inside workings of the industry from the back rooms of coliseums to the bar rooms of hotels all across the country. In the absence of the public, when everyone's guard is down, the roadies witness it all. They are underpaid and poorly treated. They are used as gofers and scapegoats. They feel powerless and disenfranchised. The wrestlers, announcers and administrators receive acknowledgment for their work in the form of a healthy paycheck. A roadie's proof of power is the information that he possesses, knowledge, unbiased and free of self-interest. Proof that he is a friend of the headliners. Proof that he really belongs. Proof that he is important. Young star-struck kids and female fans who are snubbed by the performers soon realize that befriending the ring crew is as close as they are ever going to get to their TV heroes. They are a roadie's dream audience.

The storytelling roadies fascinated me during that first season in Wildwood. At times, their anecdotes were more exciting than the wrestling show to follow. They went something like this:

Ya should have seen what happened at TV on Tuesday. McMahon (the announcer and son of the boss) threw that fat drunken manager out of the fuckin' building! He was so smashed! He called Vince a goddam momma's boy!

George 'The Animal' Steele didn't show in Philly. Heard he went back to Detroit. Had to go to some teachers' meeting. Shit! Imagine if he was your teacher! What a pisser!

Ya know that blonde broad in Philly? Ya know the one that dyes her pubes green and shaves them in the shape of a shamrock on St. Patrick's Day? The boys were bangin' her all night long! Forget about tryin' to sleep. The hotel security was up to the room three times. Better find another place to stay.

The stories went on and on.

35

As entertaining as they were, I was confused by many of their anecdotes. So much of what they said conflicted with my naive perception of pro wrestling from a fan's perspective. I quickly learned to keep my mouth shut and my ears and my mind open. And with time, I discovered that the roadies' accounts were the most consistent with the truth.

The first revelation that had an enormous impact on my future in wrestling concerned the Manchurian Giant, Gorilla Monsoon.

He had been wrestling in the WWWF for the better part of twelve years. As a fan I knew him as a four hundred pound, main event wrestler who had challenged the hugely popular Bruno Sammartino in a moneymaking series of matches. One legendary contest in the early sixties at Madison Square Garden lasted one hour. For many years, his manager, Wild Red Berry, did all of his talking. During interviews, Monsoon stood behind him scowling and growling unintelligibly. As a kid, I believed that Monsoon was a wild man who spoke no

My employer, my mentor , my favorite monster.

English. I headed for the balcony every time he made his way to the ring. As the subject of the first magazine article that I authored, I discovered that Monsoon was actually a 1959 Ithaca College graduate earning letters in wrestling, football and track. As an announcer I was even more amazed to learn that the guy who was introduced to the public as a subhuman beast, had evolved into a minority owner of the WWWF. He was responsible for promoting New Jersey, Pennsylvania and

Monsoon came to the pros from college.

Delaware and supervised all television production. Darwin would have had a field day with this gorilla. While Willie administered business in public view, Monsoon controlled the operation from backstage. I was soon to learn, in fact, that the Gorilla was my boss.

From monster to management ..... only in America!

Chapter Two
"The Bunkhouse Stampede"

What gives an act its great entertainment value, is its
spontaneity. It's the way an actor seizes on something that happens
unexpectedly and turns it into a laugh. The public loves that.
William Morris, founder of the William Morris Talent Agency

After the Labor Day show, I thanked my mentors and headed back to the real world. I was preparing to enter the classroom for my first year as a high school Spanish teacher. Shortly after settling into a New Jersey lakeside rental home, I received a call from my mother. After exchanging the latest family news for an update on the progress of my new teaching assignment, my mother hesitated, then continued with uncertainty in her voice.

"Gary, I have a message for you."

"Really?"

"Some man called for you tonight."

"It's okay to give him my number, Mom. He's probably a friend from college."

"No, a man called. Do you know someone by the name of *Gorilla*?"

"Gorilla? What's his last name?"

"Do you know *more* than one Gorilla?"

"Naw, I was just kidding. That's Monsoon. You know, the four hundred pound bearded guy that grunts and groans on TV every week."

"So, what does he want from *you*?"

"Bananas?"

"That's not funny. He left a number for you to call."

My return call began an eleven year association with Gorilla Monsoon and the WWWF. Working for Monsoon was always a pleasure. He was an intelligent guy who was respected by the workers both for his athletic accomplishments, as well as for his fair and even management style.

Gino, as we called Monsoon, was an enterprising promoter who brought wrestling to tiny hometowns throughout his three-state territory. In addition to promoting wrestling at high schools and colleges, as well as the traditional armories and summer vacation destinations, Gino booked alternative venues like skating rinks, shopping malls, army bases and night clubs.

Even though I was teaching all through my years with the WWWF, I was working as many as five shows a week. It was understood that if Gino promoted a show, I was the announcer. The experience that I received from working continuously during my early years was invaluable. My way of showing appreciation for his loyalty to me was to give my all every night. My pay was only twenty-five dollars per show. But the money didn't matter. I was starry-eyed. In order to work with all of the personalities that I had grown up watching on television no distance was too far.

One of the more unconventional sites where Gino promoted was the Cowtown Rodeo Arena located at the southern tip of New Jersey, just north of the Delaware state line. The ring was positioned in the center of the dusty outdoor arena. The fans, mostly Hispanic farm workers, loved to watch my arrival to the ring. I entered from the far end of the field where the bulls were corralled on rodeo nights. I gingerly tiptoed over mounds of freshly deposited bull dung in my three-piece suit so as not to ruin my carefully polished dress shoes.

One stormy evening, while making my way to the ring, I was startled by the sudden sounds of snorting and moaning coming from the direction of the bullpen behind me. Nervously spinning around, I lost my footing and felt the bull manure warmly settle around my ankles. It was like sinking in quick sand. I slowly shook one foot at a time to free myself of the excrement, which had been softened by the summer rain. The farm workers began to whistle and wildly shout their approval. Suddenly I spotted preliminary wrestler, Eddie Gilbert, the sound effects expert of the troupe, doubled over in laughter as he stood inside the empty coral. I was not amused.

Ribbing each other was a way of life on the road. It would not have been farfetched for one of the pranksters to unleash the bulls for the fun of watching the rookie announcer dive out of the way of a charging animal. The boys would have enjoyed such an entertaining diversion. But it didn't matter. Although I might have gotten to the ring much quicker, nothing would have kept me from doing my job. I was loyal at all costs.

Why else did I forge ahead, holding a hot wired microphone, beneath the towering, outdoor ring lights, in the middle of an electrical storm? Anyway, I accepted such periodic pranks as my rite of passage into the wrestling fraternity. I was receiving an elementary education in Wrestling Subculture 101 and I didn't have a clue.

Every month when I asked Monsoon for the dates of my future bookings, he cautiously wrapped his oversized date ledger around his head, partly because he suffered from poor vision, and partly to keep the information it contained hidden from me. The large black book listed the dates, towns and matches for each night through the following month. He felt that there was more information in his booking ledger than I needed to know, since finding out the line-up so far in advance would tip his hand as to when the title belts were scheduled to change hands.

Continuing my apprenticeship, I happily roamed from town to town. I taught high school each day and became a traveling journeyman, perfecting my craft, each night.

In late June of 1976, exactly two years to the week of my Wildwood debut, I got another call from my guardian angel. Monsoon asked me to drive over to the Philadelphia Arena the next Tuesday where the WWWF taped their primary television show. Buddy Wagner, the ring announcer for *Championship Wrestling* was sidelined and Monsoon wanted me to fill in for him. Having no idea what to expect, I readily agreed. All I remember Gino saying was that he wanted to put me on TV!

Chapter Three
"The TV Challenge Match"

Television is a very peculiar medium — even more revealing in many ways than film. Because there are no retakes, you've got to be sharp. What you are inside comes out over the tube more forcefully than through a camera on a set.

Bette Davis, "I'd Love To Kiss You ... Conversations"

The cavernous Philadelphia Arena at 45th and Market was an intimidating brick structure reminiscent of the ominous penitentiaries so often the setting for mobster movies of early Hollywood. Every third Tuesday hundreds of wrestling fans congregated on Market Street, impatiently waiting for the arena's front doors to creak open. Spilling onto the busy Center City street, the colorful crowd clutched posters, cowbells, air horns, stuffed monkeys and other assorted props. Although the show wouldn't start until 6:30, devoted fans from all walks of life routinely gathered outside the arena hours before show time, buzzing about the latest wrestling gossip. Some traveled hundreds of miles, leaving the daily grind behind, to make their pilgrimage to the WWWF television tapings. Their dedication and passion was similar to party delegates at our national political conventions. This community of the faithful was eager to support its incumbent champions and campaigned on behalf of its favorite challengers for the various WWWF championships. With the outcome of every contest pre-determined, and knowing their attendance merely served as window dressing to enhance the TV product, the delegates of every faction were simply there to be heard and to have a good time.

Reporting for my first TV assignment, I found the stage door off a narrow back alley behind the arena. Cautiously stepping inside, I was instantly overwhelmed by the nauseating odors of urine and cooking grease, which had simmered all day under the hot summer sun. Decayed after decades of thunderous mat action, roller derby games, small time boxing cards and inaugural balls of city politicos, many memories lay beneath the peeling red and blue striped white paint that covered the walls of this stifling monument to years gone by.

In the center of the steamy arena floor, the white canvas surface of the eighteen foot square ring, appearing much smaller in person, reflected the intense television lights. Between the ring and two stationary cameras, Vince McMahon, Jr., the show's host, was conducting interviews with WWWF headliners. The interviews, in which the baby faces pleaded for the fans' support and the heels arrogantly hurled insults and threats at their opponents, have always been most effective in generating controversy surrounding upcoming live house shows. Since the same main event routinely topped the cards in all major cities along the WWWF circuit, identical interviews were repeated for each city in order to bring them local flavor. When the villains ridiculed New York's Puerto Rican community, Pedro Morales angrily responded in Spanish. When they assailed the Italians in Boston, Bruno Sammartino expressed outrage in his native tongue. By the time the show hit town, the angry fans were provoked to the point that they filled the major sports arenas throughout the Northeast ready for revenge.

Four versions of each market specific interview were recorded so that the intensity could slowly build with each week. The effect of saying "Next Saturday I'm coming to Madison Square Garden to show all you New York wetbacks that Morales isn't man enough to shine my shoes!" or "Tonight you'll see once and for all, how I'm goin' to beat up your meatball hero Sammartino and bounce him back to the Italian slums!" brought an urgency to each event. All of the market specific interviews were later posted in the show for each city's edition. Producing four sets of interviews for as many as twenty-one cities where recurring events ran was a lot of work, which made TV days seem never ending.

Vince, Sr. was the brains behind the old WWWF.

When I entered the oversized communal locker room, Gino, who was huddled in front of a tiny TV monitor with WWWF owner, Vince McMahon, Sr., waved me over for a hurried, but polite introduction. On television nights, the two partners scrutinized each interview and all of the matches. When a wrestler flubbed his lines or a match failed to portray the desired intensity, Gino and Vince ordered a retake.

On nights when television was taped, the fans in Philly sat through three one-hour broadcasts. Taping the weekly show every third Tuesday was a cost-effective way of doing business. The one time arena rental, production expenses and payroll yielded three weeks of TV wrestling at a third of the cost.

While this arrangement was economically sensible, the live arena audience often witnessed events that made little sense. Such was the case when the combatants of an unacceptable match were sent back to the ring to duplicate much of their performance from only minutes earlier. In addition, taping three weeks of television in front of the same audience meant that the fans saw a wrestler, battered and bloodied, carried out on a stretcher in the first hour, only to return, fresh and energetic, for revenge in the third.

While this seemed plausible to the viewer at home, since the events were separated by two weeks, the audience in Philadelphia saw him miraculously recover the very same night. The fans wanted so much to believe that they conveniently overlooked these improbable circumstances. To challenge the authenticity of pro wrestling would threaten their one retreat from the difficulties of daily life. The enjoyment that they received from wrestling and the community of which they were a part was central to their lives. It was cause enough to suspend their belief.

As the arena began to fill up, Monsoon took me aside to tell me that I would announce the first and third hours, while a "candidate" who was sent by the Pennsylvania State Athletic commissioner would work the second hour. The promotion was obliged to at least portray us as having an equal chance at getting the job. However, I later learned that there was never a doubt that I was the heir apparent to be the lead TV ring announcer.

This decision, as are so many talent acquisitions in pro wrestling, had less to do with my abilities and more to do with a shrewd business maneuver. Since I worked all of Gino's non-televised shows, he knew that when I became a regular on TV, I would add an importance to all of the events that he promoted. With my stature elevated through weekly television exposure, I would become a valuable asset to all of the towns that Gino claimed for himself.

In many parts of the country, pro wrestling was under the auspices of state athletic commissions. Gino and Vince, Sr.'s decision to treat the alternate announcer as a serious candidate was calculated to appease the Pennsylvania Chairman, who was entrusted with far reaching powers such as licensing wrestlers, referees, announcers, promoters, box office personnel and time keepers. It would have been easy to legally prohibit me from announcing in Philadelphia since the Pennsylvania statutes barred out-of-state residents from securing a license. Without the Chairman's approval, I would not have worked. He had the authority to sabotage a promotion by enforcing routinely ignored regulations that could cause the cancellation of a show or declare a wrestler unfit to perform. The absence of advertised main event wrestlers will kill a town in short order. The Chairman, well aware that he always held the trump card, flaunted his advantage over promoters to gain favors.

Rarely did regulatory boards govern our events by the book. Most sent representatives for the sole purpose of collecting the state's taxes on box office receipts. The commissioners and their deputies were often moonlighting government workers who looked forward to a night away from the wife with a fifty dollar pay off and a few autographs for the kids as justification. Others became arrogant and over-impressed with the leverage of the law at their disposal. The autographs and their fifty-dollar stipend just weren't enough. Private audiences with the television personalities and a little extra consideration might suffice to overlook an infraction of commission rules. Their entire identity was based on this patronage position with the commission.

Over the years, the relationship between Vince, Sr. and state athletic commissions throughout the Northeast had been cultivated with care. It was not recommended to buck the state boards if you wanted to continue conducting business without interference. You were forced to do whatever it took to present your show with the personnel of your choosing. I was unaware at the time that my promotion to the *Championship Wrestling* program was a politically sensitive issue. This was a matter that Vince, Sr. and Gino took care of. I never asked what price was placed on my head. Such dealings are rare in today's environment, since athletic commissions, in the few states where pro wrestling is still regulated, have been stripped of much of their authority.

Waiting for Gino's signal to start the show, I realized that this was an opportunity for me to become more than the kid at the local New Jersey matches. If I passed this test in front of Vince, Sr. and the tough Philadelphia fans, then my voice would become the ring voice for the WWWF television network. Finally, grasping the importance of this one performance, my stomach began to churn. My throat felt like sandpaper.

I was saying a little prayer as the house lights went down. When the television lights came on, Gino waved me out to the ring. Nervous tension propelled me down the aisle in a jog, which became my signature entrance for many years. Like a frightened deer charging through throngs of bloodthirsty hunters, I received an immediate reaction.

"Who the hell are *you*?" "Where's Buddy Wagner?" "Who dressed *you,* your mother?" (I don't know whether it was my over-sized velvet bow tie or the carnation boutonniere that they objected to.) "What's this, kiddy night?" None of it was positive, but at least they noticed.

I nervously hopped through the ropes. As someone on the floor handed me the mic, I jerked it up with such force, that I popped myself in the mouth. As I had done in so many embarrassing situations in the past, I forged ahead and welcomed the crowd as my lower lip began to swell. Vinnie and his broadcast partner, wrestling legend, Antonino Rocca, strolled out to their positions. Vinnie didn't seem pleased that no one noticed.

Gino had told me to look straight ahead into the camera and when the bell rang, like Pavlov's dog, I was to begin. After introducing the first wrestlers, I calmed down and settled into a comfortable rhythm. Two years of working in local clubs was finally paying off. I tuned out the catcalls, insults and television cameras to focus on what I was saying and how it was being received.

During the second hour I changed clothes and watched the action from backstage. Augie Weil, who helped Gino to promote his New Jersey towns, had wandered back to tease me, as was his way. Eyeing my swollen lip he snickered, "You're not supposed to eat the damn microphone." Not the most encouraging words, but I understood him and somehow felt comforted. If anyone else thought that I was doing well, they weren't saying. The only indication from the top brass as to my performance thus far came from Mel Phillips, one of the office gophers. He handed me the line-up for the third hour with a challenge, "They think you can handle 'The Animal'. Let's see."

The initial impact of my move to TV announcing was magnified by the encounter I was about to have with one of the most grotesque looking characters in the WWWF, George "The Animal" Steele. Weighing 290 pounds, his body was completely covered with dark, thick hair. His clean shaven head revealed a creviced skull layered with excess cartilage jutting over his forehead. When he wrestled, he was uncontrollable. In the '70s he never spoke English. He only bellowed and howled. George's eyes darted from side to side as he erratically charged his opponent, the referee, and the fans. After The Animal won the match he comforted himself by shredding the corner turnbuckles with his teeth and proceeded to chew the foam padding. He appeared on the scene in June and disappeared in September because, oddly enough, he was a schoolteacher in the

Although The Animal scared the hell out of me, his constant attacks made this kid announcer famous among fans who feared for my safety.

Detroit area. I wasn't aware of this at the time. George scared the hell out of me and he knew it. So I became his favorite target.

Waiting my turn to announce the third hour, I couldn't decide how I'd handle George on camera. I thought my prayers had been answered when his manager, Captain Lou Albano, approached me. Lou told me to stay in the center of the ring when George ran out. He assured me that Steele would run through the audience until I finished my announcements and then charge the ring, leaving just enough time for me to escape. George's killer instinct would be preserved in the minds of the fans, I would be safe and everybody would be happy.

I approached the ring for the third televised hour feeling much more at ease. When it was time for George's match, he ran down the aisle like a raging bull. Hairy arms flailing, fleshy head bobbing, he charged the audience as women screamed and children ran to their parents. Just as Lou had promised, "The Animal" stayed on the floor, circling the ring, as I began to make my introductions.

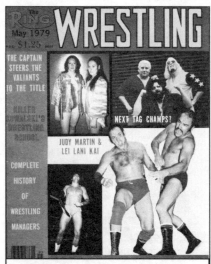

I was able to concentrate on what I was saying, as it seemed that Lou had successfully communicated our game plan to George. Or so I thought.

Without warning, I was knocked down from behind and lay on the mat in darkness. Struggling to get to my feet, I could not move. Reaching up, my fingers became ensnared in matted fur. The Animal had attacked and the Philadelphia fans were in an uproar. When I freed my head, I noticed that George was chewing on my carnation boutonniere. Captain Lou was straddling Steele feigning shock and horror in a disingenuous attempt to pull him off me. I struggled to get away, leaving my sports coat with the salivating beast.

"The only fan club in the world for a wrestling announcer is one for Gary Cappetta. The club is quite unique in that it gives a lot of information on its honorary through the pages of the club's official publication, "The Magical Microphone". George "The Animal" Steele was shown a copy of the bulletin and quoted to say, 'Great bulletin, but the Kid (meaning Gary) is ah #%&@%#. . .!"

When I finally returned to my position at ringside, I sank into my seat and looked over at Vinnie. He rolled his eyes. A look of absolute disgust covered his face. I felt that getting myself in yet another embarrassing situation had destroyed all of my best efforts. I failed the promotion. I failed Vince, Sr. And worst of all, I failed Gino.

At the end of the show, I started to make my way down the aisle. Some of the women in the audience came up to console me. "Are you all right, honey?" The men were shouting, "Why the hell didn't you deck the bastard?" A little boy grabbed for the carnation. I was a pathetic sight. My suit was a crumpled mess, the boutonniere swayed from the lapel of my sports coat and a dreary look covered my face. I dreaded the thought of facing Gino.

As I reached the dressing room, Lou was all apologies. "Are you okay, kid? I had no idea that things would get so out of control." Even *then*, I doubted his sincerity.

When I entered the near empty room, I was met with congratulatory words from some of the wrestlers. "Hey, that was fuckin' great! It really looked like ole George was scarin' the shit outta ya!."

I tried to avoid Monsoon and McMahon. Feeling shamed and alone, I faced the wall and began to change my clothes.

Suddenly, I felt someone standing behind me. I looked over my shoulder and saw Vince, Sr. With a concerned look in his eye, he shook my hand.

"Are you coming back next month?"

I couldn't believe what I was hearing.

"Do you want me to?"

"Sure. The people really took to you. Don't worry about the boys. They'll calm down."

"Thank you. Um ..... I'll check with Gino next week to be sure."

At first, I wondered why Vince felt the need to question me about continuing. Was he kidding me? Why would I have passed up such an opportunity? Since then I have realized that he knew how frightened I was. He recognized that I wasn't acting before the television cameras. I was reacting. Reacting to danger. My only thought on that fateful night was to survive. And that's why my television debut was so successful. My genuine fear communicated to the audience how dangerous it must be for a non-wrestler to step into the ring with the big boys.

In the years to come, I drew from that experience to maintain my effectiveness as a supporting player to other "dangerous" wrestlers such as Abdullah the Butcher, Jimmy Superfly Snuka, Stan Hansen and Bruiser Brody.

It didn't take long for me to recognize the importance of this evening. With the notoriety that appearing on weekly television brought, I entered a new phase of my announcing career.

Chapter Four
"The Triangle Match"

But they (wrestling matches) are good burlesque. They say in effect, 'All right, if you want violence, we'll give you some. But it will be make-believe, and no one will get hurt, at least not on purpose.' Half the fun is the glib-tongued announcer who appears to take the wrestling nonsense seriously. He reports it deadpan straight, appalled by brutality, exhilarated by the unexpected move so carefully rehearsed, outraged by unsportsmanlike behavior, and always sympathetic with the referee who goes through the motions of trying to keep order while the contestants are gouging, hitting one another with chairs, chasing opponents up and down the aisles, and committing various other forms of mayhem. . . . I like my violence that way, in a make-believe world

James A. Michener, "Sports In America"

The instant notoriety that I experienced when my first shows aired was proof positive that a huge and tremendously loyal audience viewed *Championship Wrestling*. People were intrigued by simple soap opera scenarios played out by homegrown pretty boys and grotesque monsters. The basic ingredients were elementary. With clearly defined good versus evil themes, feats of strength, athleticism, violence and a bit of mystery, the show became must see TV for millions.

My contribution to the production was to supply a direct contrast to everyone else who appeared on the show. I was slight of build. The athletes were enormous. I was conservatively attired with bow tie and carnation boutonniere. The competitors wore outlandish costumes or skimpy briefs. I announced in clear, understandable English. Many wrestlers ranted unintelligibly or spoke with foreign accents. I maintained a calm composure while surrounded by chaos. Aside from lending credibility to the performance, the fans ultimately related to me as a trustworthy representative of the promotion. I developed a rapport with the audience. They believed me. And in years to come, this perception of credibility and sincerity became my greatest asset to The World Wrestling Federation and to Ted Turner's World Championship Wrestling.

In the sixty-minute television program, I used the scant twenty seconds of airtime that I enjoyed each week to the best advantage possible. Following the broadcast's open, the camera captured a close-up of me in center ring where I introduced the officials. Before I became comfortable with the cameras, my nervous tension gave way to an unbridled, over-enthusiastic announcing style, which brought forth the false impression that I was offering an endorsement of the matches to follow. Since I was unable to restrain my overly exaggerated delivery, it was lucky that the decision-makers were pleased with the excitement that this style produced. But when I settled into my role, and began to understand the effectiveness of this style, those energetic introductions became a calculated effort to fire up the crowd. Since Vince, Jr. never allowed his various broadcast partners throughout the years to refer to me by name, I shrewdly took advantage of my few seconds to shine at the start of each show by rounding out my welcoming announcements with ....*and I'm your ring announcer, Gary Michael Cappetta!.*

The viewers never knew that Vince, Jr. was the boss' son. He portrayed himself as the lead announcer with no connection to management. The World Wide Wrestling Federation was held out as being structured very much like boxing. Willie Gilzenberg portrayed the president and ultimate authority, referees and the attending physician were assigned by the state athletic commission.

Vince, Sr. had nurtured his business from its infancy, and meticulously cultivated it into one of the most successful wrestling territories in the United States. The brains behind all that took place, Senior was a second generation promoter. He was an unimposing, soft-spoken gentleman. The immaculately groomed, impeccably dressed wrestling impresario's attention to detail carried over to his wrestling business. The son of long time Madison Square Garden boxing promoter, Jesse McMahon, Vince, Sr. was raised in the world of ring sports. Although at first, Vince refused to bring Junior into the family business, by the mid '70s he had a change of heart and began to groom his son to some day assume control of his Northeastern wrestling empire.

When he died in May of 1984, most of his contemporaries had kind words to say about Vince McMahon, Sr. During the years that he ran the WWWF, he often combined forces with various promoters both in North America and abroad. Each tailored his individual wrestling product to tweak the sensitivities of their local fans taking into account the cultural differences in each region. They regularly traded talent to keep their rosters fresh, to perpetuate interest in their promotions and to keep the top wrestlers working. In the United States alone, there were as many as twenty territories with thriving wrestling promotions. It was a beneficial arrangement for all. The promoters and top wrestlers made money while the fans were always introduced to fresh faces that brought new challenges to each region's hometown and "world" champion.

Vince, Jr. towered over wrestlers like Bulldog Brower. That's why the guys often stood on boxes, hidden from the cameras, for television interviews.

I announced the *Championship Wrestling* TV bouts at The Philadelphia Arena every third Tuesday from 1976 through 1978. Then I was reassigned to the WWWF's alternate program, *All Star Wrestling*, which was taped in Hamburg, Pennsylvania every third Wednesday. I worked through that program's final episode when the WWWF went national in 1984 with its new *Superstars* show.

Although I announced for the WWWF a total of eleven years, Vince McMahon, Jr. rarely acknowledged my existence. When he wasn't conducting pre-show interviews, huddling in a corner with one of the main eventers or holed up in the tiny box office with his dad and Monsoon, he strutted about the arena like a peacock on display. Watching him shuffle around the darkened building in his worn terry cloth bedroom slippers, he never left any doubt that this was his home turf.

I decided very early on that Vinnie's demeanor was only a facade. By maintaining a distance from the "underlings", he exerted a form of passive control. The message was clear. It was Vinnie's way of letting you know: "You are unimportant, so don't dare bother me." The more insecure he could make you feel, the higher he elevated himself, thus keeping the workers and their concerns at a distance. It made his life as the boss' son easier. And while we're talking about the boss' son, here's an anecdote to prove true my analysis of Junior's use of psychological warfare as it was confirmed by a kid sitting at ringside during a jam packed Meadowlands Arena show in the early 1980's.

I was emceeing a WWF show at the Meadowlands Arena (now Continental Airlines Arena) on a particularly hectic evening. The building was close to capacity. Hulk Hogan was defending his heavyweight championship in the main event. I believe it was a Bodyslams Challenge Match against Big John Studd. As usual, Vinnie was on hand to personally deliver the instructions for Hogan's important matches because he was in the process of grooming Hogan to represent The Federation before a national audience.

The wrestlers on the undercard had been fighting all around the outside of the ring, which caused added confusion at my ringside position. There was a youngster sitting at the announcer's table. I didn't know who he was with, but he was continually getting in the way. He demonstrated an attitude that conveyed the impression that he was more important than the wrestlers who were working their butts off. Guessing that he was a guest of the state athletic commissioner, I was working around him, the politically safe thing to do.

During one of the calmer matches the kid began to ask me a series of business related questions. Thinking that this interrogation was peculiar coming from such a young kid, I responded with caution. Impatient with my guarded answers, he finally revealed that he was Shane McMahon, that he had come to the show with his father and that he was asking so many questions because he was interested in learning more about the business. I couldn't resist. I decided to test him with the following loaded question: "From everything your dad has told you about the business, what's the most important thing that you've learned?"

Without skipping a beat, he confidently answered, "Don't let your workers know how important they are so you can get the most out of them for the least amount of money."

Talk about a chip off the old block!

In 1976, I was paid sixty-five dollars for one night of television announcing. Sixty-five dollars for three one-hour programs. Nothing extra. Travel expenses, food, and costumes (which for me were "makeshift" tuxedoes) all

51

were considered ordinary expenses for which I was responsible. It was a take it or leave it deal because while a payoff of sixty-five dollars for a month's worth of televised performances was meager, we were prohibited from belonging to AFTRA, the performers' union.

Wrestling companies will never allow their "hired hands" to organize. I use the term "hired hands" because wrestlers are not considered employees by management. The performers are classified by the front office as self-employed contractors. Essentially, most on air personnel receive no health benefits, medical coverage, stock options, or pension plans. There was a time when Turner Broadcasting offered to sell me employee benefits for $10,000 a year. The Turner organization was fearful that the IRS was about to dispute a self-employed status for someone who was told when and where to work, as well as exactly which tasks would be performed for the agreed upon compensation. And when the "hired hand" is prohibited from working elsewhere within the industry, it all adds up to the IRS definition of an employee. Needless to say, as soon as Turner's accountants thought they had escaped the government's scrutiny, the offer was withdrawn. And McMahon, he doesn't even consider the issue worthy of discussion.

So wrestlers will be stuck with the self-employed contractor classification until someone challenges the promoters. But don't hold your breath. It is not likely to happen. If challenging the front office on the workman classification issue doesn't kill your career, it will greatly reduce any chance of seeing your action figure on a Walmart toy shelf any time in the near future.

During my first years on television, I made the mistake of asking why I didn't have to belong to the union. I innocently thought that everyone on television did. The comeback was creative. I was told that a wrestling event came under a special AFTRA provision allowing a sporting event (which pro wrestling is not) that is broadcast live (which we weren't) to be exempt from union supervision. While I knew better, I kept my mouth shut and pretended to accept this ludicrous explanation. Those who worked for the McMahons sensed that anyone who challenged the system would quickly be replaced. So like everyone else who valued his job, I didn't question what I was told. I went about my business and began to seek out associations with co-workers who could help me to better understand this crazy business.

The first of those who offered encouragement was The Grand Wizard, Ernie Roth. Along with Lou Albano and Fred Blassie, The Grand Wizard was one of the WWWF's three lead managers. The condescending arrogance of the slightly built Wizard always guaranteed disdain from the fans. His shark skin suits accented by his trademark turban and slotted, wrap around sunglasses effectively added to the menacing countenance of his weasel-like character. Ernie was so effective in his role that he was given the top heels to manage.

Before entering wrestling, Ernie worked in Canton, Ohio delivering weather updates for his hometown television station. Later he supervised ticket sales and public relations for The Canton Theater, where he was discovered by the road manager of 1950's crooner Johnny Ray, a friend of heavyweight wrestling champion Buddy Rogers. Ernie's first involvement in wrestling was as an announcer. He advanced to his initial managerial position as J. Wellington Radcliffe, managing Moose Cholak and Mr. Kleen in Detroit. He led his wrestlers to the ring wearing a bowler hat, spats and carrying a walking stick. In the late sixties he completely changed his identity to manage The Sheik, using the name Abdullah Farouk. The barbarous Sheik, best known for throwing fireballs at his opponents, was involved in many savage and bloody battles.

In the early '70s, Vince McMahon, Sr. brought Ernie to the WWWF. Although his character stayed the same, Ernie's name was changed to The Grand Wizard. He managed Mark Lewin and King Curtis as well as Tarzan Tyler and Crazy Luke Graham. Ernie was also paired with

Ernie with Superstar Billy Graham

Beautiful Bob Harmon who became his life-long friend and companion. Vince Sr. became impressed with Ernie's ability to incite the fans. As a result, he managed two WWWF World

Heavyweight Champions: Stan Stasiak, a transitional champion, and Superstar Billy Graham who held the title from April 1977 to February 1978.

Away from wrestling, he was the complete opposite from his arrogant Grand Wizard persona. He always had time to help the newcomers. Ernie was a generous individual who was one of wrestling's most interesting characters. With his reassurance, I became comfortable around the wrestlers and was ultimately accepted. Except for monthly events at Madison Square Garden, and an occasional house show, Ernie only worked at television tapings once every three weeks.

I learned a great deal about the business from Ernie. We always tried to get together when he was in for the Garden shows. Sometimes he stayed at my apartment for a couple of extra days. This is when I began to smarten up to the wrestling business. He'd get out his pot, light up and we'd talk for hours and hours. We'd take long drives or spend the afternoon at a Broadway matinee constantly chatting about the business.

During the summers of 1980 and 1981, I vacationed at Ernie's Fort Lauderdale, Florida residence. His bedroom, equipped with television and phone, was where he conducted his business. On the telephone all day, Ernie counseled many of the wrestlers who called from the road with a myriad of problems. Between periodic dips in his in-ground pool situated a couple of steps outside his bedroom door, Ernie stretched out on his bed with the phone propped up to his ear, the television always on in the background and a cigarette dangling from his mouth. In between calls he churned out press releases for the WWF.

Each day we drove over to Vince, Sr.'s home in a neighboring waterfront community to pick up Senior's mail. Ernie sorted the parcels and forwarded Vince's personal correspondence to his summer home in Maryland.

He loved for me to prepare dinner during these stays. Ernie would send me around the corner to Smitty's Butcher Shoppe where I picked up the groceries for that evening's meal. While I cooked, Ernie entertained me with stories about performers who had inspired him. One such talent was early 1900's vaudeville and nightclub singer, Sophie Tucker. He admired her professionalism and perseverance. He was impressed by her skill at self-promoting. Whenever Sophie Tucker was booked to play the Canton area, she dropped Ernie a line so that he knew in advance that she was coming to town.

He showed me a an old, discolored postcard that simply said something like, "Look out for me. I'm coming your way with a brand-new show. New songs. New clothes. Don't miss it! Love ya, Soph." During World War II, Ernie was stationed in the Orient where he bought her bolts of satin fabric (a scarce commodity during the war), which Sophie used to line her performance gowns.

Ernie was the first to trust me with an insider's view of pro wrestling. He fondly spoke of the McMahons as his family. He told me many stories of the plans that Vince, Sr. was making for Vinnie to one day succeed him. And just as Vince, Sr. was grooming Vinnie to take over The WWF by promoting towns in the northern part of his territory, Junior likewise was

This rare, backstage picture of The Grand Wizard out of character and a 29-year-old Vince McMahon, Jr. shows that despite Senior's reluctance to allow his son decision making power, Ernie looked upon "his boy" with fondness. He was confident that Junior would one day be successful.

preparing his teenage son, Shane, for the future.

About this time, Vinnie bought The Cape Cod Coliseum in Massachusetts, where he set up his base of operations. In the same way that Senior insisted that Junior learn every aspect of the business from the bottom up, Junior sometimes drove Shane to the Coliseum late at night to work with the clean up crew after the concert crowds had gone home. This was yet another sign that the foundation was being laid for the McMahons' to reign over the first and most dominant national wrestling promotion ever in the United States.

Chapter Five
"The Ladder Of Fame Match"

A lot of people who don't have it, lust after fame . . . People don't relate to you as the person you are, but to a myth they believe you are, and the myth is always wrong. You are scorned or loved for mythic reasons that, once given a life, like zombies that stalk you from the grave, live forever.
Marlon Brandon, "Brando, Songs My Mother Taught Me."

Following my inauspicious debut on *Championship Wrestling*, fans along the wrestling circuit perceived me in a strikingly different light. Instead of seeing me as a hapless, but determined kid, trying to be a part of the show, TV had turned me into a celebrity who added an importance to all of the live events where I announced. It was just as Monsoon had anticipated when he put me on TV. People began to ask for my autograph. Some even brought me gifts. Those, who wouldn't give me the time of day before, now wanted to buy me a Rolex. They judged me based on just twenty seconds of airtime every week. I could have been the most despicable ingrate on earth. It didn't matter. I was rubbing elbows with their TV wrestling heroes for which they thought I earned great sums of money. If they only knew that my price tag was just $21.67 per TV show!

With time, my identification with the WWWF spread to the general public. Whether I was shopping, out to a movie or walking down Theater Row in New York City, people regularly stopped to ask about the show and inquire about the wrestlers. The routine remained the same. After hesitating momentarily, they first approached to confirm that I was indeed Gary Michael Cappetta. Once convinced, my curious inquisitors invariably asked, "What are you doing *here*?". I always took that question to mean that they knew where I was supposed to be and wherever we were wasn't it. As if I spent the week in their TV sets and with a touch of the remote control, I'd spring into action every Saturday night. During my first year on the WWWF broadcast, I enjoyed the attention. But after the unhealthy attraction of a fan one year later, I would forever tread carefully when approached by strangers. I learned early in my career that this wonderful opportunity could indeed become very dangerous.

After an event in West Orange, New Jersey, I was signing autographs for a few of the youngsters at ringside, when I noticed a young woman waiting on the fringe of the crowd. As I made my way back to the dressing room, she sidestepped in front of me and Esther, as I came to call her, eyeballed me face to face. After a few uncomfortable moments, I stepped to the right and she followed. A couple of steps to the left and we were still nose to nose. Since ballroom dancing was not my forté, I thought it would be best to find out what she wanted so I could waltz back to the dressing room as quickly as possible.

"Did you enjoy the show?"

My attempt at small talk was met with giggles. No words, just giggles. So I continued.

"Well, this is always a good crowd. The show's usually better when the fans are enjoying themselves." The monologue continued pointlessly until finally I blurted out, "Can I do anything for you?"

She appeared stunned at my expectation that a successful dialogue takes teamwork.

"I think so," she tittered timidly. "I think I'd like to start a fan club."

"That's great. What kind of a fan club?"

"A fan club for you."

She gazed at me longingly like a kid asking for two bucks in advance of her allowance. I was stunned.

"What do you mean?" was the only thing I could say to what I thought I had heard.

"I'm going to start The Gary Michael Cappetta Fan Club."

Suddenly she switched from what she'd *like* to do to what she *was going* to do. The first thought that came into my mind came out of my mouth.

"Who would join a club for *me*?"

"I've been talking to people at ringside and a lot of them are interested."

It was 1977, a time when fan clubs for wrestlers were commonplace, but an organization to honor a ring announcer was unprecedented. No one ever noticed the ring announcers. Our role was an expected formality, which, until The Animal and I collided, added little to a wrestling event other than to introduce the performers.

So I shied away from the idea as being improbable until months later when Esther resurfaced at many of the New York area WWWF events. She renewed her unrelenting requests for my permission to form the club. But now, she was a little more forceful. Each time, she embellished her sales pitch with different ways that a fan club could be beneficial, always emphasizing that there was no down side to her idea. Eventually, her words began to stick with me until I seriously considered the possibilities.

"There's nothing to lose," I thought to myself. "If it turns out to be a bad idea, it'll just die a natural death." At the time, I had no idea how prophetic those words would be.

Despite my anxiety that being the honoree of a fan club could make me the laughingstock of the wrestling world, my ego gave way to better judgment and ultimately, I agreed to endorse the project. My naiveté prevented the healthy skepticism that someone more worldly than myself would have had.

As soon as I gave her my blessing, Esther quickly began to enlist young and old alike from every corner of McMahon's territory. For a nominal fee, each member received a monthly, state-of-the-art fan club bulletin. In no time, Gary Michael Cappetta T-shirts, photo buttons and mugs became available.

Would you believe Davy O'Hannon vs Gary Cappetta?

News of the club hit pro wrestling periodicals, bringing an immediate and positive reaction:

Our good friend Esther _____, President of the GARY CAPPETTA FAN CLUB, tells us that membership is increasing by leaps and bounds. And it's no wonder. It's a great bulletin -- professionally printed and chock full of current stories and news -- for a great honorary, ring announcer GARY CAPPETTA ..... This club is first-class all the way, and has RASSLIN' WONDERS strongest endorsement.

**Mike Omansky,
RASSLIN WONDERS 1978-1979 ANNUAL**

And there was more . . .

58

Bodyslams!

He is not a wrestler, manager or even a referee, however, he happens to be one of the most popular wrestling personalities in the World Wide Wrestling Federation. He is Gary Michael Cappetta, the official ring announcer of the WWWF television tapes. Gary happens to be an ex-writer for Ring Wrestling. The bulletin for the club is called The Magical Microphone. Professionally printed, this publication is filled with stories not only on Gary, but various wrestling personalities. Photos fill the pages of the bulletin which sells for 75 cents an issue or $3.50 a year. Members receive photos, membership card and periodic bulletins. Esther ____ is the president of the fan club and is really a sincere fan.

Tom Burke RING WRESTLING, April 1978

"Wow, he's talking about *me*! Just a few years ago, I wrote for that magazine. Now they're writing about me!"

On December 10, 1977, due largely to Esther's lobbying efforts, I was named announcer of the year at the New York City Wrestling Fans Convention. Then The Wrestling Fans International Convention named the Gary Cappetta Fan Club "Rookie Fan Club of the Year" and *The Magical Microphone* was named bulletin of the year for as long as Esther presided. Reporters began calling for interviews. Hosts of radio sports shows invited me to field questions from callers. Two page profiles were printed in national wrestling magazines. The attention that I received was unprecedented for a ring announcer. One headline read: "The 'Magic Microphone', Gary Cappetta: Inside the Voice of Wrestling". Here's an excerpt from the introduction of that article illustrating the attention that Esther's one woman publicity campaign had initiated.

There are many ring announcers in the United States - literally hundreds upon hundreds. But other than a select few, like Jimmy Lennon, in Los Angeles, very few are known, remembered, and sought after by fans and promoters alike.

The most recent entry into this special, elite circle is the youthful Gary Cappetta, who beams into the living rooms weekly as announcer for CHAMPIONSHIP WRESTLING. And when you talk to Gary Cappetta, there's just no wonder as to why he has captured the imagination of so many rooters of the squared circle.

Gary Cappetta is now recognized by millions of viewers as his weekly announcing is seen across the Northeast, from Bangor, Maine, to Washington, D.C., and from New York to Baltimore. His live appearances have taken him from New York to Pittsburgh, and he has appeared in over 200 arenas, always complete with carnation and bow tie.

And, no doubt, those fans who do have the opportunity to meet Gary Cappetta will find him to be as happy, knowledgeable, and congenial as we found this great young ring announcer to be!

Mike Omansky, WRESTLING REVUE, June 1980

It was an exciting time. It seemed as if my notoriety had skyrocketed overnight. The Pope, in his infinite wisdom, never hired a public relations team that could hold a candle to Esther's single-minded crusade. She labored nonstop as would a religious fanatic in the name of St. Gary Michael. The steaming presses never stopped rolling. Center this headline and justify the margins. Enlarge this picture by 25%, shrink that one by 52%. Her unending use of copy machines may have been the reason that 24-hour copy centers were invented.

All signs indicated that her campaign to familiarize the wrestling public with my work was successful. But little by little, I began to hear stories that just didn't add up. Esther booked personal appearances that I knew nothing about. I was told of times when she claimed that I was with her when I wasn't. Before I knew it, more stories, horror stories, surfaced among the club members. Eventually, there were allegations that Esther began soliciting money from fans beyond regular membership dues. Before I could make sense of it all, troubling reports emerged that female club members were receiving threatening letters and obscene phone assaults from a mysteriously disguised caller.

When I questioned Esther about these rumors, she brushed them off as gossip and skillfully swayed the conversation elsewhere. She only worried about the damaging effect that such rumors could have on enlisting more fans. When I told her that I was more concerned for the well being of our terrified club members, Esther quickly

SHE LIKES GARY

I wanted to write to you about your article on that fine-looking young man, Gary Cappetta (June 1980 Wrestling Revue). I watch Gary here on T.V. each week as he announces the best wrestlers that I have ever seen.

It was very interesting to see another side of a man involved with a rough sport like wrestling. Gary's interests in music, theatre, and the Spanish language go to show how diverse people invilved with this sport can actually be.
Mrs. J. L. Hughes
Boston, Mass.

changed the subject, bemoaning the countless illnesses from which she suffered. She had begun wrapping her legs with gauze and ace bandages to treat what she referred to as a rare skin condition. Addressing the threats that upset club members proved futile.

Finally, what should have been obvious much sooner became crystal-clear when people began to congratulate me on my recent engagement to Esther! I was shocked and then outraged to learn that it was my fan club president who was jubilantly spreading these absurd lies about our supposed union.

Quickly moving to distance myself from the monster that I had empowered, I informed her that our collaboration had to end immediately. Expecting hysteria from my unpredictable "fiancée", I was instead struck by her dreamy gaze upon hearing the news. Esther was lost in an eerily hollow stupor. But if I thought that I had put this dangerous chapter behind me, once again, I was naively mistaken.

For several months following Esther's ouster, she continued to show up at all of my public appearances. While everyone's attention was on the mid ring action, her piercing eyes never left me. With a fixed angry glare, her eyes all but singed the velvet from my oversized bow tie. She began to dress in black and wore dark tinted eyeglasses. Somehow, she was always able to secure first row tickets, which were strategically positioned across the ring from the announcer's table. So we sat face to face, night after night. If her bizarre behavior was intended to scare the hell out of me, she was doing just fine.

The last time that Esther was seen at a wrestling event was in Asbury Park, twenty miles from my home. She was bound in somber black from head to toe like a bitter widow attending the funeral of her backstabbing bridegroom. She floated through the crowd, self-absorbed in the forbidding fog of a far off planet.

As was customary, I went out for a quick snack with a few friends after the Asbury show and then headed directly home. Turning onto the street where I lived, I noticed a shimmering ball of light on my front lawn. As my car rolled up to the curb, a crackling bon fire spit charred embers in all directions. My heart began to pound with the force of a vicious Chief Jay Strongbow tomahawk chop. I flew out of the car and trounced the simmering embers like the Chief on a warpath. As the flames slowly died down, I could see scorched remnants of club newsletters, press clips and publicity photos. Something, which started so innocently, had spun so far out of control.

The last time I heard from Esther was perhaps the most bizarre. She sent a letter to me with a warning about the evil that lived within the soul of Gary Michael Cappetta. She never addressed her comments to me directly, but instead talked *about* me, as if she was alerting a third party about the treacherous Gary Cappetta. She signed the letter, "Esther Navalek of the Philippine Islands".

Esther never surfaced on the wrestling scene again. Like a misguided meteor, she vanished in a ball of fire.

Sadly, Esther's mental and physical ailments ultimately led to her early death. It wasn't until much later that I discovered the extent of her illnesses. The bandages that covered her legs concealed self-inflicted pencil point wounds resulting in recurring cases of lead poisoning. When her body was discovered, well after her tenure as president had ended, authorities found a shrine to the fan club in the corner of her bedroom. It was adorned with fan club memorabilia surrounding photos that documented my announcing career. Her bedroom walls were covered with writing samples, including my signature, where she perfected her skill of forgery to disguise bogus letters and to sign unauthorized checks.

It was now clear to me that the purpose of Esther's work was to win my attention and approval. When her efforts failed to be rewarded with my affection, she became intent on distancing me from all others. If she couldn't claim me for her own, then nobody would. Anyone who stood in the way of Esther's fantasy relationship with me was at risk. It was all very sad.

B ack in the arenas, there continued to be a buzz about the TV attack that I had survived some time ago at the hands of The Animal. Following my embarrassing experience of being flattened in center ring on national television, I remained cautious of George. Some nights I was as fearful of the hairy beast as were the paying customers. Uneducated to the inner workings of the business, I was still a "mark" as we'd say in wrestling. From the day that our televised confrontation aired, whenever George entered the ring, at live shows or on TV, he wildly chased me into the crowd. In my search for safety, I'd wind up in the fourth row, sometimes I'd scramble up to the balcony and one night I even found myself at the hot dog stand. The people loved it. For the first time in the

WWWF, a ring announcer was actively involved in putting over a wrestler's persona. Never before had a wrestling pitchman added to the entertainment value of a live wrestling show on a nightly basis. While George only appeared on the scene during his summer months away from teaching, the image of our constant cat and mouse game stayed vivid in the minds of the fans throughout the year.

I n the late seventies, my home base shifted from the dingy Philadelphia Arena to the newly constructed Spectrum. The WWWF was more popular than ever before. Our monthly shows at the Spectrum regularly sold out. In 1977, the marquee match between Superstar Billy Graham and Bruno Sammartino attracted 19,500 fans three months in a row. The WWWF was not only outdrawing the 76ers and the Flyers in Philadelphia, but wrestling became a trendy night out all over Vince, Sr.'s northeastern United States territory. It was commonplace to see sports stars like Dr. J., Julius Erving in the VIP section with their children. Everyone wanted to be a part of the action.

The most exciting series that I ever announced was
Sammartino vs Graham,
The Philadelphia Spectrum, Sept. 17, 1977

Through my monthly appearances at the Spectrum, I became friendly with the building's administrators. Often serving as the contact person between the Spectrum publicity department and the WWWF, I was offered easy access to all Philadelphia theatrical events. Whether it was The Academy of Music, The Shubert Theatre or The Spectrum, choice seats were just a phone call away. Even if the show had sold out, additional seats were set up for my guests and me. I never deceived myself into believing that these privileges were warranted. I simply considered these perks as added compensation to the modest $65.00 that the McMahons had determined was a fair wage for these events which grossed more than $250,000 a night. I wasn't getting rich, but I was having a great time. From tripping into the wrestling scene only three years earlier, I was now hobnobbing with Philadelphia's entertainment and sports hierarchy.

The valuable training that I received during my eleven years with the WWWF came about by stumbling into the spotlight on a whim, completely unaware of its inevitable rewards and hazards. Oblivious to the extent to which I was sharpening my ring announce skills and defining a performing persona, I unwittingly developed a presence far more important than the announcing for which I was hired. I became a credible spokesman with whom the paying customer identified. The fans witnessed my slow progress over the years. They lived through my public predicaments, empathizing with me as I was harassed by The Animal and in later years by Jimmy Snuka, and together we formed a bond of trust. But it was never a calculated process. My center ring talent and my behind the scenes camaraderie with the wrestlers grew gradually and free from any plan or design to carve out a long-lasting career. The communication skills that I learned so well were not studied. It was a process of learning by doing and the rest was acquired through osmosis. I was beginning to understand how the game was played and to recognize how my role could best enhance the wrestling characters who were responsible for drawing people to the box office. The rest came naturally.

I learned that most matches are just loosely outlined, with just a few high spots planned before hand. Only the chain of events leading up to the bout's conclusion and any event along the way, which lends logic to the finish, are carved in stone. For instance, if a wrestler is to submit to his opponent's back breaker, it makes sense that throughout the match, his back becomes a target leading up to the finishing hold. Aside from the wrestlers' signature moves, along with a tone and a pace that fits whatever history exists between the two, the wrestlers talk their way through the match as it unfolds. The best workers craft their matches based on the response of the fans.

The referee follows the wrestlers through their unspecific plan, careful to be on hand when it counts and looking elsewhere when necessary. The ring announcer's words are fixed, but his demeanor is unrestricted.

Each is afforded ample freedom to make choices that should reinforce the personas of fellow performers and achieve the desired effect through the finish of the match. The effectiveness of every bout is often determined by how well you can think on your feet.

It is within this framework that certain rules, and they're only my rules, will make the difference between capturing the audience's attention and creating a crushing stampede to the souvenir stand. My recommended guidelines can never be comprehensively recorded in a textbook. Aside from the intangible of natural talent, three basic practices serve as a starting point to believability. While some are easily defined, most are implied. Beyond inborn ability, my blueprint for a successful ring career starts with logic, camaraderie and respect.

The first simple principle from which all others flow: use logic. With every movement, by every facial expression and through every word, use logic. It may sound easy, but when tens of thousands are watching your every move, listening to your every word and inflection, there is a natural tendency to overact, overreact and overstate. The fans cannot be fooled. People are keenly aware of both the genuineness of a performer and a genuine performance. They are two very different, but equally significant qualities.

Early in my career, I was fortunate to actually feel fear in the face of George Steele. At the time, I didn't have the skills to feign terror. If I had pretended to be frightened, the audience would have seen through the schtick. It would have come across as a cheap attempt to attract attention, which most certainly would have been met with distrust for all else that I portrayed in the future. In years to come, after smartening up to the game, I drew on those feelings of fear. Whether I came face to face with Bruiser Brody, Jimmy Snuka, Stan Hansen or Abdullah the Butcher, I allowed myself to relive the anxiety that I felt years earlier with "The Animal". And then it seemed genuine.

As an announcer, another genuine feeling that I never overcame was my passion for the art of pro wrestling and my respect for the extraordinary skills of the sport's top athletes. I never lost sight of the talent possessed by the many performers who risk their physical well being to excite and to dazzle.

It is unfortunate that much of the public never seems to recognize the superior athleticism of pro wrestling's elite. These men are the most underrated athletes in the world. They offer the total package of physical conditioning, strength, agility and endurance. They execute amazing athletic feats, which most other pro athletes would never dare to attempt. And yet, because pro wrestling is not a true competition, the skills of the top workers in the sport are often overlooked.

My part was to lend seriousness, an importance to these men's abilities in the midst of a circus-like atmosphere. Even my most cynical detractors recognized that I never took the opportunity to work beside wrestling's greatest workers for granted. I never undersold their performances and I gave my best effort every time I stepped into the ring. And that speaks to the second principle: the camaraderie necessary to pull it all together.

Everyone should be working in unison to carry out what the booker needs to accomplish in each match. Camaraderie among the performers is essential. Everyone should be striving to carry out the booker's master plan.

When a match falls short of producing the required results, sometimes it is a personal issue between the participants that is to blame. A fellow performer can undermine so much of what goes on in the ring. It is not uncommon for the outcasts of the troupe to find themselves and their performance diminished by his opponents' carefully timed action, inaction or inappropriate smirk to the crowd. It is most damaging of all to find the guys you're working with to be unresponsive to what you are trying to accomplish. The veterans know all of the underhanded ploys better than anyone. It is therefore equally important to respect the seasoned pros while developing an understanding for the rookies. And that brings us to the third principle: respect. Respect for your fellow performers and respect for the art of the game.

When the guys recognized the respect I paid to them and the appreciation I showed for their craft through the way my work enhanced their believability, we began to develop a different kind of relationship. A new level of mutual admiration, sometimes unspoken, but exhibited in so many implied manners. Both inside and outside of the ring our shared respect inspired us to watch out for each other.

So beyond one's natural talent, the three principles upon which I believe a successful pro wrestling career is built are logic, camaraderie and respect. And if you can stay out of trouble while developing some solid political contacts, then you surely will be on your way to stardom.

Chapter Six
"Beat The Champ"

As for me, I felt a change in myself - more confidence, more energy, a greater sense of direction. When an audience laughed, I felt fulfilled. It was a sign of approval, of being accepted - it was nourishment. The more I heard, the more I needed. There was never enough.

Neil Simon, "Rewrites, A Memoir"

The wrestlers, who for six years had censored their every word within earshot of this rookie announcer, were finally beginning to let down their guard. The cryptic vocabulary and cautious glances that the brotherhood used to cover up the family gossip when I was nearby gradually dwindled. My acceptance began with early signals, so gradual, so subtle, that you'd have to study the scene from a distance to notice. The boys became less cautious when telling colorful tales about their escapades, the likes of which had never before been uttered in my presence. Little by little, they began venting their frustrations about the business side of wrestling with thinly veiled criticisms of the WWWF's leadership. Now, Gino gave me my upcoming bookings by unceremoniously tossing over his big black bible of secrets, without worry that I'd leak upcoming title changes to outsiders. Each step was a signal that it was safe to carry on unguarded conversations "if Cappetta is in the room". When the coded messages ceased, I knew that I had gained the trust of my fellow performers. Regardless of how connected I had been perceived by the public during my early years on television, my evolution into a self-assured performer was now finally complete. In this era when baby faces and heels were forbidden from socializing in public, when the business was protected at all costs, my role was transformed from gate crasher to gate keeper.

While I was gaining a level of intimacy with the wrestlers, my distant relationship with the McMahons, who never encouraged or even acknowledged the public notoriety that I enjoyed, remained unchanged. Except for my pleasant, on-going rapport with Monsoon, the McMahons' continued their indifferent, impersonal style of management to keep everyone insecure. At first I thought the cold shoulder was reserved for supporting players like me. But it soon became clear, as I gained the confidence of both the headliners and the preliminary talent alike, that *everyone* was kept at arm's length, off-balance and ultimately intimidated.

The McMahons controlled the future of all locally based wrestling talent. For part-time performers who lived in the Northeast, the WWWF was the only wrestling promotion where one could work. The touring wrestlers, who weren't confined to the New York based territory, watched their step for fear of McMahon's power to blacklist them in other promotions across the country. It was customary that whenever a boss considered one of his wrestlers "uncooperative", a simple phone call to his fellow promoters dried up the "troublemaker's" work everywhere and, in effect, put him out of business. The result of the owners' united front rendered their workers defenseless in a climate in which you dare not question pay-offs, performance schedules or working conditions. If you think that The Undertaker's spine-jarring choke slam is an effective finishing maneuver, you'd be mightily impressed with the way in which wrestler after wrestler's backbone was weakened by the promoters' strangle hold over their performers.

The monopolistic maneuvering that wrestling's power brokers flaunted in the faces of their athletes had existed for decades. This practice was addressed in the autobiographies of two respected former world champions.

B runo Sammartino led the WWWF through two extraordinary title reigns as Vince, Sr.'s champion. He was the cornerstone of McMahon's empire for more than eleven consistently successful years. Back then, Bruno sold out Madison Square Garden more times than any other headliner in the history of the storied building. Not for just wrestling events, for *all* events.

"The Living Legend", as he became known, was the reason that many kids like myself became lifelong fans of pro wrestling. Without Bruno, the WWWF would have been just another wrestling territory. But he *made* the WWWF. He *was* The Federation. You would think that the long relationship between the McMahons and Sammartino was a match made in heaven. But there was always one nagging problem. Bruno possessed a personal trait that Vince, Sr. tried to correct early on, but for once, McMahon was unsuccessful. One character flaw that both father and son begrudgingly tolerated in their franchise player in order to keep him in the fold; in order to keep millions of faithful fans filling the arenas year after year. Sammartino, a man of principle, was never afraid to speak out when he thought the McMahons' grip on him had become too tight. True to the classic Tinsletown struggle between an entertainment mogul's attempt to control and a superstar's self-determination, the stage was set for a heated tussle. It was a struggle, which spurred intense resentment from both sides that existed to the day of Bruno's bitter departure and to the present.

Bruno learned about McMahon's game of manipulation years before reaching headline status. Dating back to his first months in pro wrestling, the rookie Sammartino fell victim to what I like to call the McMahons' "in-Vince-ible" vengeance. In his

Bruno's emotional connection to his fans was the reason that McMahon's business thrived for many years.

1990 autobiography, Sammartino writes about his introduction to the wrath of Senior thirty years earlier, in an otherwise guarded account of his legendary career

As I mentioned before, McMahon held a grudge against me for leaving him and going with Kola Kwariani. When things didn't work out with Kwariani, McMahon had reluctantly agreed to put me back on his roster. The catch was that I only worked the curtain opener. He made me into the opening match against the worst opponents and always in the smallest club. Then even these miserable dates would be spread so far apart that I couldn't make a living.

With bills mounting and finding it increasingly difficult to support his wife and newborn son, David, Sammartino gave McMahon notice that he had found work elsewhere. After fulfilling his remaining WWWF obligations, Bruno moved on to wrestle in San Francisco. Sammartino continues.

"It was at that point that McMahon decided that Capitol Wrestling (the corporate name of the WWWF) was going to teach this 'young wop' a lesson.

"What McMahon did was book me in Baltimore for a match and then just didn't tell me about it. When I finished my two remaining matches in Pittsburgh and left for the Coast, to the best of my knowledge I was through with Capitol.

"Of course, I didn't show up in Baltimore. I didn't know about the match. McMahon then contacted the Commission and asked them to take disciplinary (action) against this punk Sammartino."

The effect of McMahon's tampering was to render Sammartino unemployable. When Bruno arrived in San Francisco, California commission representatives informed him that he was suspended for not appearing on a Maryland card about which he knew nothing. You see, if promoters weren't able to convince their fellow owners to freeze a wrestler out of work, many of the state athletic commissioners were readily available to do the dirty work. Commissions from state to state worked together. You'll never find these arrangements in their by-laws, but it happened all the time.

"And I'm sure the Commission listened well to what McMahon had to say . . . especially since they were being taken care of by the promoters.

"I don't know what the Commission members are like today, but in those days, as far as I'm concerned, they were corrupt, corrupt, corrupt. Look at my suspension. It was an illegal suspension. Before they can suspend you, you must be given a hearing where evidence is presented. You have to be given a chance to defend yourself against your accusers. You can't just be blackballed like I was. They had suspended me with no explanation . . . no reason. I never received a notice detailing the charges. I was never given the chance to appeal."

If these tactics strike you as illegal, you're right. But with the cozy arrangements among owners, between owners and commissions, and among commissions from state to state, wrestlers didn't have a fighting chance. If you were to assemble all of the parties and ask them about their underhanded practices, they would act as if they had all fallen under the spell of one giant sleeper hold.

In his autobiography, "Hooker", six time NWA champ Lou Thesz addressed similar occurrences throughout the United States in the 1950's. Thesz's career spanned six decades with his last match taking place in December of 1990 at the age of seventy-four.

"By 1956, a total of 38 promoters belonged to the organization, effectively giving the NWA, of which the WWWF (McMahon) was a member, control over virtually every wrestler in North America and Mexico [sic].

"Essentially, what the NWA founders agreed to do was share talent within the Alliance and withhold them from rival promoters in their territories. They also agreed to respect each other's territorial boundaries and to actively police the industry by blacklisting any wrestler who did 'anything detrimental to wrestling'. It was those three points that eventually got the NWA in serious trouble during the mid-1950's with the US Justice Department. The blacklisting provision, for instance, was obviously designed as a means of keeping the boys in line; it usually came into play when a wrestler had the gall to complain about poor payoffs or to wrestle for a promoter who was in competition with an NWA member. The feds ruled the NWA was engaging in illegal restraint of trade, and the case would have gone to court, with all kinds of embarrassing disclosures resulting, if the Alliance members hadn't signed a consent order, agreeing to eliminate those illegal bylaws. Of course, being wrestling promoters, some of the Alliance members resumed their old practices as soon as the feds lost interest in the case."

Sammartino's scuffle with Vince, Sr. five years later corroborates Thesz's claim.

Naturally, like everyone else who valued his job, I fell in line in order to preserve my position. It was reasonable to assume that with the threat of the top wrestlers' careers being off-handedly sabotaged, that anything a supporting player like myself did to fall out of favor; anything which could be interpreted as uncooperative, would surely ban me from the profession that I valued so much.

By the end of the decade pro wrestling was beginning to undergo a facelift. In April of 1979, McMahon shortened the name of The World Wide Wrestling Federation to the more manageable World Wrestling Federation. In addition, by loaning their wrestlers to promoters of other territories for single shot appearances, the allied owners finally began using their influence constructively. Vince, Sr. began sending his top performers to wrestle outside of the WWF while frequently booking talent from other territories to appear on his monthly cards at Madison Square Garden.

Although I was never fool enough to believe that my presence on a card sold a single ticket, I continued to cultivate a loyal following among the paying customers. As a familiar figure, I provided a comfort, continuity, air of importance and seriousness to the show. I developed many friendships along the way not, only with fans, but also with the people who covered wrestling for the trade magazines. Bill Apter, Frank Amato, Georgiann Makropoulos, George Napolitano, Mike Omansky and Paul Heyman, who went on to make his mark as a manager and then promoter of Extreme Championship Wrestling, were always friendly faces up and down the WWF circuit

In the dressing rooms and makeshift offices in arenas throughout the territory I maintained a quiet presence. I'd speak only when spoken to, otherwise I minded my own business and never took part in the routine locker room horseplay. There has always been a distinction between wrestler and non-wrestler. Always a different set of rules, a different standard allowed to one of their own. Unless you've wrestled, never believe that you'll ever enjoy 100% confidence. It was therefore a source of great fulfillment to have gained such a level acceptance.

While I was seen as the most dispensable and the least connected of the group, I was the safest target of the ribs that the guys routinely played on one another. But luckily, I was rarely the foil of their pranks. I suppose that my understated presence and outward actions fit into the boys' definition of what it means to be a professional. I gained their respect. They knew that my heart was into making a contribution to the show, so the more powerful guys, both in pecking order and in street toughness, had the tendency to protect me.

To some I became a safe haven when things weren't going well on the road or at home. They began to approach me with stories and concerns, both professional and personal. I learned more from listening, than you could ever imagine. Aside from the performers' condemnation of the insensitive treatment they received from management, it was during the quiet, behind the scenes discussions that the wrestlers' veil of unity unraveled.

Inside of the brotherhood, with enormous egos and considerable payoffs at stake, there are bound to be family feuds. But ongoing grudges are rarely carried into the ring. Since you could be matched with any other individual on any given night, it would be foolish to antagonize the guy who might some day be entrusted with your physical well being. You don't want to "feed" yourself into the arms of an opponent who at will, can easily toss you head first into the ringside fans. You want to feel confident that you'll receive protection when he's in control of your body. The dangerous nature of the athletic feats performed in the ring demands cooperation between performers to maintain a certain level of safety during a match. The need to get along guarantees more peace behind the scenes then you might expect.

Nevertheless, I began to see how even inside of the tight-knit wrestling brotherhood, the performers segregated themselves into a number of smaller sects. When I worked at the TV tapings, the wrestlers on the inside track separated themselves from the TV jobbers who, although were often more talented than the headliners, had the unenviable job of putting over the established players in convincing fashion. The stars had the run of the communal locker room, while the struggling journeymen withdrew to its remote corners awaiting their assignments for the evening.

Another division was between the more serious guys who conducted themselves in a friendly, but business-like manner as opposed to the carefree carousers and partygoers who were forever joking, scamming and ribbing each other.

The professionals often expressed their embarrassment by the shameless behavior of a few of their co-workers who habitually demeaned the preliminary performers. On any given night in the late '70's and early '80's, there were undertones of dissent caused by the over blown ego of "Polish Power" Ivan Putski and the wicked humor of Mr. Fuji. For whatever their reason, they felt the necessity to humiliate the powerless undercard wrestlers simply because they could get away with it. Since both had achieved a certain level of success and therefore favor with the front office, they were protected and consequently spared any retaliation from their offended victims.

But as berating as they could be to each other, there was no greater disdain than for fellow wrestlers who undermined the covenant of the community. The deep-rooted loyalty among the boys allowed no tolerance for traitors in the ranks. Spies and stooges, thieves and performers that undermined the work of others often became the target of ruthless ambushes, both physical and political.

The anti-social behavior of the Putskis and Fujis was not representative of the majority of the WWF wrestlers who were there to make a living in a game that they loved. Most had no axes to grind and no need to impress. Away from home for weeks at a time, they were more interested in the real world that they had left behind. And that's what I represented behind the scenes, the real world. The fellows, who managed to keep a level head in the midst of their vagabond existence, resisting the temptation of drugs and easy sex, welcomed the normalcy that I brought to the locker room. They were the individuals that gravitated to me.

One of the WWF athletes that I most respected was Tony Garea. Combining the carpentry skills that he learned in his native New Zealand with his flair for real estate, Garea's astute business sense led him to the property resale market. During his run as co-holder of the WWF tag team championship from 1973 to 1981 with partners that included Haystacks Calhoun, Dean Ho, Larry Zbyszko and Rick Martel, his focus reached beyond the insecurity of wrestling. Garea bought run down houses, fixed them up and sold them for a healthy profit. He understood that the short-lived money-producing span of a wrestler's

Garea won the WWF tag team belts with his 601-pound partner, Haystacks Calhoun in Hamburg, Pa. May 30, 1973. Tony held the tag championship five times with four different partners.

career can be cut back even further by circumstances over which he has no control. If a missed step in the ring leads to an injurious fall, that night's paycheck could be his last. If he's out of step with the promoters, that paycheck might never come. With no medical benefits or retirement plans offered to any of the wrestlers, Tony wisely prepared for his future.

When I was ready to buy my first house, Garea's advice was of great help. When I finally decided on an income producing beach house, Tony gave his approval as he was among the first to visit. Although he's now retired from wrestling, Garea stays close to the business through his role as a WWF road agent.

Gorilla Monsoon is the one person most responsible for my start in pro wrestling. Gino was the first to hire me, he was the first to put me on TV, and most importantly, he was the first to show that I was valued as an individual and not just for what I contributed to the show.

One rainy night, I found myself with Monsoon in the back of a cab after a big show at Madison Square Garden. My ears were still ringing from the clamor of the crowd as the taxi sped across the rain swept streets of New York City. Gino began to make small talk until he realized that I wasn't tuned in to what he was saying. Gazing through the taxi's water streaked window, I was hypnotized by the bright neon lights of Broadway. Feeling the absence of his audience, he casually looked over.

"What's the matter?" he prodded.

"Nothing's the matter. Why do ya ask?"

"Because you haven't heard a word I've said. Is it that girl?"

"Gino, I told you that everything's okay. I took care of things."

"Are you still worrying about her?" Gino just wasn't going to give up.

"No, that's not it."

"Then why are you acting strange? What is it?"

Unable to conceal my nervousness, I gave in.

"Gino, where are we going?"

"We're going to dinner. What's your problem with that?"

"I don't know if this is a good idea. I don't have much money on me."

"*That's* what's bothering you? Forget about it. You're not going to need money. The old man will pick up the tab. You just go and smile and eat and drink. There's nothing to worry about." He chuckled a little, then added, "Hell, wouldn't matter how much money you had in your pocket. You wouldn't be able to get in this place on your own anyway."

After every monthly Garden event Vince, Sr. invited his top operatives to Jimmy Weston's, a trendy club on the Upper East Side of Manhattan, for a feast at the boss' expense. We were on our way to dinner with the upper echelon of the WWWF and this twenty-six year old rookie was feeling intimidated. Monsoon's well-intended words didn't help any as the cab glided up to Jimmy Weston's canopied entranceway where a uniformed doorman waited attentively to usher us inside. Gino leaned over with his final words of encouragement.

"It'll be okay. Just follow me."

As soon as we entered the swank eatery, Vince, Sr. called Gino over to the other side of the room. Following Monsoon's advice, I trailed closely behind until Senior waved me away with a polite, but firm gesture. "Excuse us. This will only take a minute." Suddenly, I was forced to focus on Vince's dinner guests. The next sixty seconds felt like an eternity.

It was a particularly important night. Vince, Sr. was hosting a contingent of promoters who flew in from Japan to see the show. Although these special occasions were customarily off limits to the wrestlers, Bob Backlund, Vince's world champion at the time, was there along with the Asian contingent's top wrestler. Vince, Jr., his wife, Linda and Willie Gilzenberg were also along with Vince's promotional partners, Arnold Skaaland, his wife Betty and Angelo Savoldi who were already cracking crab claws at the long, formal banquet table.

As I approached the party no one looked up, no one said hello. The frolicking conversation continued before me. I didn't know where I was expected to sit. I didn't even know if I would be *allowed* to sit. I was lost and it must have been obvious. Monsoon never told me that one half of the guests didn't have a working knowledge of the English language and the other half seemed to be ignorant of the basic rules of etiquette.

Maureen, Gino's wife, picked up on my predicament, called me over and invited me to join her. For the rest of the evening she did her best to make me feel comfortable. I was grateful beyond words for her kindness.

The consideration that Maureen showed me that night along with the times that Gino invited me to join the guys at his house enriched me in ways that a huge paycheck could not. Their friendship meant more to this rookie than they could have known. Their hospitality more than overcame the inferiority that was instilled in me by the aloof McMahons. Without Gino's encouragement, I might have been driven out of the wrestling business before I had a chance to prove myself. And you can't put a price on that.

A unique by-product of my involvement in pro wrestling has been the opportunity to befriend stars whose luster shined far beyond the bounds of the squared circle. Andre the Giant was such a celebrity.

One of the good-natured of the lot, Andre, billed at seven feet, four inches, with a weight of four hundred and seventy-five pounds, was featured in many movies and TV shows. The stories of Andre's eating and drinking habits are legendary. His ability to put away enormous amounts of food and beverage has been the topic of many a locker room tale. He delighted in my gullible nature with stories that started off sounding like real life experiences, but concluded with an "I gotcha" kind of punch line. In his early years, Andre was rare beyond his size due to his impressive agility and more importantly, his command of ring psychology. Whether taking on the role of baby face or heel, Andre was convincing and he knew how to evoke the desired reactions from his audience.

The last time I saw Andre was on September 2, 1992 in Atlanta, Georgia for the celebration of twenty years of wrestling on Ted Turner's TBS. After the live broadcast, WCW hosted a post-show reception in a restaurant adjacent to the shoot where I joined Andre and Bruno, who reminisced about their intertwined and storied careers. By now, Bruno only came out of retirement for special events and Andre, who supported himself with the aide of a walker, was suffering from failing health.

Suddenly, George Napolitano, one of the most published wrestling photographers of the past twenty-five years, asked us to pose for a photo. Andre and Bruno looked incredulously at each other as their performance faces kicked in.

"I don't know. I'm usually careful who I associate with," snickered Bruno with a friendly elbow to my ribs.

"Now, come on guys. Cooperate!," I playfully pleaded.

"Gary's right," Andre bellowed, shooting a devilish grin across to Bruno. "Let's do it."

Just as George snapped the first shot, Andre placed his enormous mitt in front of my face and pawed my head as if it was a baseball.

"Let's do it," he repeated, "but only if he pays us fifty dollars!"

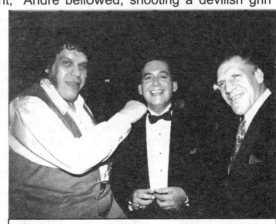

Andre & Bruno, two legends. What more can I say?

"Now you're testing my patience." My schoolteacher posturing and threatening tone had us laughing for a treasured moment indicative of my relationship with the pros with whom I proudly associated.

This was Andre's last public appearance in the United States. He died on January 27, 1993 (real name, Andre Rene Roussimoff) at the age of forty-six from a heart attack while in France to attend his father's funeral.

Bruno, on the other hand, is thriving in retirement. Thirty-seven years after gaining the WWWF world title from "Nature Boy" Buddy Rogers, the Sammartino allure lives on. He regularly receives offers for personal appearances, guest referee spots and color commentating assignments for both broadcast TV and Internet on-line appearances.

This prolonged relationship with my childhood hero, has been the most personally satisfying. With all of the fame that he has achieved, Bruno remains one of the most genuine professionals with whom I've had the pleasure to work. Most importantly, like Monsoon, he cared about me personally, as an individual.

Early on, because my personal contact with Bruno was limited, I assumed that he was unaware of my existence. After all, I figured that he was preoccupied with a non-stop travel schedule, pressured by the attention of his devoted fans and obliged to deliver a performance which lived up to his reputation. I was soon to learn that there was much more to "The Living Legend".

In July of 1978 Monsoon booked me on the Pittsburgh Civic Arena house show. Arriving late in the afternoon, I took a cab to the arena directly from the airport, as it was my practice when working in an unfamiliar building so that I could scout out the ringside area well before bell time. It was about five o'clock and the locker room was empty. As I approached the ring, I noticed three teenagers working out, exchanging holds and tossing each other across the mat. Assuming that the kids were with the ring crew, I didn't pay much attention. I tested the mic and inspected my ringside position, before wandering back to the dressing room to lay out my ring attire for the evening performance. As the commission officials began to arrive, they suspiciously questioned why I traveled all the way from New Jersey when the Pittsburgh announcer, who for years had emceed at the Civic Arena, was quite able to get the job done. Since I avoided athletic commission politics at all costs, it was time to escape the interrogation of my predators.

As I reached the dressing room exit, the teenagers, having completed their workout, brushed by me on their way from the ring. One familiar face paused before me as if he had something to say. As he grew uncomfortable, his eyes hit the floor. So I led the conversation.

"Don't I know you?"

"Oh, no. No, I don't think so."

"But your face just seems so familiar."

"Well, Mr. Cappetta, I'm David Sammartino."

Frozen in time, his words whirled around in my head as he bashfully continued.

"My dad and I watch you every weekend on television."

Did he say Mr.? Is Bruno Sammartino's son calling *me* Mr.? And did he say his father watches *me* on television? Feeling old beyond my mere twenty-six years, I was overwhelmed.

Throughout my career, I have treasured my sporadic encounters with Bruno. His concern and ease in relating to people must have been the source of the sincerity and humility that he effortlessly communicated in his early TV interviews.

One last personal anecdote about Sammartino occurred in my years with WCW. Whenever I was off the road, I took advantage of every opportunity to work in the voice over industry. This is the art of laying a commentary over a visual for television commercials, providing the narration for a radio spot or in this case, recording the phone announcements for a telephone hotline service.

I booked the job directly with the agency for what was scheduled to be a three-hour voice over session. It was a beat the champ format in which callers listened as I introduced their match against Sammartino. In my ring announce voice, I recorded a separate message for over one hundred cities, in addition to recording several ring weights in five pound increments from seventy-five to two hundred pounds and a list of special rules for different styles of matches (no disqualification, loser leaves town, etc.). When the caller punched his self-descriptive parameters into the push button phone pad, a computer automatically strung together my ring introduction by selecting the prerecorded announcements to match his hometown, weight and the wrestling event in which he was participating.

As I effortlessly soared through the scripts, my technician was dumbfounded. What was supposed to have taken three hours, was completed in forty minutes. I explained to him that ring announcers, never having the luxury of a second take, are accustomed to precision the first time through. In less than an hour I was on my way $500.00 richer.

The agency quickly booked me again during my next hiatus from the road to be the announce voice for the Lou Duva boxing hotline. This time they were set on getting their money's worth. When I arrived back at the New York recording studio, the technician was waiting with enough material to fill the Manhattan phone book twice over.

At one point we reached a question in this multiple choice boxing quiz which required the caller to supply the hometown of a former middleweight champ whose name was like an Italian tongue-twister that no one in the studio could pronounce. That's when I decided to call upon Bruno for help.

When we reached him at home in Pittsburgh, he was as obliging as always. He had heard that I was steadily working with WCW and true to form, Bruno was more concerned for me personally than with the business at hand.

The first words out of his mouth were "Are you okay?"

"What do you mean, Bruno?"

"Well, you're still teaching, aren't you?"

"No. I work for Turner's Atlanta wrestling office full time now."

"You left teaching? Are they treating you well?"

"Yeah, I'm happy with the way things are going."

"You be careful. Don't let them get the better of you."

I am fortunate to be among the very few to have known and worked with their childhood hero. The Bruno Sammartino that I grew up with every weekend on TV wrestling was gentlemanly, sincere, and. approachable. The Bruno that I came to know as a friend lived up to every bit of his press.

The end of an era occurred on October 4, 1981 when I announced Bruno's farewell victory over George Steele at the New Jersey Meadowlands Arena.

I t was during the final phase of Bruno's career when my future in wrestling was altered by events that I could not have predicted. It was a recurring pattern that repeated itself through all of my years in wrestling. Whether I was too blind to see it or too much of a fool to know the difference, at every critical crossroad, it took circumstances beyond my control to propel me in the right direction. It was without purpose or plan. It was inadvertent and uncalculated. You can call it dumb luck. But I think the Lord had his hand in this. I think He was telling me that enough is enough. And that's when I became sidelined by a debilitating case of hepatitis.

The illness was exacerbated I'm sure by the exhaustion of a never-ending schedule. For months I remained bedridden, reflecting on the many hours I spent traveling from town to town, through summer traffic and winter ice storms, at the expense of my core sources of income which provided the stability that announcing could not. While my colleagues in education furthered their studies in masters and doctoral programs, my after school goal was simply to get to the next show. As their paychecks increased, mine lagged behind. It was time to reevaluate all of the time and energy I was expending for a payoff which barely covered expenses. And the only conclusion to be made: if my role was considered valuable to the McMahons, then they would have to start paying me a reasonable fee for it. No longer would the comfort of future bookings serve as confirmation of the importance of my work. It was time to determine the real value that management placed on my contribution to the promotion. It was time for the owners to show their appreciation for my loyalty and consistent performances where it counted, in my payoffs. It was time for me to break away from the control to which I had become so vulnerable by what I finally understood as their premeditated disregard for my work "to keep the kid in his place".

Throughout my months of recuperation, only Monsoon took the time to call, concerned about the progress of my rehabilitation. He probably wasn't too surprised by my request for higher house show payoffs upon my return to the promotion. And without blinking an eye, he came through by doubling my nightly performance fee. Throughout my remaining four years with the WWF, Monsoon subsequently tripled my income for live events without further prodding.

Dealing with the McMahons was an entirely different matter. There had been no change in my sixty-five dollar fee for TV shoots since I began working the tapings four years earlier. This was my first request for a raise. It was also the first time since hooking up with the WWF that I approached Vinnie beyond the passing smile, nod and brief "hello" for which I was usually ignored. Sending the clear message that his time was reserved for important matters and my concerns weren't among them always seemed to make his day.

Junior's response to me was short and to the point. Without breaking his stride as he walked by me early one afternoon before we began taping a month's worth of TV, Vinnie's contempt dripped from the biting words he spewed forth. "A raise?," he smirked. "For you?" sarcastically grimacing even more. "It's not my department. Talk to my father." I wanted to search his eyes hoping to uncover a trace of humanity, but the much taller McMahon never looked my way to afford me the opportunity.

Senior's simple retort stopped me in my tracks.

"I can't afford it," he bristled.

"But Vince, I'm only asking you for a raise to cover my TV and Spectrum shots. That's less than thirty dates a year."

"And where do you think the money's going to come from?"

What can you say to the man who singularly controls the northeastern monopoly of a multi-million dollar industry, in the richest territory in the country? Today, I'd say, "Bullshit!" Back then, I pleaded my case and wandered away disheartened. The irony of the entire scene was that McMahon then instructed Phil Zacko, his Philadelphia promoter, to increase my pay from then on out. But he never afforded me the satisfaction or recognition of a job well done face to face.

I came away from that experience with so many lessons in the ways of the wrestling world. And maybe it's the way of the world, at large. The McMahons taught me that in their world, loyalty is a one-way street. It's a quality expected by management for which, in return, the faithful should be happy with whatever the owners might slip your way.

Another lesson that I learned after returning from my illness was that there's something to be said for the strength of inaction. Many times in the course of my career I saw that my contribution to the promotion was appreciated only in my absence.

Perhaps the most vital lesson from pleading my case for more money was how good I felt about myself when it was over, even before knowing that the extra money would follow later on. Yet it took a sidelining illness to finally grow up and speak out for myself.

Finally, I had broken the aura of intimidation that had controlled me for so long. In doing so, any hope I might have had of enjoying a lengthy career with the McMahons and The World Wrestling Federation was shattered.

Chapter Seven
"The Loser Leaves Town Match"

....show business is a business, and a hard-boiled one. If you are in it, it's up to you to protect yourself. No one else is going to do it for you. And there's no room in show business for hurt feelings, resentments, or self-pity.

Sophie Tucker, "Some Of These Days, The Autobiography"

I had done the unthinkable. As the low man on the talent roster, I dared to confront the McMahons with what was considered a brazen request for more money. With this one move, my long-term prospects for a lengthy future with the WWF had been undermined. The months ahead were sure to be more uncertain than ever. With a simple request for payoffs to reflect my contribution to the company, I was branded a potential troublemaker. The message was clear: talent, professionalism, dependability and loyalty alone were not valued qualities for which one could expect to be rewarded without dependence and blind faith added into the mix. I knew it was just a matter of time before I'd be gone. For those who spoke out for fair treatment, for those like the unknown Sammartino of 1960, who rejected anything less, nothing much had changed. Twenty years later, the only remaining course of action was to sustain the visibility that I had established for as long as I could, in the face of the continued, off-handed snubs from the McMahons which had become commonplace.

With the arrival of the new decade, Vince, Jr. began positioning himself to assume control of the entire operation. As his father's health started to fail, he would ease out some of the established players who did not fit into his vision of a WWF that would extend beyond the McMahons' established northeastern domain. If Junior was to have it his way, the WWF of the future would be transformed into a national organization, breaking across all of the promotional boundaries that had been respected by wrestling's ruling class for years. Vinnie's global view of the WWF, as indeed would come to pass, would revolutionize the wrestling business. And it was clear as he started to maneuver that there would be no place in his new world order for me.

Speaking out did result in an immediate rise in my performance fees. Between my bout with hepatitis in 1979 and the end of 1983, my yearly earnings from pro wrestling doubled. Announcing now equaled one third of my overall income. The subsequent raises came in small increments, without having to ask a second time. My income from pro wrestling stabilized with *All Star Wrestling* continuing to tape every three weeks, monthly Spectrum events generating a profitable payoff, as did shows at the newly constructed Meadowlands Arena which opened its doors to pro wrestling with the Bruno Sammartino "retirement" match. In addition, an abundance of hometown fund-raisers kept me active on nights in between. Without a competing wrestling promotion in the Northeast, where I could capitalize on my reputation to position myself for the future, I continued announcing in the WWF towns along my established circuit.

In the Spring of 1982 there was one last flurry of activity that once again brought me widespread TV attention. My latest nemesis, Superfly Jimmy Snuka, was portrayed as a savage native of the Fiji Islands. Just as with George Steele, the wild man's manager was Lou Albano. And

Snuka went for my tie.

once again, I was used as a prop to get over Snuka's uncontrollable rage. It had been six years since the Steele incident and now a new generation of young viewers could see how the entanglement of a wrestler with the impartial ring announcer could effectively advance the careers of both.

My first encounters with Snuka took place at the *All Star* taping. In each of the three shows that we shot that night, he made it his business to become inexplicably distracted by my ring announcements. Halfway through introducing him for the first hour, he snatched the carnation boutonniere from my lapel, shoved it into his mouth, chewed it into a milky pulp and spit it back in my face. Albano acted embarrassed with apologies for not being able to control the beefy brute, and then gleefully taunted the crowd to generate heat. During the introduction for his match in the second hour, Snuka unfastened the tie from around my neck and delivered it to Albano as a symbol of his conquest. As I declared him at the conclusion of the third taping, Snuka plucked off my bow tie and then stalked me with his glazed-over eyes fixed on the rest of my clothing. I back peddled from his menacing advances, as he began to paw at my jacket and shirt. Snuka then unfastened my belt with his sights set on my loose fitting pants. Unlike the way I handled the Steele incident, I ignored Albano's whispered direction, "Run, run! Get out of the ring!" With little more to lose (except my pants and the respectability resulting from being exposed on national TV), I decided to stand my ground to see how far he would go. As The Superfly continued his pursuit, with only seconds left in the show, I positioned myself on the side of the ring where the stationary cameras stood.

.... *Oh no! Help!*

This was important since in these earlier days of TV wrestling, hand held cameras were not yet used. Two stationary cameras, both on the same side of the ring, captured all of the action. One was floor mounted, the other was elevated on a platform. A small range of horizontal and vertical alignment limited their scope. Today, roving cameras will catch all of the action anywhere in the arena. But in 1982, if you weren't within camera range, the action was lost. And I was intent that our performance would not be squandered on the live Hamburg audience without TV coverage.

As the salivating Snuka hovered over me, I wedged my

He's after my pants!

ankle between the bottom two ropes, spun myself out toward the floor and thus hung myself up side down over the side of the ring. As the show's theme music pounded and the credits began to roll, we went off the air. Our home viewers were left with the image of me dangling upside down from the ring ropes with Albano frantically blocking the wild eyed Snuka from attacking his fallen prey. I guess my melodramatic tendencies surged out of control. My impromptu contribution to the entertainment value of the show now caused the program to go off the air with an unscripted cliffhanger. Would the savage succeed in tearing apart the hapless announcer? Tune in next week and find out!

Despite the absurdity of continuing to face off with the Superfly, the unplanned attacks were effective in portraying the unpredictability and danger that surrounded him. I was only too happy to go along with the charade, knowing that the residual effect was to once again draw the spotlight my way . . . oh that unfortunate ring announcer!

As in the past, Vinnie was not amused. He didn't have to say a word. The grimace on his face spoke volumes. "Who does Cappetta think he is, showboating on my broadcast?" McMahon was rightfully upset with what he helplessly witnessed just ten feet in front of his broadcast position.

Granted, I knew what I was doing. I had orchestrated an incident that made me the focus of the broadcast. But by then, I didn't care what management thought. I had finally come to realize that the spotlight was dimming on my WWF career and whether Vinnie pulled the plug sooner than later, I was way beyond trying to accommodate his ever-forbidding temperament. And any way, although admittedly it wasn't my call to make, I thought it made for good television. It gave people something else to talk about throughout the week. The portrayal of Snuka, so out of control, so blood thirsty, that he would attack the hapless announcer, enhanced his barbaric persona for his upcoming feud against WWF champ, Bob Backlund. Incidentally, the incident was never mentioned during the following week's broadcast.

I was losing ground fast. Not only for my on air stunt, but because in June of 1982, when Senior relinquished his corporate control to Junior, Vinnie made a daring move to overthrow the minor partners, thus empowering himself as the sole owner of the company. He exercised an option that existed in his father's partnership agreement with Monsoon and the secondary shareholders to purchase their shares and thus assume full control of the entire promotion. By eliminating his father's cohorts, Vince, Jr. took the first step in making the WWF a household name in every neighborhood throughout America.

Monsoon, feeling undermined by Junior, was understandably rattled by the takeover. The magic carpet, which had promised a long, comfortable ride toward ensuring his future involvement in pro wrestling, was suddenly pulled out from under him. Gino became dejected and bitter. His authority was revoked and he suddenly tumbled from power. In the months following the legal maneuvering, Monsoon settled into a state of despondency. At house shows, when wrestlers came to him for the finishes to their matches, he waved them off. "I don't know. Why ask me? I'm just another worker here. Just another hired hand." Like those who only days earlier looked to him for guidance, now Gino was also on shaky ground. Not that his financial security was uncertain. His compensation from the buyout was substantial over the long term. But in the business for which he had so much invested, as an artist whose life was his work, as a performer who displayed his love of the game in every nagging battle wound that he carried, there was no telling what his future role in pro wrestling was going to be. The nature of his active involvement, if any, in the WWF was now in Junior's hands.

I understood the delicate situation in which Monsoon found himself. He had to declare his allegiance. He had to position himself for the future. And at this crossroads of his career, that meant distancing himself from friends who would soon be distant memories of WWF history. No one's future was safe. It was politics. And with Senior out of the picture, the man responsible for my entry and survival in pro wrestling could no longer shield me from Junior's disdain.

A full year passed before the lights dimmed on one of my two most publicly visible platforms. The incident that in all probability triggered my final downfall took place at the Spectrum in early June of 1983. The headlining event, former WWF champion, Ivan Koloff versus the current champ, Bob Backlund, was scheduled to be the last match of the show, preceded by a bout involving Iron Mike Sharpe. Sharpe was known backstage as Mr. Clean. He spent hours at the sink washing his hands before wrestling and several hours more in the shower after each of his matches. One night, after wrestling in an early bout at the Spectrum, he was still soaping up in the shower long after the matches had ended. Luckily he found a night watchman to let him out of the locked building long after everyone had gone home.

Mike was a middle card tough guy who often was used by McMahon as a stepping stone for future contenders of the WWF championships. He wore a leather band on his arm that extended from wrist to elbow. Although it was made of nothing more than thin black leather, once nailed with an ordinary forearm smash, Sharpe's opponents senselessly collapsed to defeat. Iron Mike also slid weapons under his armband which he used when in trouble, concocting more controversy than his harmless gimmick ever deserved. He squashed lesser opponents on television only to be thrashed by up and comers at live events in Philadelphia and all of the major venues throughout the WWF territory. Once getting past Sharpe, the wrestler who was receiving the push gained credibility en route to presenting himself worthy of a title shot.

Ordinarily, I announced the next month's Spectrum lineup immediately before the final match. It was perhaps my most important task in cities holding monthly WWF events. Much like a prophet, my dramatic presentation of the upcoming card was designed to lure our ticket buying public back for an extravaganza that they wouldn't want to miss. When the next show offered little out of the ordinary, the boys teased me for my ability to "make chicken salad out of chicken shit". But thanks to a freak accident with the iron man following his semi-final match in Philadelphia, the fans never witnessed my culinary wizardry.

After losing to a referee's fast count on the night in question, Iron Mike began to storm around the ring in protest. Ferociously flailing his arms, he charged his victorious opponent in a post match flurry, only to be sent flying back across the mat

Iron Mike Sharpe

to the opposite side of the ring. Sharpe was flung head first, to the same corner of the ring, at the exact moment, in the exact spot where I was about to enter, with the intention of announcing the official decision. It was as if we had preplanned a perfectly choreographed collision. Landing in his typically over-exaggerated fashion, Mike's arms were flapping wildly as his leather covered forearm popped me in the mouth. The force of his unintentional shot to the jaw propelled me backward. My prepared notes flew in all directions as I soared through the air in reverse motion. It oddly seemed like super slow motion, as I glided over the steps and to the floor driving the back of my head into the steel barricade which separated the front row of spectators from the ringside area. I lay motionless, sprawled on the floor for several minutes. The ring doctor, who believed that every action in pro wrestling was plotted out in advance, was nowhere to be found.

When the fans saw me fly through the air, they rose to their feet to follow my flight to its crashing conclusion. They were bellowing their approval for this post match skirmish, which was much more entertaining than the lackluster match that preceded it. The roar of the fans was deafening as this unexpected scene unfolded before them.

Lying at the feet of the first row of startled onlookers, I floated through a remote inner world of darkness. Little bursts of light flared in all directions against a black backdrop of nothingness. They faintly sputtered back into black only to be replaced by several more sparkling spurts. It was like the Fourth of July one month early. But as unpredictable as pro wrestling often is, the real fireworks were just about to begin. And that's when the local promoter got into the act.

I began to regain my wits as the slow moving ringside physician kneeled over me waving smelling salts beneath my nose. As if he held a magic wand, the haze began to clear. And that's when I first detected a frantic scene, a sense of desperation, from the huddling, blurred masses that swirled overhead. The commotion was more frenetic than one should have expected surrounding a fallen ring announcer. Looking up from the floor, my concerned attendants were nothing more than shadowy silhouettes before the bright ring lights that glared behind them. The first vision upon which my eyes focused was the individual I least wanted to see.

Phil Zacko, the foul tempered Philadelphia promoter, stood just a hair higher than our tallest midget wrestler. This guy was the model caricature for the rotund, cigar champing, old time fight promoter that movie lore has depicted as typical, but in my experience was the exception. Phil was a scoundrel, with a temperament so vile, that his miserable disposition was protectively excused by his associates with "That Phil, he's such a character. But once you get to know him, he's really a sweetheart." I never had the masochistic desire to search for his well-concealed sweet heart that I doubt ever existed. But there he was, huffing and puffing, wheezing and upset that I could be so derelict of duty as to abandon the show before my all important hype for the next Spectrum event.

"Jesus Christ! What are you doing? Get up kid. You're holdin' the fuckin' show up." Phil paced back and forth, intermittently waving the next month's lineup in my face. The more irritated he got, the more crumpled the paper became. "Here. Take this and get back to work," he panted. "Announce this next card before it's too goddamn late."

I lay sprawled out in the midst of 15,000 fans, who by now grew silent with concern about the seriousness of my injury. While it was likely that I could have carried out Phil's cold-blooded command, I nevertheless remained still, growing more and more galled at his indifference for my well being. This was a guy who stood silently by while Vince, Sr. cried poverty upon hearing my request for a measly thirty-five dollar raise, and now all of a sudden he regarded my role so important, that I should ignore a concussion to prove my loyalty, that one-sided loyalty. I peered up at Phil one last time and the decision was easy. I would deliver to the fans what they least expected. In those days when protecting the business was still in the best interest of wrestling, I would do nothing. I would just do nothing.

After all of the years of running away from The Animal, and enduring the taunting pranks of Baron Scicluna and the body slams dished out by Peter Maivia, and the recent Superfly attacks, along with the menacing sneers of hundreds of wrestlers in between, I had always managed to regain my composure. Like a trouper, I pulled myself together and continue for the sake of the show. This time was different. This time I had come closest to real danger. At this point I wasn't even sure if my injury was serious. So tonight's performance would be set apart from all of those in the past. This time it was best to just do nothing.

This is a happy look for Phil with former WWF champion, Bob Backlund.

Besides, it made sense. It was logical. I had just been clobbered by the dreaded leather armband which had defeated so many titans in the past, flown over the ring steps and crashed head first Into the steel barricade. But there is nothing in the imaginary pro wrestling rulebook that says that management has to be logical. Especially when I was to make the big announcement to sell tickets for next month's show. This is when all of a sudden, protecting the business was secondary to doing business, to making money. It was a shortsighted concern at the expense of long term credibility.

When it was apparent that I wasn't going to move, the Spectrum security hoisted me up and carried me around the ring, down the aisle and to the dressing room area. The fans were on their feet cheering encouragement for my safe recovery. This is the kind of a scene that makes live events memorable. That's the reason for enticing people to pay for a ticket. Unless your audience can witness something in person that it is not going to see otherwise, there's little reason for them to make their way to the arena. Wrestlers sell tickets. Announcers do not. Fans are not attracted to the arena to see an announcer get knocked out. But when such an out of the ordinary incident occurs, it's an extra bonus. It becomes part of the report carried back to those who didn't make it to the arena. Such a mishap sets a live event apart from the overly programmed television show. It is a different experience. It has to be. Why bother paying for something that you can for free on TV?

After a thorough examination, the ring doctor determined that I had indeed suffered a concussion. He gave me his number with instructions to call in the event that I noticed any abnormal aftereffects. But while he addressed the physical consequences from my little misadventure, he was powerless to prescribe a remedy to cure the trauma that my announcing career would soon suffer.

Vinnie made a rare appearance at the Spectrum ten weeks later. Ordinarily, aside from the television shoots, he only surfaced at Madison Square Garden. Whenever he showed up at live events, the entire locker room took on a somber tone. Everyone was on his best behavior, knowing that something was up.

For me, the night was like most others. The huge, volatile crowd had assembled in eager anticipation of the hottest feud of the summer, Sergeant Slaughter challenging Backlund for the heavyweight crown. As the preliminary contests continued to set the stage for the main event, the moment arrived for the build up to the next live Spectrum show. As I began to bill the Spectrum card as a "super spectacular", one that no fan in his right mind could miss, I was stopped in mid sentence and waved from the ring. Mel Phillips, the same guy who fiendishly enjoyed my initial TV clash with The Animal (but not the resulting hype that it generated), entered the ring, took the microphone, and whispered, "Vince told me to send you to the back." He then continued with his version of the announcement that I had started.

My first thought was that there had been an emergency call from home. Someone had been rushed to the hospital. Who was it? What else could have been so urgent to stop me in mid sentence? My mind raced as I rushed back to the promoter's suite to find Vinnie standing in the middle of his henchmen.

"Vince, you wanted to see me?" I gasped. "Is there something wrong?"

"No, nothing's wrong." He was as calm and as poised as I'd ever seen him.

"Then why did you call me from the ring? I was in the middle of my pitch for next month's card!" Everyone's attention was on this conversation that wasn't making any sense to me. What was going on? Was this some kind of a joke?

"We're not going to be needing your services here any more." He managed to hold back a smile that settled into a smirk. "This is your last night."

"My last night? Why? What's wrong?"

"You didn't do anything wrong. Things are going to change. If we need you, we'll call."

I was stunned. "So you're canceling all of my bookings?"

"No, just here at the Spectrum. You'll continue to work all your other dates."

Monsoon and Zacko looked on in silence. It was as if they expected me to have more of a reaction. But there was nothing more to say. Encouraging Junior's insensitive flaunting of his newfound power served no further purpose.

One year later, Memorial Day of 1984, Vinnie delivered a second sucker punch that like the first, caught me completely off guard. Not only because this night marked my final WWF broadcast, but because of the callous manner in which I was told the news. It was as sudden as had been my departure from the Spectrum.

With the first shows completed, we were about to begin taping the third hour of television. On Monsoon's cue, I began to make my way to center ring. All of a sudden, as I was half way down the aisle, one of McMahon's lieutenants tugged on my shoulder from behind. He held out a yellow piece of legal lined paper.

"Here. Take this. Vince said to make this announcement now."

I naturally began to read over the copy before continuing to the ring.

Impatient with my hesitation, he persisted, "Vince said *now*! He wants you to make the announcement *now*!"

His words echoed hollow in the background as I suspiciously scanned the memo. It was simple and to the point. *Thank the fans for their support. This will be the last TV taping in Hamburg. Tell them to watch for local upcoming events in the future.*

Momentarily paralyzed, I reviewed the announcement in disbelief. Just minutes before the fans, I learned that the *All Star* program had reached the end of its run. For me, the message carried more of a meaning. After ten years, I was as valued to the promotion as the guy who sat in a three-dollar bleacher seat. Both of us learned of the final television taping at the same time.

The news was not altogether unexpected. But while McMahon repeatedly had shown a heartless streak throughout my lengthy tenure with his family's promotion, I nevertheless was once again taken back with his indifference. I wasn't a stranger. The McMahons held me out as their primary ring announcer on more than five hundred hours of TV wrestling and nearly a thousand live events over a decade. I deserved better.

I respected Vinnie's right to assemble the talent roster of his choosing. I have never disputed that. My problem with him had nothing to do with the decisions he made, but with the insensitivity he displayed toward the individuals who were affected by them. For the second time Junior had fired me in the middle of a performance. I was like a tightrope walker getting the hook half way across the elevated high wire. For me it was an emotional tight rope and Vinnie seemed to enjoy standing on the side platform jiggling the taught wire in gleeful anticipation of my long fall to the arena floor below.

It was all about humiliation, insecurity and most importantly control. My college degree and a managerial position in my dad's business provided more financial security than McMahon would ever be prepared to offer. And since Junior acted as if loyalty could only be guaranteed from those who could be easily intimidated, he would never gain the leverage over my life that he felt was necessary for me to be deferential to his every whim.

It was different for most of the other talent. Keeping the wrestlers insecure in their positions was easier to do since unfortunately the vast majority of the boys didn't have an alternate means of support. While my consistently solid performance could not be denied, the McMahons knew that my need for the job was emotional, not financial. I announced because it was fun without expecting to get rich in the process. It was as if since he couldn't buy my loyalty, then it didn't exist.

During the months leading up to the final *All Star* taping McMahon found something that he *could* buy. It wasn't loyalty that he bought though; at least not directly. No, he added to his existent debt from the WWF partnership buyout to purchase airtime on television stations in many of the country's major markets to showcase his new program, *Superstars of Wrestling*. It was commonplace for promoters to buy TV slots. They used the airwaves in the same way, as do producers of infomercials. In return, promoters counted on the income from arena ticket sales and concession stand profits to more than compensate for the investment.

Until now, these outlets aired only hometown wrestling shows, which allowed local promoters to monopolize the wrestling business in their areas. Vinnie's was about to play the same game in the promoters' own backyard. He was not content to compete on an equal footing. Wherever possible, he not only wanted to *introduce Superstars* in cities that were previously off limits. His goal was to entice station managers to *replace* the established wrestling program with his.

It was therefore an expensive proposition for McMahon to line up a solid network of affiliates in his quest to broadcast the WWF to every corner of the country. Some believed that he made a deal with the devil to arrange the financing. He has always maintained that a simple second mortgage on his home funded the deals. The truth probably lies somewhere in between.

In certain cities Vinnie offered to buy the local wrestling promotions in their entirety. In others he extended no such courtesy. They were established promotions who had long enjoyed uncontested success in spite of their provincial way of doing business. They offered recycled rasslin' angles on poorly lit TV shows set in small studios and dingy arenas. Produced with limited budgets, the quality of these local programs was no match for what the television industry of the 1980's was capable. But without competition, these stale wrestling shows were enough to do big business for years. There was never a reason to stray from the formula, which had for decades made regional promoters wealthy. Until now, if fans wanted to see wrestling, the home team was the only team in town.

When some of McMahon, Sr.'s NWA colleagues cried foul, he insisted that they were overreacting. By taking advantage of his close working relationship with many long time associates, Senior managed to soothe their insecurities. With a wink, he pacified his contemporaries' fears by assuring them that the McMahon family would never trespass on their home turf. "Come on boys, there's nothing to worry about, this is my son you're talking about."

Other old school czars weren't as bothered. Some even smirked at the thought that this audacious upstart could ever topple the established base that had been their cash cow for as long as one could remember. The prevailing mindset among those who had rejected McMahon's buyout offers was that undoubtedly the kid would run out of money sooner or later.

But Vinnie was sailing on uncharted waters. No one knew for sure how fans across the country would react when, for the first time in US wrestling history, the nation as a whole would be presented with one heavily hyped, national wrestling product via a television program which boasted state of the art production values. The battlegrounds were set as the WWF war ships surrounded the independent brigades on all sides. By the time the smoke cleared, many promotions were capsized and several others scurried for the safety of dry land.

Junior's new program was so revolutionary for its time, that it evoked strong reactions from both supporters and critics alike. There was no middle ground. The fundamental facelift that McMahon's wrestling product underwent combined the hipness of cartoon satire with outrageous counter culture themes. In appearance, his show emulated the glitz of the youth oriented music industry. It was slickly packaged and promoted with the bravado of a fast talking Hollywood press agent.

In no time, Vinnie contacted the most popular wrestlers from those regions that he intended to invade. He sought the services of solid performers such as Mike Rotunda, Barry Windham, Junkyard Dog, the Von Erich brothers, Ted DiBiase, Paul Orndorff, Randy Savage, Roddy Piper, Ric Flair and Hulk Hogan.

Junior was sure that the wrestlers he plucked from competing territories, those who dared to switch their allegiance to the WWF, would remain under his control. With one-sided contracts which would have insulted an indentured slave of the Civil War era, the wrestlers who broke away from their unsuspecting mentors, had nowhere else to work if Vinnie's plan failed. Now that these ex-patriots had declared their loyalty to the WWF, there was no turning back.

On January 23, 1984, twenty months after taking full control, Vince McMahon, Jr. was now ready to crown Hulk Hogan his standard bearer for the new generation of the WWF. Hogan was fresh from a tour of Japan after being groomed for headline action by Minneapolis promoter Verne Gagne. With his defeat of The Iron Sheik in Madison Square Garden, Hogan began a barnstorming campaign across America, in the media and at live wrestling events, as the symbol of the revitalized WWF. The message was clear. It was now cool to be a wrestling fan again.

But success for Vinnie's new concept did not come easily in many parts of the country. Like consumers of any other product, wrestling fans are creatures of habit. It was not easy to lure them away from the established brands. Many were comfortable with the style of wrestling that they had supported for years. McMahon's attempt to draw them away from the wrestling that they had known since childhood proved to be an uphill battle. With few exceptions, the WWF's first live events outside of his Northeast territory failed miserably.

However, in 1984 and 1985 Junior was not content to sit back and wait for the public to discover his new WWF. He was determined to grab their attention by using a variety of media accomplices who were willing to hawk what he proclaimed was a revolution in sports entertainment. With the shamelessness of a carnival huckster that would have made PT Barnum blush, McMahon sold America on the perception that he was a visionary who single-handedly revitalized a stagnant wrestling industry from a listless slump to respectable profitability. What no one seemed to notice was that he used the only statistics available as proof of wrestling's earning power - the cumulative national figures of 1983. These figures did not reflect McMahon's influence on the industry, but rather the national success of pro wrestling as a whole when it was still a territorial business. An all too willing media, caught up in McMahon's grossly exaggerated portrayal of a nonexistent WWF phenomena, reported his bogus claims as fact, creating a perception of hipness and success. If not for Vinnie's masterful manipulation of a news hungry media, his new brand of wrestling might never have gotten off the ground.

McMahon was perceptive in his understanding of America's susceptibility to being on the cutting edge of society's latest trends. He knew that everyone wanted to be involved in the latest fad. More importantly, he wisely targeted the audience which held enormous influence over America's entertainment dollar, its kiddy consumers. Demographically, impressionable young people controlled an enormous segment of America's disposable income. By manipulating the youth oriented media outlets, he convinced those who were always looking for the next hip breakthrough that WWF wrestling was it.

With the advent of cable, expansion was certain. It was Vince, Jr. who was the first to identify cable's value for pro wrestling, the first to recognize the opportunities and the first to act on what he believed would be a revolutionary period in American pro wrestling.

In 1984 Vinnie brought WWF wrestling to the USA Network and then produced a wrestling talk show, *Tuesday Night Titans,* also for USA. *TNT*, as it was nicknamed, became one of the highest rated shows on cable.

Elsewhere on cable, he invaded the MTV generation by signing the music industry's newest recording sensation, Cyndi Lauper, to manage the teen oriented lady wrestler, Wendi

Wendi and Cyndi Lauper, Rock n Wrestling

Richter. The flamboyant Lauper, with her hit "Girls Just Wanna Have Fun" topping the pop charts, was at Richter's side when she dethroned the women's champ, Fabulous Moolah, who had held the belt for decades. The Madison Square Garden event became an MTV special, which delivered its highest ratings to date. The highly publicized event was invaluable in exposing the prized audience of youthful trendsetters to the WWF. The success of the special won Hulk Hogan a guest VJ spot, placing the embodiment of the WWF alongside not only Cyndi Lauper, but the music videos of Van Halen, Prince, ZZ Top, Rod Stewart and Def Leppard.

Not content with his success on MTV and the USA Network, Vinnie began acquiring the stock of Georgia Championship Wrestling's minor shareholders. The promotion had long been cable's wrestling heavyweight on Ted Turner's Superstation TBS. McMahon engineered a surprise takeover of Turner's wrestling program, which he shrewdly snatched from under the inattentive watch of promoter Ole Anderson. The takeover lasted only nine months before an irritated Turner recaptured the timeslot. McMahon's unsuccessful maneuvering on this one front came back to haunt him a decade later when Ted Turner, who did not forget Junior's brazen raid, bankrolled an aggressive challenge to the dominance of the WWF..

By the time 1985 rolled around the media couldn't get enough of McMahon's beefy, bawdy ambassadors who were embraced by reporters and talk show hosts from coast to coast. The rebellious image of the WWF's new cast of characters was reinforced beyond the weekly wrestling programs with wrestlers flexing their jaw muscles on prime time TV shows. Among the most reported incidents was bounty hunting wrestler Dr. D David Schultz's ear ringing slap of ABC correspondent, John Stossel on the news magazine show *20/20* when Stossel questioned the authenticity of pro wrestling. In addition, Hulk Hogan's front face lock on Richard Beltzer resulted in the comedian collapsing to the studio floor with a concussion-causing thud. Lawsuits followed both incidents and the WWF made headlines.

The print media was also in the fray with the *Sports Illustrated* cover feature, "Hulk Hogan, Wrestling's Top Banana", outselling all other issues of the year except for SI's swimsuit annual. *Newsweek* along with several of the major big city newspapers also ran features on Hogan and the World Wrestling Federation. It was as if the public could not escape the word that not just pro wrestling, but the WWF was fashionable.

All of the hype led to the first Wrestlemania on March 31, 1985. In this pre pay-per-view environment, 400,000 witnessed Hulk Hogan and TV celebrity, Mr. T defeat Paul Orndorff and Roddy Piper live from Madison Square Garden at more than 135 closed-circuit locations.

Six weeks later, McMahon, in partnership with NBC executive producer, Dick Ebersole, brought pro wrestling back to network television after a thirty year absence with the premiere of WWF *Saturday Night's Main Event.* As a monthly replacement for the NBC late night mega hit, *Saturday Night Live*, the 11:30 PM time slot on NBC was a familiar hangout for the college crowd and young parents who had become accustomed to off beat humor every Saturday night. Another coup for McMahon.

Ultimately, Vince, Jr. had not only established that the WWF was the major league of professional wrestling, but that the World Wrestling Federation was major league entertainment.

Part Two

THE
INDEPENDENT
YEARS

1985–1989

Chapter Eight
"The 'I Quit' Match"

In 1946 boxing and wrestling and roller derbies were still taken seriously, but when they began to grab for the nearest dollar, the quickest laugh, the most grotesque parody of violence their credibility was destroyed. When enough people begin laughing at the exaggeration of any sport, it is doomed. The custodians of the game refuse to heed the first warnings, because the people who are ridiculing the sport don't appear to carry much weight.

James A. Michener, "Sports In America"

In May of 1984, Vinnie, with his updated vision of what he coined sports entertainment, was about to steam roll across the US wrestling terrain. He was indifferent to territorial traditions and condescending to the rich wrestling heritage, which was unique to each region.

That month also marked Vince, Sr.'s death to cancer. His was the one voice, though growing fainter in the face of the inevitable, that could have tempered his son's growing rift with fellow promoters. In his final months, the patriarch of the WWF battled the disease that ravaged his body, while continuing to deflect his colleagues' claims that Junior intended on putting them out of business. Though the cancer was deadly, it was the latter battle that gutted his spirit.

However disingenuous Vince, Sr.'s defense of his son's actions may have been, history will look back favorably on the wrestling impresario. Aside from the enormity of Senior's lengthy success in the most populous region of the country, he will be remembered as a gentleman of high standards in an often low brow world. Many of those who knew better than to defy his authority were rewarded with steady work in an unstable environment. It was a very different world from the new era that was about to begin.

By the start of 1985, the new rules of the game were in place. Vince, Jr. concentrated on making his campaign a success. In order to offset the money spent on TV timeslots each week, it became necessary to run live arena shows on a regular basis nationwide. Since his wrestling talent could only be spread out so far, the minor towns of the original WWF region were eliminated from the tour schedule.

It was a matter of survival that united the two groups that Vinnie left behind: former WWF stars and Northeast-based promoters. They cooperated with each other to bring wrestling back to the schools and community centers that Junior no longer ran. It was their only hope of staying in the wrestling business.

Local promoters depended on the name recognition of former WWF stars to sell their shows. Sergeant Slaughter, whose failed attempt to unionize the wrestlers prompted an unappreciative McMahon to boot him from the The Federation, was the number one draw on the independent circuit. Others who Vinnie terminated to make room for fresh faces included Bob Backlund, Jimmy "Superfly" Snuka, Wendi Richter, Afa and Sika, The Wild Samoans, "Polish Power" Ivan Putski and Dr. D. David Schultz.

As Vinnie began driving smaller regional promotions out of business, there were few places for free agent wrestlers to work. Under the old system, wrestlers were forewarned that their run was about to end and could prepare for an easy transition to another bustling region. In fact, wrestling moguls often took care of the top talent by lining up their next deal with fellow promoters. But in the mid 1980s, with smaller territories being gobbled up by McMahon, promotions where a wrestler could make a decent living outside of the WWF were quickly disappearing.

In addition to the local promoters, Charlotte-based Jim Crockett, Atlanta promoter Ole Anderson and Puerto Rican kingpin, Carlos Colon also set their sights on the Northeast. This unlikely partnership brought the National Wrestling Association (NWA) back to the New York area after a twenty-year absence. On May 29,1984, they drew a crowd of more than 12,000 for "The Night Of Champions" to see Ric Flair defeat Ricky Steamboat at the Meadowlands Arena.

This success, which was only promoted on the strength of Colon's weak UHF Spanish language station in Paterson, New Jersey, made Crockett hopeful that he could continue to do business in the Northeast. He spent the summer reworking his strategy, which resulted in his promotional collaboration with Verne Gagne, who ran the American Wrestling Association (AWA) from his Minneapolis headquarters.

More than Crockett, Gagne had been hard hit by the WWF talent raids when McMahon hired away Hulk Hogan, who since his start with the AWA in 1981, had become its top drawing card. Crockett and Gagne were representative of promoters across North America who finally accepted that Vince, Jr.'s master plan was taking hold in their own backyards, spurring them to finally respond to the WWF tidal wave. But although McMahon's success was slow to take hold, by the time they mounted any kind of offense, it was too late to stop him.

So more out of revenge than with any real hope of capturing the Northeast, McMahon's outmaneuvered rivals decided to give him a dose of his own medicine. By late summer of 1984, the NWA and the AWA, calling their joint promotion Pro Wrestling USA, teamed up to produce their own television program featuring headliners from both groups.

With the program's New York debut on September 29th on independent outlet WPIX, the tables were turned, as McMahon's backyard fans were able to enjoy a non-WWF product for the first time in many years. The new show was an ideal vehicle to introduce headlining wrestlers from both promotions while advertising forthcoming live events to a growing home audience.

As soon as *Pro Wrestling USA* settled into its Saturday morning time slot, the program began to develop a loyal following of New York fans. While most viewers remained devoted to the WWF "home team", many enjoyed the alternative personalities that before they could only read about in national wrestling magazines.

With all oaths of loyalty a thing of the past, I watched the many players jockeying for position in a free for all environment, the magnitude of which had never before been seen in the North American pro wrestling business. The media's ground swell of support for the WWF unleashed tremors beneath the feet of everyone in the business. It was time for me to decide where I might land when the wrestling world would eventually settle into place. Once again, conditions beyond my control took over and my rapidly deteriorating relationship with the World Wrestling Federation made the decision easier.

From the end of the *All Star* show in May and through the remaining seven months of 1984, I was booked on just eighteen WWF events. It didn't take long for me to realize that the time had come to free myself from the one-sided loyalty which I had observed for so long. As the battle lines were drawn, the timing of the promotional war coincided perfectly with my need to find another announcing position.

At the beginning of 1985, I sent word through the wrestling grapevine that I was now available to announce at non-WWF events. Before long, I began to receive bookings from independent promoters throughout the Northeast. My existing work for McMahon, combined with a growing number of requests from the indie promoters, kept me as busy as I had been during the height of my WWF TV exposure.

But the independent circuit soon became a natural feeding ground for the unscrupulous trend chasers who saw fund raising organizations an easy target for their underhanded cons. To avoid this seedy element and to maximize my job security in an insecure business, I needed to align myself with another major league organization. And once again, I was led to a pot of gold by pure luck.

With their new TV program off and running, Crockett and Gagne decided to run house shows in WWF-owned cities on a regular basis. In the New York area, they set up a two-week tour of smaller venues on both sides of the Hudson River to showboat their wrestlers, thereby developing the momentum needed to carry them forward to another major Meadowlands event. Finally, they assumed an aggressive stance. Their raid, in the heart of enemy territory, was a bold move. It was their second attempt in a year to challenge McMahon in his most valued metropolis.

Unfamiliar with the area's wrestling trade, it was natural that Gary Juster, Pro Wrestling USA's Northeastern representative, turned to the independent promoters to tap into their established contacts for these initial tours.

Eight shows were booked in all. Four were booked through individual promoters in New Jersey, while the four to be held in the New York boroughs were all placed in the hands of one promoter, Tommy Dee. Juster left them in charge of lining up the support personnel for their shows which included hiring ring announcers. Each of the promoters had me at the top of their list and within a few days, I was hired to emcee all eight shows.

I was thrilled. This was an opportunity to showcase my work in front of the only company, other than the WWF, that produced a national TV program. Since my travel was limited by a teaching schedule, which tied me to the classroom every weekday, this was my only chance to sustain my announcing income while maintaining a widespread following. Confident that my days with Vince were numbered, my future as an announcer would be determined by my performance on the upcoming Pro Wrestling USA tour. The shows were so important to me that I would have worked without pay.

But before long, as quickly as I had been booked, everything began to fall apart. One week before the start of the tour, the New Jersey promoters began calling. One by one, each apologetically scratched me from their shows. And each of their stories was identical. When Juster checked in to monitor advance ticket sales, he learned that I was booked as the announcer. Although my home state promoters believed that my involvement would add to the event, Gary thought otherwise.

While my past association with the WWF was attractive to smaller independent promotions, Juster considered my high WWF visibility a drawback. He wanted to present Pro Wrestling USA as a complete departure from what the fans were accustomed to seeing. He reasoned that with me on the show Pro Wrestling USA would look like it was imitating the WWF. Sending such a message could have undermined his attempt to make the statement that Pro Wrestling USA was not only different from, but superior to, the customary wrestling with which northeastern fans were familiar.

While I had been absent from McMahon's TV shows for almost a year, I couldn't argue with Juster's concern. Not only was I announcing at the occasional WWF house show, but also WWF video tapes, many of which contained my past work, had become top selling items. The video tape sales and rental market served to perpetuate the perception of my strong, continuing association with Vince McMahon, Jr. In fact, I no longer had a relationship with Vinnie and the WWF.

After the rapid succession of cancellations, I nervously waited for Tommy Dee to pull me from his New York dates. But the call never came. So when I arrived for the first New York show, it was no surprise that I was not welcomed as a member of the team.

I was early for that first show in Brooklyn. About an hour before show time I began to change into my tux. By the time I was finished, Juster entered the dressing room. As we stared at each other across the locker room, it was evident that he was not happy. Expecting that he would pay me off and send me home without working, I decided that my best move would be to introduce myself and let him get to know me. In retrospect, this one decision added ten years to my career in wrestling.

Surprisingly, after the initial discomfort of my forced introduction, Gary and I quickly settled into an easygoing conversation. I don't know what I said to change his mind. I can't explain why he allowed me to work the rest of the tour. But we became so chummy, that after the final show at Hunter College in Manhattan, we found ourselves breaking bread like two long-time friends at a Greek eatery in Manhattan.

My best guess is, that by the end of the week, I was able to demonstrate that my skill as an announcer and my credibility with the fans could be used to bolster the Pro Wrestling USA product. It is likely that until he watched me work, Juster wasn't aware that I had become a WWF personality in my own right. Maybe he decided that by appearing on his shows, I was making the statement that Pro Wrestling USA was the wrestling of choice. Nevertheless, it was clear by the end of the week that he was convinced that my strong identification with the WWF could be used to his advantage. Shortly after the end of the Pro Wrestling USA mini-tour, Gary hired me to work the big follow-up show at the Meadowlands Arena.

Eight months after Pro Wrestling USA first beamed into the homes of WWF fans throughout the Northeast, my opening announcements to a receptive Meadowlands audience were significant beyond the obvious. My words would trumpet the triumphant debut of Pro Wrestling USA to the New York area. My presence would signal that, as the ring voice of the WWF for the past eleven years, I now endorsed the competition. My ceremonious declaration of independence from Vince McMahon could not have been more public.

As I approached the Pro Wrestling USA ring, my act of defiance stemmed from the shabby treatment that I could no longer tolerate. As I addressed the home crowd on behalf of the opposition, my vigor was bolstered by memories of my public humiliation when Vince yanked me from the middle of the Spectrum ring back in 1983. As I interacted with this new cast of characters, with the skills that I had developed in WWF rings, I remembered the snub of learning about the cancellation of the *All Star* show just moments before informing the public one year earlier. My performance carried an added purpose. My words resounded with conviction. My self-respect prevailed over the fear of never working in pro wrestling again.

While I expected McMahon to dismiss me the morning after my Pro Wrestling USA debut, that was not to be the case. Oddly enough, Monsoon continued to call me to emcee at charity events and to announce at the WWF's own monthly Meadowlands shows. I never understood why Vince didn't fire me on the spot. He certainly knew that I worked the rival show since it was his practice to send spies to scout his competitors whenever they raided his home turf. But neither McMahon nor Monsoon said a word about working for Crockett and Gagne. So without anyone objecting to my participation at the rival shows, I continued to work for both companies.

As it turned out, it was my decision to disassociate myself from the WWF that terminated our eleven-year relationship. I was uncomfortable proclaiming the superiority of the wrestlers who worked for Pro Wrestling USA one week and the virtues of the WWF the next. I began to feel that my appearances at the Meadowlands for both organizations began to compromise my credibility.

At all of the live shows, I was the promotion's spokesman. I broke the bad new to the fans when a headliner didn't show up, delivering fabricated explanations in a convincing manner. I set the stage for main events with exciting buildups and lent realism to the show by establishing a tone of sorrow when an "injured" baby face was carried from the ring. I was the approachable figurehead who tempered the fans' anger when they felt the need to voice a complaint.

I knew that my believability as a performer was my most marketable attribute. My announcing style and mannerisms could be imitated, but the years of trust that I had developed with the fans were uniquely mine. And it was this most valued distinction that I needed to preserve.

It was a second chance to make the same choice. I thought my fate had been sealed the moment I broke ranks. But when the WWF kept me on their booking sheets, I began to have second thoughts. Even after declaring my independence, I remained confused. Should I stay with Vince, hoping to be included in the WWF expansion? Or should I attempt to parlay my reputation as a credible wrestling personality into a position with Pro Wrestling USA?

107

Once again, a crucial decision was made easier when Verne Gagne's son Greg asked me to join the AWA announce team for their new TV program. It was to be the first pro wrestling show ever on ESPN; my first opportunity to perform before a national audience on a bona fide sports outlet. From that point forward, I never worked for Vince McMahon, Jr. again.

As Gagne headed for ESPN without Crockett, the co-promotion's ambitious plan to run monthly shows in the New York area ceased. Because of scheduling conflicts, astronomical expenses and clashing egos, Pro Wrestling USA's tours were scaled back. The only regularly running city where the renegade promotion continually held its own against the WWF was Baltimore.

Every Tuesday night ESPN presented two American pastimes that bordered on the outer limits of sport, pro wrestling

and roller derby. A quarter page ad in USA Today advertised *Tuesday Night Slams and Jams*, a three hour block set aside for two activities which had long been considered fringe or pseudo sports.

The roster of performers who wrestled for Verne during the years that I announced for the AWA is noteworthy, both for the legendary names, as well as for those who have gone on to become today's industry leaders. During my tenure with the AWA, Rick Martel, Stan Hansen, Nick Bockwinkel, Curt Hennig, Jerry Lawler and Verne's son-in-law, Larry Zbyszko, held Verne's version of the world heavyweight belt. Among those who held the AWA tag team straps while I was with the organization were the teams of The Road Warriors, Scott Hall and Hennig and Marty Janetty and Shawn Michaels. Also featured on Verne's cards were Sergeant Slaughter; Gorgeous Jimmy Garvin with his valet, Precious; Michael Hayes, Terry Gordy and Buddy Roberts, The Fabulous Freebirds; David Sammartino; Stan Lane and Steve Kiern, The Fabulous Ones; Rick Steiner and Sherri Martel.

We went into production in July and the American Wrestling Association debuted its first ESPN program on August 27, 1985. But although the AWA had assembled a formidable team of wrestlers to perform on a legitimate sports network, Gagne's unimaginative, out of date promotional tactics quickly weakened the initial impact that this new program briefly enjoyed.

Verne, who had retired from regular mat action by the time we met, had always been widely respected for having won both the Big Ten and NCAA heavyweight titles in 1949. Immediately after college, he turned pro.

After twelve years on the wrestling circuit, Verne formed the AWA when he crowned himself champion in 1960. He liked being the champ. Must have. By the time we met for the ESPN experiment, he had given himself the AWA title on nine different occasions defeating Gene Kiniski, Dr. Bill Miller, The Crusher, Fritz Von Erich, Mad Dog Vachon and Dick Beyers in the process.

Gagne, the eternal champ!

When Gagne retired in 1981, he did so with the belt still around his waist. At the age of 53, he just declared himself unbeatable. It didn't seem to matter that the future of his own company would have been better served if Verne, the legend, fell to a charismatic up and comer whose guts and determination could carry the fans' support into the post-Gagne era. That would have been a plan geared for the future. Instead, by walking away with the belt, Verne was saying, in effect, that no one else in his company, no matter how big, how strong, how young or how expert a wrestler could take down the 53-year-old icon. "So folks", Verne was seeming to say, "I am retiring with my belt around my waist because legitimate wrestlers like myself can never be beaten by today's talent." And then he went on to build his company around the wrestlers who were not good enough to beat the guy whose first title reign began twenty-one years earlier.

I am in no way lending this insight into the psyche of Gagne to ridicule him. He gave Minneapolis fans believable performances and solid wrestling for many years. He has been credited with teaching the basics to such stars as Ric Flair, Bob Backlund, Ken Patera and Ricky Steamboat. He was good to me during the years of our association. But understanding the mentality of Verne Gagne is essential in order to comprehend the mindset of his generation of promoters as well as to explain some of the decisions that are inconceivable to the average viewer. They are judgments that are contrary to what would seem like common sense from a fan's perspective because they have more to do with politics and outdated thinking and huge egos of the powers that run pro wrestling than with doing what's best for business, what's best for wrestling. My favorite personal anecdote about Gagne clearly shows how out of touch he was.

The ESPN tapings were held every few weeks in the main ballroom of the Tropicana Hotel and Casino in Atlantic City. It was mostly a local New Jersey crowd with some fans traveling from Philadelphia and New York to see the wrestlers who had never before performed live on the East Coast.

It was an easy gig for me in all ways. The casino was just an hour from my home, which allowed me plenty of time to make the shows following a full day of classes. And the perks were great. The Tropicana staff generously comped the performers with rooms, meal vouchers and other amenities.

Throughout the run of the show I had no idea how large our viewing audience was or whether the ESPN executives were satisfied with our ratings. I was aware only of the casino's gradual dissatisfaction with the makeup of our audience. The Tropicana had spotters positioned outside the ballroom to monitor the flow of the crowds. Unlike boxing, whose patrons dropped big money at the gaming tables before and after the fights, wrestling was a family affair. After buying a wrestling ticket and a hot dog, our fans headed home at the conclusion of the last match to get their kids ready for school the next morning.

By the end of October I sensed there was trouble. Verne was telling me to pep up my ring announcements. He wanted me to smile more when I was on camera. He insisted that I keep the wrestlers facing the cameras for their introductions. I did what I could to please him, but I ignored his impractical request that Stan "The Lariat" Hansen or The Mongolian Stomper could be prompted to adhere to television etiquette. While the suggestions were typically Verne, his tone of voice and his demeanor were not. He always had presented himself in a sincere manner, though with the backslapping ease of a gregarious politician. But after the show had run for a few months, he developed uneasiness, an edge, and an uncharacteristic uncertainty.

He cornered me after a show in late October. I had just entered the banquet hall that we used as a dressing room.

110

"Gary, do you have a minute? I want to ask you a question."

"Sure Verne, what's up?"

"What do you think of the show?"

I stopped for a few seconds to carefully consider the question, which had come out of nowhere and more importantly, I needed time to measure my response.

"Well, Verne, do you really want to know the truth?"

"Sure. Just tell me what you think."

"I think that your talent is strong and your commentators are effective with what they have to work with. But the problem is that you haven't given them a whole hell of a lot of interesting scenarios. You've got wrestlers jumping others for no apparent reason and matches booked without any build up. Except for the fans who know about your wrestlers' pasts, most of the audience doesn't understand why one guy's beating on another. There's no depth to their personalities. The viewers don't understand why they should root for your faces other than to put the heels down. That wears thin after a while."

Gagne just looked at me in disbelief. I didn't know whether he was shocked that I answered truthfully or if he was having trouble understanding what I was saying. To break his silence, I followed up with a question of my own.

"Verne . . . what do *you* think?"

He paused for a moment before answering.

"I don't know. I've never seen the show."

This time *I* looked at *him* in disbelief. Certainly, I must have misunderstood.

"You've *never* seen your *own* show?"

"Just what I said. I don't know. Never saw the show. I don't get cable where I live."

"Oh."

That was about all I could think to say as I wandered off replaying the conversation back in my mind. Some time later, Precious Paul Ellering, manager of The Road Warriors confirmed that Verne did indeed live in a remote lakeside region that was not yet wired for cable. But this didn't explain why Gagne didn't take the time to review the show at his studio where Mike Shields, his full time director, could cue up whatever Verne wanted to watch.

I started to wonder if Verne understood the importance of his ESPN opportunity. Did he realize that this was his last chance, although a long shot, to be a player in the game that was quickly being monopolized by McMahon? What would it take for Gagne to see that without a national platform, any hope of countering the WWF tidal wave would have been foolhardy? Did Verne realize how high the stakes were? Was he incapable of booking a show outside of the formula that had for years served him so well in Minneapolis? Was this the best he could do? Was he trapped in a time warp? Did he know any different?

It is fair to question just how difficult it really was for Verne Gagne and Ole Anderson and Don Owen and Gene La Belle and Paul Boesch and McMahon, Sr. and Eddie Graham and Fritz Von Erich and Crockett, Sr. and Joe Blanchard and a dozen other regional promoters to have attained such heights of success in their heyday.

Is it so difficult to believe that a company with little or no competition, a business which dominates its employees with a take it or leave it attitude, an entertainment form in which the corporate arm has complete creative control over its product with the ability to quickly modify it until its audience will buy it has a better chance than most to thrive?

Which brings one to wonder how spectacular was Vince McMahon Jr.'s coup in closing down wrestling office after wrestling office when he invaded their territories. And that is not to undermine the enormity of Vinnie's success. It is just to ponder that maybe the promotional dinosaurs of wrestling had become so complacent after years of big business, without the need to deliver a creative product, that maybe they were ripe for the picking. If not Vince, it could easily have been the next guy in line with the audacity to break the barriers in which the sport had been entrenched for decades.

Verne, with legitimate wrestling credentials to back up his championship belt and his refusal to allow the title to stray far from around his waist, epitomized the mentality of his promoting colleagues. He was the personification of a company, which had always promoted the same Midwestern mat traditions that have delivered so many winning teams on the university level. The AWA was the glorification of the American work ethic. Train hard, learn your craft well and the public will always be in your corner. This basic, no nonsense approach that had worked for years was no longer relative to the wrestling business as it had been redefined by McMahon. And outside of their tried and true formulas, the industry's pioneers were lost.

I think that McMahon, himself, gave the most accurate answer in an interview with *Icon* magazine in August 1997 when he was asked why he was able to overtake the more experienced, better financed regional promoters. His answer was simple: "They didn't have the balls to do it."

It is unlikely though, that most of the others had the flair to deliver a wrestling product glitzy enough to capture the imagination of the casual fan for the long run. It has been Vince's innovative marketing of pro wrestling that has sustained the WWF's dominance for so long. While he had the chutzpah to frame the basic wrestling formulas with all of the trappings of a Hollywood production, Verne, like many of his contemporaries, had chosen to preserve wrestling's past by living in it.

I remained with the AWA until December 1985 when the tapings moved to Las Vegas. In retrospect, while my role on the show lasted only six months, bolting from the WWF to ESPN was the right move for me to make at the time. There was no reason to believe that Junior's treatment of me was going to change. In addition, the exposure that I received from my work on national television brought me even more offers to work for independent promotions across the country.

For the first time, I was left without the backing of a major office. In effect, I became my own agent. But after an initial flurry of job offers, my phone stopped ringing. With my teaching duties curtailing my freedom to travel, landing another TV opportunity was a long shot. I needed to continue teaching for the core income that education had always provided, since it was impossible to earn a living from the money that the unreliable independent groups were offering.

Despite the adversities that I had weathered during my first eleven years in the game, my love for the wrestling spectacle had not waned. I had elevated the role of ring announcer to where I was a recognized and relevant part of the show. The performance bug had bitten and was still a large part of how I defined myself.

As the low man on the talent roster of wrestling performers, I was like the circus laborer who constantly squawked about the disgrace of scooping up elephant droppings for a living. Finally, a co-worker, tired of the never-ending complaints, turns to him and says, "Stop bellyaching. If ya don't like the work, then quit." Defiantly dropping his shovel, the laborer indignantly snaps, "What? And leave show business?"

Chapter Nine
"Barely Legal"

I'd rather be a failure at something I love than a success at something I hate.   **George Burns**

B ranching out into the unknown was a difficult step to take. While my early years under the guardianship of the WWF were at times filled with anxiety, continuing outside of its custody was terrifying. Throughout the early years, under the watchful eyes of even an abusive guardian, at least there had been the security of television exposure, which guaranteed steady work at live events. Now, without the assurance of mass media visibility, my public voice was sure to fade to a whisper. Even for a long running cast member like myself, I was fearful of soon being forgotten. I knew that the longer I remained off TV, the less valuable I would seem even to the upstart promotions.

But while I was realistic about the instability of my status, I couldn't anticipate the predicaments of announcing for the independents. After years of working for a professionally run outfit like the WWF, I was about to receive a crash course in how to survive the treacherous existence of a gypsy announcer.

It is common for outsiders to make the false assumption that announcing for a major league, under the scrutiny of a vast viewing public, is much more challenging than working a little-noticed spot show at a rinky dink roller rink. Nothing can be farther from the truth. While my work at noteworthy events is forever open to scrutiny via video, there are built-in safeguards that protect my high profile performances from flagrant blunders.

Whenever I worked for an established organization, the performers, for the most part, understood the importance of everyone on the show looking good. We protected each other. We worked together to put each other over. On the other hand, at hit and run shows, everyone is working cold. Aside from the past reputations of a couple of headliners, there is no rhyme or reason to most of the matches. Everyone just tries to get through the night.

Behind the scenes, the support staff for a televised broadcast is the same experienced team that regularly work together to make an event run smoothly. With little discussion, everything easily falls into place. Spot shows are staffed by anyone who can be enlisted for the night, from the promoter's mother-in-law to his neighbor's kids.

After years of working comfortably at the major events, I soon experienced the many headaches of announcing for the mom and pop shows. I quickly learned that maintaining a semblance of professionalism on the indie circuit was much more difficult than even the greatest of challenges presented by performing before millions on television.

At a local show, while the main eventers are usually seasoned pros, the undercard is filled with kids breaking into the business. While many possess the natural talent and professionalism to become stars of the future, there is also an abundance of self-important rookies who have a lot to learn, too much to say and expect everyone to listen. They're rookies looking to make a name for themselves whose placement on the card is often dependent on the number of tickets they sell to the event, instead of based on how talented they are.

While I encountered a good number of questionable characters during my years on the independent circuit, I consider myself fortunate that even the most unrealistic entrepreneurs, those, who expected to make a fortune in the wrestling business, were often well-intentioned. But my most vivid memories surround the unlikely predicaments and disreputable scoundrels that have always plagued the indies.

The Convention Hall in Asbury Park, New Jersey has always held many memories of my first romance with wrestling. At one time Asbury, the Queen City of the Jersey shore, swelled in the summer with fun loving family vacationers. But pillaged by the race riots that tore through its streets in 1969, the brief resurgence of nightlife, which brought Bruce Springsteen to the forefront, proved to be the city's last gasping breath of life. The convention center was a sad remembrance of the glory days when so many of the top touring rock groups and family shows were included on its summer schedule of events. The tattered yellow handbills decorating the faded walls of its box office offered a haunting reminder of a bustling wrestling palace that now, in its declining years, had become a cheap rent opportunity for small time promoters to run low budget shows.

I always looked forward to my Asbury bookings. The hallowed hall held so many childhood memories of the drama and the thrills that captured my imagination as an impressionable youngster. And best of all, the beachfront auditorium never failed to draw a most curious cross-section of characters. The three thousand fans, who often packed the house, were a mix of inner city toughs, lily white suburbians and carousing New Yorkers all looking for a wild night of fun. Throughout my years on the independent scene, I returned many times to the storied building. It was during this period that I came upon one of my most bizarre experiences.

Arriving at the once majestic hall early one balmy evening in late Spring, Billy Dello, a personable promoter and good friend, greeted me in the front lobby with a little more enthusiasm than usual.

"Yeah, we're goin' to have a good crowd tonight. The phone hasn't stopped ringing since this morning. Put my son in the box office so I don't have to worry about the money disappearin'. It's Slaughter ya know. The kids go wild for him. He charges a bundle, but he's well worth it. Brings the little ones with their moms and dads. Never fails."

Throughout his non-stop babbling, his eyes never met mine. His hands dug deep into his pants pockets as he shifted his weight from side to side. The few times he'd pause for a breath, I filled in with an "Uh huh", "I know" or "You're right".

My attention wandered away from his ramblings as I became lost in the decor of the hall's grand lobby. Many times over the years I had survived the crush of the crowd, guardedly pawing my ringside ticket, caught up in the contagious anticipation that filled the air of every wrestling show in Asbury. The stained red velvet ropes, which somehow managed to restrain the mob that always crowded into the lobby, still swaggered from their gold tarnished metal posts.

"Tried to get the midgets on the show, but the trans from Canada was more than I wanted to spend"

The oriental design of the tattered carpet of the outer lobby had faded along with the memories of so many concerts, athletic events and expos that had rolled through the building over the years.

"A midget tag match, now that would have been perfect with Slaughter on top!"

My eyes scanned the paint chipped walls as voices of the boisterous ring crew echoed from inside the hall. My attention settled on the show poster advertising that night's card.

"But the kids are goin' to get a big kick out of the undercard. Wait 'til they see him."

The placard was printed in the same ruby red that sent tingles down my childhood spine each time I spotted one posted in a storefront window on Asbury Avenue. The square jaw of the fatigue-clad Slaughter seemed to protrude from above the bleeding letters that blazed beneath his out of focus picture.

"They're gonna be talkin' 'bout this for a long time."

Scanning the names of the supporting players, my attention was drawn to another fuzzy photo. It was a shot not only blurry, but furry. My peering eyes quickly darted back to the promoter. And then back to the poster. And then back to Billy. Our eyes finally met.

"Have ya heard who I booked for the kids?"

As soon as I realized where his one-sided conversation was leading, my immediate reaction could not be contained.

"Don't tell me you expect me to get in the ring with Victor! No way!"

I had read a lot about Victor over the years. He gained much attention as a novelty act, wrestling mostly at summertime state fairs and carnivals throughout the South and Midwest. Victor was a one of a kind performer. Weighing in at over 700 pounds, he was such a feared and awesome sight, that few wrestlers ever agreed to work with him. From the second he slumped into his assigned corner, he was known to direct an angry but guarded glare at his foe. At the sound of the opening bell, Victor unleashed a fierceness, the likes of which had never before been seen in a wrestling ring. He never listened to the referee. He never sought the crowd's approval. He never wasted any time to get the job done. And he almost never lost. The curiosity that surrounded Victor was that he was a bear. He was billed as Victor The Wrestling Bear, 700 pounds of grisly grizzly.

No human wrestler, regardless of how ill tempered, could ever get away with the privileges that were afforded to Victor. His single-minded goal was to win at all costs, in the least amount of time, knowing that the true reward for his labor awaited him in his private quarters. The faster he could end his match, the sooner he would slurp down the dinner that was simmering backstage.

Each of his matches followed the same pattern. His opponent was always his trainer who had taught him every hip toss, leg dive and bear hug that he executed with confidence. Victor often flattened his ill-fated pseudo-foe in five minutes or less and then gleefully dashed back for his dressing room feast. All very simple. Very straight forward. Very entertaining. However, on this occasion, if Billy got his way, Victor's act would be expanded to include me.

"Now, Gary, there is absolutely nothing to be nervous about," Billy bravely continued. "He always wears his muzzle you know."

"And for a very good reason, Billy."

"He's as tame as a teddy bear."

Victor & Billy Graham, two pros.

"A teddy bear? I don't think so. Don't you remember the story about how Victor got out of control? I think it was in Tennessee. They had to shoot him with a tranquilizer gun to restrain him. Billy, you've got to be out of your mind if ya think I'm goin' to get into the ring with that beast."

"Now listen, do you think I would ask you to do this if I thought there was a chance that you'd get hurt?" Knowing better than to wait for a response, he continued. "The kids will get a kick out of seeing you feed him before the match."

"Feed him? What are you talking about? I thought you said Victor was always muzzled."

"Well, he will be . . . . . except for when he shares his Coke with you. The kids will go wild."

"The kids will go wild? You're insane. Billy, whose idiotic idea is this?"

"Well, it wasn't really anybody's idea. It's just a perfect tie in for our promotional sponsor, the Coca-Cola Bottling Company in Neptune. The public relations guy at Coke says that this gimmick can't miss."

"And I'm sure he'll get a big kick out of Victor smashing the Coke bottle over my head too. That is if he can make out what's going on from the safety of his balcony seat. How much are they paying you to have me share a coke with the bear?"

"Hey look. I'm not going to force you to do it. It was just an idea that they thought you'd go along with."

An hour and a half before the start of the show, a contingent of animal-rights activists from the ASPCA, along with a police escort, showed up at the box office demanding to see Victor. The show posters with the blurry, furry photo of Victor had not escaped the critter crusaders. They had been gearing up for this raid from the day Billy had filed for his permit with the Asbury Park Board of Health. But Billy, an ex-Asbury cop, had been tipped off in advance. He knew it had been a long while since these die-hard defenders of animals had reason to spring into action and he was ready for them.

With most of the oceanfront amusement concessions boarded up, there was little to keep the area's militant advocates busy. Chester, the dancing chicken, who had performed his final pirouette at a local arcade years before, had been a seasonal concern of the group. Chester was boxed in an elevated cabinet, securely encircled by a chicken wire mesh. When your quarter entered the coin chute a jazzy tune blared from a speaker on the side of the cabinet, a corn pellet-filled bin opened and faint electric shocks heated the platform beneath the chicken's feet. Chester danced to the music, then feasted on the corn pellets as his reward for a captivating thirty-second performance. Chester's final curtain fell the day the Monmouth County chapter of the ASPCA was formed.

After retiring Chester from show business, their only remaining purpose had been to free the hundreds of gold fish, swimming in water filled plastic bags, which were offered as boardwalk prizes. It was no surprise that the liberators of livestock were primed when Victor ambled into Asbury. Much like the big game hunters they opposed, they silently lay in wait until just before show time for the surprise attack.

At each stop on the fury fighter's tour, inspections of this sort were routine. His handlers knew what to expect. Having completed a swing through New England just days earlier, the 700-pound grizzly was fresh from successfully sparring with the impassioned members of the New England chapter. He had maintained his winning streak and was ready for another challenge. So when the Asbury authorities found Victor's dressing room cleaner and more spacious than Sergeant Slaughter's, his diet more well balanced than their own, his training more complete than most of the preliminary wrestlers and his pay certainly topping mine, they backed off and did what any well-intentioned humanitarian would do: they gave Victor the green light to annihilate of a fellow human being.

By match time Billy and I had sorted out our differences. The plan was for me to present the challenger while Victor waited in the wings. When I began the build up for the bear, the trainer's wife would lead him down the aisle. By the time they reached ringside, I would be long gone thus relinquishing center stage for Victor to guzzle his bottle of Coke. Simple. Safe. Effective. Everyone would be happy.

When we reached Victor's match, everything began as planned. From the middle of the ring, I introduced his nightly nemesis, constantly looking over my shoulder to confirm that the bear was cooperating as promised. I was relieved with each glance back at the stage to find Victor docilely peering from behind the curtains. Spinning to face the entrance aisle, I began the stirring intro that would bring forth the grappling grizzly.

The creature appeared on cue before the awed assemblage. He towered over his lovely blonde escort who carefully gripped the harness that kept him close to her side. But no more than a few words had passed my lips when Victor bolted from the side of his diminutive handler, snapping his leash from her delicate grasp. A squadron of middle-aged, overweight policemen, their caps flying in the air, dove out of the unruly animal's way. His attendant, seemingly annoyed by Victor's rewrite of our agreed upon script, was hot in pursuit. Using the severed leash as a whip on the bear's back side, her desperate actions only accelerated Victor's mad dash toward me. Like a startled deer in the middle of the night, blinded by the headlights of an oncoming truck, I was defenseless.

My heart pounded inside my immobile body when the big brown brute reached the end of the aisle and abruptly screeched to a halt. He stopped short of entering the ring, deciding instead to remain on the floor. Violently flailing his gigantic paws at the crowd, the unharnessed beast sent our terrified ringsiders running for cover. Occasionally sticking his snout through the ring ropes, Victor calmly peeked at my tense form from behind his leather muzzle. Oddly enough, the threatening advances of the intimidating bully contradicted an attentive and knowing sparkle in his eyes. Through all of the commotion, I recognized a familiarity in his glance. I had seen the gleaming look before. It was the look of George "The Animal", the Superfly and other beastly brawlers from my past.

I then noticed that he never strayed from where the ring lights illuminated the floor. He kept a safe distance from the closest taunting fan. He was causing havoc without endangering anyone's safety. I finally realized that Victor knew what he was doing. He had the timing of a well-trained veteran. He had everything under control. Victor was now running the show.

Somehow comforted by the realization that I was working with a seasoned pro, my rousing introduction resumed with confidence. When his handler caught up with him at ringside, she tugged once on his harness whereupon he gingerly mounted the ring steps and then paused. When she joined him on the ring apron, she tugged twice and he dutifully entered the ring. Victor slowly slumped into his corner and patiently glanced at me. I was beginning to think that if he wasn't silenced by the muzzle, his proper upbringing would have prompted a heartfelt thank you for my rousing fanfare that added excitement to his entrance.

Within ten minutes Victor was back in his dressing room, feasting on his reward for a stellar performance. He had stirred up the crowd, dutifully chugged down the Coke and pinned his friendly foe in short order. Unlike many that I worked with along the independent circuit, I developed an instant respect for the good-natured professionalism of my new colleague, Victor.

Victor The Wrestling Bear turned out to be one of the more honorable figures that I encountered over the following three years. Unlike the underhanded charlatans that sought out my services, my burly bud lived up to his promise.

By the end of 1986, many of the job offers I received were from front men determined to get rich in the midst of the pro wrestling explosion. Their pockets were stuffed with the money of unwitting investors who schemed to carve out a piece of the wrestling pie for themselves. If Vince dropped any crumbs along the way, there was a long line of eager investors with outstretched hands behind him. For some starry-eyed marks, bankrolling a wrestling event was their opportunity to rub elbows with the stars. It was my first experience of distinguishing between the reputable entrepreneurs and the thieves. In the same way I learned my craft, it was a trial by error process to separate one from the other.

In December of that year I received a call from a fellow who was lining up talent for an all-female fight video. From the start of his pitch, as soon as he laid claim to being George "the Animal" Steele's nephew, I should have seen the con. Unfortunately, I allowed him to continue to tell me that the show's producer, Tor Berg, who usually promoted Verne Gagne's AWA events in Alaska, had made arrangements to shoot the action in Houston. I was offered a $350 guarantee, plus Berg would pick up the tab for my private hotel room as well as the round trip airfare between New Jersey and Texas.

The direct to home video footage would be shot at an event co-promoted with long time-wrestling impresario, Paul Boesch. Berg's troupe of lady wrestlers would supplement the local talent Boesch always assembled for his regular Friday night cards at the Sam Houston Coliseum. The matches of local interest would alternate with the female free-for-alls.

The Berg-Boesch arrangement seemed like a perfect marriage. Teaming with Boesch's successful promotion guaranteed Berg the excitement of a rousing house for his video. As far as Boesch was concerned, the deal appeared to be a no lose proposition. In addition to the extra revenue from Berg, his loyal Houston fans would be treated to an unusual lineup of wrestlers. This was especially attractive since holding on to his local fans had become more difficult of late now that the WWF had begun competing in the Houston market.

Although unfamiliar with Berg, I was assured that he was on the level. And from what I knew of Boesch's success in Texas, I took the job on the spot

Immediately, I began to meticulously map out my trip to the Lone Star State. It was the first road trip that I had ever booked for myself, so I was careful to line up everything to my liking. I would arrive early on the day of the show. A car would be waiting to scoot me over to the hotel. I would spend a restful day in the hotel room to prepare for my Houston debut. I would meet the production crew late in the afternoon for an organizational meeting. We would all be whisked off to the Sam Houston Coliseum to coordinate our efforts with our Houston based hosts. Every base was covered. Everything was in place. Every detail was confirmed. And nothing went according to plan.

When I arrived at the hotel, the desk clerk informed me that my name was not on the private room list. Instead, there was a double room registered to "Cappetta / The Samoan". I told him that he was mistaken. I tried to explain that I was traveling alone and neither Afa nor Sika, the only Samoans that I knew at the time, was with me. With an innocent shrug of his shoulders he insisted, "Mr. Berg personally approved the room list. He has made it clear that he will not pay for any changes, whatsoever!"

I snatched up my luggage and made my way to the room. Slipping the key into the door lock, a shuffling could be heard from within. When I swung open the door, there was a squat, thickly muscled islander propped up on one elbow on a bed at the far end of the room. The lifelessness of his bloodshot eyes disguised his self-protective instinct, as his outstretched hand reached beneath the bed pillow for what I later discovered was the dagger-like blade that he always carried for protection. Realizing that my unexpected intrusion caused the Samoan to spring into a defensive stance, whereby it was now my life that was in danger, I reached for the words to put this attack dog at ease.

"Hi. Uh . . . think you must be my roommate for the night. I . . . uh . . . I thought I had a private room, . . . but . . . uh . . . it looks like they switched things around. Hope ya don't mind. We can get this all straightened out later if ya want."

Eyeing his partially exposed paw, protruding from beneath the pillow, I slowly made my way to his side of the room. Extending a hand in friendship I introduced myself with the hope that my five fingers would be returned to me unbroken.

His deadened eyes coldly floated across my form with no attempt to mask his scowling sneer. Slowly, he withdrew his hand from beneath the pillow to offer a clammy, but gentle handshake. It was the handshake of a fighter. Ever so light. Fingertips touch. A faint and always so gentle squeeze of hardened tissue. Wrestlers never offer a firm handshake. A limp-wristed press of the flesh always sufficed. The workers have nothing to prove. It was an undeniable sign that the massive Samoan held himself out to be one of the boys.

Without even a word, he nonchalantly turned away, instantly sinking back into a sleep so deep, that the gasps of his guttural snore drowned out the clattering fan of the hotel's ventilation system. His protective mask melted into a dreamy grin. Unlike the past aggressors who faced the brutality of which he was capable, he was satisfied that his roomie posed no threat whatsoever.

By 3:30 I had showered and readied my tuxedo for my Houston debut with a half-hour to spare. As I watched the local newscast, the Samoan (I could never remember his Polynesian name) rolled out of bed and lumbered directly out the door on his way to "Mr. B's fuckin' suite" as he put it.

Shortly thereafter, I made my way to the large windowed lobby where I could see a flock of female fighters aimlessly milling beside a giant tour bus, which was parked on the side of the building.

The women were a peculiar assortment of leather and lace. Huddled in separate cliques, clinging close to their sponsoring agents, everyone was preoccupied with whether the show would go on. Rumors were flying that the deal between Boesch and Berg had fallen through. My eyes scanned the two groups of gal gladiators as an uneasy undertone spread among the performers.

It was natural that Luna Vachon headed the Canadian contingent. It was her father, Paul "The Butcher", who had recruited the Montreal performers for this event. Throughout her career, Luna has drawn considerable attention to herself by the physical transformation that she undergoes before each match.

From her early days in the sport, Luna carefully crafted a berserk ring persona to leave a vivid impression in the minds of all who caught her act. While she at times has modified her look, when she entered the ring that night, she was a frightful sight. Her neck was harnessed by a silver-studded leather dog collar,

The Longhorn lesbians loved the lovely Luna!

with a matching spiked armband that extended to partially cover her hands, exposing sharp clawing fingernails. A wide leather belt strapped around her waist supported thick links of silver chains, which menacingly swayed as she strutted around the ring. Another spike-studded strap latched between her legs for a reason that I have never understood. Beneath all of the adorning metal shackles, the one-piece halter top, tightly stretched around her body, was most distinctive for the suggestively positioned cut outs that revealed a gym-worked torso. Her black body suit barely extended to the upper reaches of her hips where flesh colored spandex hugged her buttocks and ran the length of her athletic legs. But strangely enough, the sadomasochistic trapping of this defiant dominatrix has never been the most eye-catching peculiarity of Luna's appearance.

In fact, the details of Luna's ring attire are often overlooked when distracted by the ghastly abnormality of her hairdo and face paint. Replacing her shaved eyebrows are glossy black thunderbolts which jut from the bridge of her nose to the top of her temples. At various times, the wild, shoulder length hair that covers half of her head is tinted a rainbow of iridescent colors. The other half of her head is shaved to reveal a tangled web of painted neon squiggles, as if the skin had been ripped from her cranium to reveal an intricate network of blood vessels and arteries that extend down across her cheeks bones.

Luna's twisted character remains faithful to the viciousness portrayed by the elders of the Vachon family of wrestlers. Uncle Maurice "Mad Dog" Vachon, along with aunts Vivian and Marie, were all well-known performers, as was Luna's father, Paul "The Butcher". As we waited to board the bus, The Butcher, who was in town to supervise the Canadian girls that he booked, was missing in action.

A second group of female fighters were huddled around Beverly Shade, a Florida based performer with many years of ring experience. The gal gladiators trained at the wrestling school that Beverly ran with her grappling mate, Billy Blue Rivers. Like a lioness, she protectively coddled her kittenish combatants. While Luna was as frisky as a wildcat, the youngsters in Beverly's entourage were withdrawn, almost bashful, as if intimidated by the daunting prospect of their wrestling debut before the TV cameras. They were an attractive assortment of pint-sized pixies, in their late teens, early

Beverly Shade {l.} led her girls to slaughter.

twenties. For some, this was their first time outside of The Sunshine State. Tonight was like their final exam at the end of a semester at Pro Wrestling U.

Impressed by the control that Shade easily exerted over her students, I was reminded of another teacher of toe holds and takedowns. She was the lady wrestler with whom I had worked most often, the grand dame of the grappling game, Lillian Ellison, better known as The Fabulous Moolah.

125

The great Women's World Champion, and undoubtedly the most famous female wrestler of all time, began her ring career as a valet to The Elephant Boy, under the name Slave Girl Moolah.   She became Women's World Champion on September 18, 1956 when she defeated Judy Grable in the final

match of a tournament held in Baltimore. Moolah held the title for 30 years until, at age 61, she was defeated by twenty-four year old Wendi Richter during the WWF's 1985 MTV special *The War To Settle The Score.* Today she has returned to WWF TV after nearly fifty years in wrestling!

As in the squared circle, Beverly Shade was just no match for Moolah when it came to the business of wrestling. The matriarch of the mat oversaw the operations of her own wrestling school. The training regimen for the girls at Camp Moolah was as rigorous as an army boot camp. But the price of sore muscles and

At 77, Moolah has now been reduced to bragging about her "puppies" aka breasts on WWF TV.

twisted ankles was a small one to pay compared to the monetary stranglehold that the champion spitfire often applied over the course of their careers.

Not only did Moolah's trainees pay the going rate to learn the ropes, but the crafty champ required them to live in dormitories at the headquarters of Camp Moolah on her estate in South Carolina. They were obliged to pay room and board until they were ready to work before the wrestling public. But it was at this point that Moolah's grip really began to tighten around the throats of her numerous proteges.

The wily businesswoman maintained an exclusive agreement with many of the ruling promoters, whereby she alone provided the female talent for their shows. Whenever one of the camp's alumni was booked by Moolah, they paid a booking fee for the privilege of being thrashed by the champ. You see, Moolah customarily matched herself with her own girls who were obliged to make her look good; those who could take the hair pulling and the stomach stomps that she loved to dish out during her title defenses. The champ had agreements with so many promoters around the country, that you either broke bread with Moolah or you were starved out of the business.

Lady wrestlers were never more than a seasonal attraction in the wrestling business. Never a mainstay in the promotions, but instead an added frill. The icing on the cake. A side show to the main event. The McMahons hired the girls, mostly for tag team matches, as a diversion to support their heavyweight drawing cards. In Florida, they were used mostly to entertain vacationers in the winter months. In short, since there was little work to begin with, only few could make a full time living on the mat and most were dependent on the veterans who trained them. If ya didn't dance with the one who brought ya, ya just didn't dance.

It was already an hour past our scheduled departure when Tor Berg, with his Samoan bodyguard (my roommate) close behind, called the Vachon and Shade camps together to announce that there was a change of plans. At the eleventh hour, his arrangement with Boesch fell apart due to their inability to work out the final details. To my knowledge, the only "final detail" that needed to be worked out was Berg's up front cash payment to the Houston promoter. I was convinced that my understanding was accurate when Berg went on to explain his alternate game plan to save the show.

Berg planned to move the event from the Sam Houston Coliseum to the Pasadena Civic Center without the cooperation of Boesch. We would be traveling by bus to Pasadena, a suburb just Southeast of Houston. The only remaining snag was that the bus driver would not let us on board until he was paid in full for his services. This was a problem since Berg couldn't come up with enough cash to satisfy his debt with the bus company.

But worry not, for Tor also had a solution to this second dilemma. His Samoan henchman would be taking contributions from the performers to raise whatever "loose change" we could spare toward the bus fare. He never promised to repay those who chipped in, not that it would have mattered anyway.

To my amazement, the girls began to gather whatever money they could scrape together as the angry-looking Samoan circulated among the talent. By the time he approached me, his hammer-like hands were stuffed with the contributions that my terrified fellow performers felt obligated to kick in. The look of outrage that covered my face did not deter my roommate from including me in his pickpocket scheme. Looking squarely in his piercing eyes, I barked, "Not a penny from me until I get my private room." It was the only time in our brief acquaintance that his scowl turned into a knowing grin.

Before long we were on our way. Zooming across the flatlands of Harris County, past petroleum refineries as far as the eye could see, the nervous chatter of the intimidated rookies was drowned out by Luna's boisterous chortle as she playfully chased the referee from one end of the bus to the other.

Aside from Berg, the Samoan, the referee and me, the only other men on board were the two play-by-play announcers. I sat with the commentators in the front of the bus reviewing the lineup for the evening's taping. After we determined how I'd dovetail the ring intros between their ringside commentary, they began to discuss the bargain they had found the day before.

"Hey, Gar, you should have flown in yesterday. We found a great deal on tuxedoes," the broadcaster beamed.

"Yeah," his partner chimed in. "Double breasted, one hundred per cent wool. Armani. The best."

This is the talk that gets an announcer's attention.

"Really? How much did you pay?"

They subtlety exchanged knowing glances until the first commentator blurted out, "Nothing. They're rentals and we'll be halfway home before they're due back in the shop!"

"Yeah, and they came with bow ties, cummerbunds and studs." His partner couldn't resist as if the theft of the accessories added respectability to their heist.

Heading southeast on Interstate 45, my eyes drifted out of the giant tour bus window. It was my only escape from the prevailing lunacy in this asylum on wheels. I envisioned the world's largest strawberry shortcake as advertised on roadside billboards publicizing Pasadena's upcoming Strawberry Festival. It would be a few months before the annual tradition would begin, but even the mud volleyball game, a favored event of the festival, sounded like clean fun compared to the slimy swindlers that were running this show.

By the time we pulled into the Civic Center, Luna, who, at the driver's request, had been restricted to the back of the bus, began gathering her many pieces of carry-on bags that were stuffed with the paraphernalia that transformed her from dizzy dame to dominatrix. Beverly huddled with the most mortified of her panicky crew for a last minute pep talk.

Although it was still an hour and a half before show time, the parking lot was noticeably empty. A few women were strolling around the barbecue pavilion while others congregated at the picnic area. As the bus pulled up to the building's rear entrance I wondered how Berg was planning to fill the 3,000-seat convention center on such short notice. After all, an all women wrestling show was a new twist to the typical event in Pasadena. This wasn't the Rodeo and Livestock Show. It was a departure from the Strawberry Festival. And this female fight affair was definitely a deviation from the Chamber of Commerce's Family Fall Festival.

Once inside, Beverly's bevy of beauties sped in one direction, the Canadian contingent in the other. You would have thought they were warring factions readying themselves for a battle between the United States and their neighbors to the North. But while this was indeed a contest between the two groups, the two factions would not be wrestling each other in center ring.

Each camp had mapped out their matches during the weeks leading up to the video shoot. There was nothing left to chance since the women warriors would be working with students from their own training camp. Beverly had her wrestlers' matches carefully planned and practiced in Florida, while the Vachons had whipped their girls into shape in Montreal. The group that could put together the best matches might impress the promoter and thereby gain future work in a marketplace where most lady wrestlers were regulars on the unemployment line. This was a tussle to score political points. And in that context, the battle lines were drawn for the only underlying competition - which group could present the most entertaining matches.

My prior experience with lady wrestling was exclusively through working with the WWF. Since Vince, Sr. always hired his female talent through Moolah, I was acquainted with Toni Rose, Donna Cristiantello, Vicki Williams, Peggy Patterson, Joyce Grable and all of the girls trained by the champ. While I had memorized the introductions of Moolah's girls, I was unfamiliar with the weights, hometowns and ring names that were required to properly introduce this evening's competitors.

As soon as I changed into my tux I began to hunt down each of the wrestlers to find out the specifics of their introductions. Many of the girls were so green that they had not yet decided on a wrestling alias. I tried to maintain eye contact with the partially clad women as they often deferred to Beverly or Luna who made up ring names and hometowns to suit their wrestling characters on the spot. By the time I finished with this lengthy process, I felt fully prepared for a long night of female fisticuffs. And once again, I couldn't have been more mistaken.

The moment I hit the ring, I became fully focused on the floor director's cues, while playing to the cameras for the delivery of my opening announcements. It was not until I took my place at ringside, after introducing the first match, that I had an opportunity to examine the spectators. I was immediately struck by how odd it was that eighty-five per cent of the audience was female. Before the nationalization of the WWF, wrestling audiences were overwhelmingly male. Back then, the women who attended only came along for the ride to please their husbands and boyfriends. This crowd was unlike any I had ever seen before.

As my eyes continued to scan the many sections of wildly enthusiastic women, one would have thought that they all shopped at the same boutique. And it wasn't Frederick's Of Hollywood. So many wore blue jeans and snake skin boots decorated by studded black leather that it was like being at a Harley Davidson hoedown. Women of all ages, sporting closely cropped butch hairdos, were adorned with tattoos instead of makeup.

They were hooting and hollering and stomping. One fan was so overcome when Beverly's dainty dames strutted to the ring, that she gave forth a deafening whistle that reverberated through her tobacco-stained teeth. The patrons who sat in the rows before her threatened a battle of their own as saliva-soaked clumps of chew sprayed into the air above them. From teenagers to middle-agers, they were on their feet, they were on their chairs, they were carrying on like oversexed teenage boys at a strip show. It was a crowd like I had never seen before. And finally it was beginning to make sense. At last it became obvious to me how Berg managed to fill the Civic Center on such short notice. By now I realized that the audience had been recruited at the eleventh hour from Houston's lesbian community.

I began to feel as if I had stumbled into the Li'l Abner comic strip. It was as if Pasadena, Texas had been transformed into Dogpatch USA. As if this was Sadie Hawkins Day, an event in Al Capp's cartoon in which the women of the town chase the object of their affection with a successful catch resulting in your claim on the intended. Mammy and Pappy Yokum would have suffered cardiac arrest to witness the Dykes on Bikes crowd heckling and hissing the dainty Daisy Mae-like dames from

Florida, while flashing the power sign at the beloved Luna. Given the choice between leather and lace, leather won out every time.

Luna Vachon's father, who booked the Canadian wrestlers and was to provide commentary for the video, was the only one with enough sense not to show up. Instead, he visited Paul Boesch, learned how Berg tried to stiff the prudent promoter and wisely decided to spend his time in Houston where he could have a chance of future bookings for the family talent. It was the advisable thing to do. It was politics.

Everything about my trip to Texas was doomed from the start. Sharing a room with the menacing Samoan. Never making my debut in Houston. Held up for bus fare. Working with the thieving announcers. I had no reason to believe there would be any change in the morning at check out time. And suspicious that I'd get stuck paying for my room, I decided to sneak out of the hotel in the middle of the night. As it turned out, this was my wisest decision of the day.

The Samoan, who didn't seem to need a sleeping aid to begin with, had visited a local gin mill where he washed away the memories of his many ordeals of the day. Upon returning to the room, he fell into bed where he rocked the room with gusts that blew out of every orifice. In the restlessness of his slumber, he twisted and turned, dislodging the bed pillows to reveal his lethal looking dagger. The blade must have measured five inches from its handle to its razor sharp tip. It was his security blanket. It would have added to my already insufferable ordeal had he felt threatened by any menacing movement on my part.

So I was cautiously moving lightly around the room, cramming my travel bags with belongings that would be sorted at home. I took care not to make a sound. I avoided any quick sudden movements. And I escaped.

The peaceful wee hours at the Houston airport supplied the necessary silence for the four-hour nap that I managed to sneak in at the departure gate. It had been a long day in which nothing that was promised ever materialized. I was lured by the opportunity to debut in Houston. I was charmed by the generous fee. But most disturbing of all, it was the first time that I was swindled out of a payday. And at the end of my twenty-one year career, I am happy to report that it was the only time that ever happened.

Chapter Ten
"Spin The Wheel, Make The Deal"

I've seen a pro wrestling stadium show live and it was stupendous, some of the best staged, coolest looking theater I've ever seen with more intellectual content in an arena show than David Byrne, Sinead O'Connor and Paul McCartney all put together (and those three in a "cage grudge match" is something I'd pay cash money to see).

Penn Jillette, "We've Made It To Big Time Wrestlin"

The Pasadena ordeal had served as a wakeup call. Now I realized that there would be no shortcuts. I'd have to start from the bottom and work my way up through the ranks all over again. After the female fight fiasco, I was a little less innocent. And I was a lot more wary of independent promoters. The experience taught me to doubt their tempting promises of big money payoffs. I became distrustful of offers, which promised to guarantee my return to the national spotlight. I was always on the lookout for the con. Always figuring the angle. I'm not distrustful by nature, but a defensive posture was necessary in order to fend for myself in the lonely world of independent wrestling.

Scamming promoters had become so common, that the New Jersey Athletic Commission instituted a policy to safeguard against the disreputable conmen. Promoters were now required to post a sizable bond, which was held by the state to settle any financial disputes that might arise. Until the policy went into effect, all personnel were paid in cash on the night of the show. Under the new regulation, the announcers and other licensees were given the opportunity to verify their fee with a state representative at the event. The promoter then cut a check for that amount to the commission, which was ultimately forwarded to the workers. In theory, many of the swindles that had become so widespread would be eliminated. In reality, promoters often preyed on the neediness of starving talent to undermine the intent of the law.

So even after the protective regulations were in place, I found myself at odds with a particularly sleazy New Jersey based promoter. He was running spot shows on four consecutive nights. The final event was a big TV shoot headlined by Sergeant Slaughter. It was a well financed venture, which was underwritten by Southland, the corporate parent of the 7-Eleven chain of convenience stores.

For each of the first three nights, I was shortchanged by twenty-five percent of my guaranteed fee. Each night the promoter promised to make it up from the next night's purse. Each time I believed him. The next night he never did. So by the time I entered the building for the finale of the mini tour, I had already been underpaid by three-quarters of my nightly pay.

Signing off with the NJ State rep on the first three nights of the tour for a fee that fell below what I had agreed to might have been a mistake. But I continued to believe the promises that my missing money would be paid by the end of the week. The big TV shoot was held out as the carrot at the end of the run and I was fool enough to chase it.

The thought crossed my mind to simply not show up for the taping, knowing that being shortchanged on the fourth night would be tantamount to working four shows for the price of three. But I was determined to make the conniving con man pay what he owed me. Without being sure of how I'd force the issue, my defensive armor was in place as I arrived at the television taping.

On this final night, I started the first of three TV hours by addressing the cameras with a rousing introduction, prompting a thunderous reaction from the enthusiastic crowd. The wrestlers, responding to the audience's rowdy approval, were on top of their game. Since the intermission was positioned squarely in the middle of the lineup, I called for a break half way through the second taping, signed a few autographs at ringside and was escorted back to the locker room.

Once backstage, I unhooked my bow tie and started to change from formal wear into street clothes. A couple of the wrestlers called over to find out where I was going.

"Home," I soberly responded. "Home, where I belong."

"Ya mean you're not going to introduce our matches? Who's goin' to do it then?"

"Whomever they pay to do it."

It didn't take long before word reached the promoter that I was about to head out the back door. Within minutes, he rushed into the dressing room, where he found me dressed in tee shirt and jeans as I secured my packed garment bag for the ride home.

"Where are *you* going?" he fumed. "The show's only half over."

The boys suddenly cut their conversations in mid-sentence as a hush came over the room.

"I didn't think you wanted me to work the rest of the matches."

"What are you talking about, Gar. You're working *all* of the matches. You know we're only half way through the second taping and there's another TV show after that."

By this time the commission representative and an official from the Southland Corporation had joined our locker room huddle. They listened intently as I continued.

"I realize that. But what I've already delivered is worth more than what you're willing to pay me."

"Hey look, we have an agreement. You've contracted to work the entire show. There are three TV tapings tonight. Don't give me any bullshit. Put your tuxedo on and get back to work."

"That's true. We do have an agreement. But there's more to our agreement than what *I'm* supposed to do for *you*. For the past three nights I've worked the entire show and you stiffed me every night. Underpaid me by twenty-five percent. I don't expect tonight to be any different. So let's see how *you* like coming out on the short end."

I reached for my gear as the rattled promoter blocked my path to the door.

"Listen to me. The commissioner is here with tonight's pay schedule. Tell him what I owe you for the tour. Then get dressed, get back to the mic and bring the popcorn match to the ring." Turning to the commissioner he added, "Pay him whatever he says I owe him."

So I totaled the amounts that were due me from the previous three nights, added my fee for the TV shoot and threw in an extra hundred bucks on account; on account of his mistaken impression that I was fool enough to let him get away with bamboozling me one more time.

A couple of weeks later I was suiting up for a show run by another indie promoter when the same promoter strolled into the dressing room to confirm future dates with wrestlers he had booked on his upcoming cards.

As soon as he spotted me, he headed in my direction and squawked, "Cappetta, I can't believe you're still workin'. After what you tried to pull at my TV shoot, you'll never work for me again."

"What makes ya think I'd ever *want* to work for someone who's not goin' to pay me? Everyone here knows what you're all about. So get out of my face. You're not foolin' anyone."

After a momentary silence, one of the boys let loose with a loud Ric Flair, "Whoa. You tell him Gar." The locker room then burst into laughter as the scumbag was escorted out of the building.

I was known for saying things that others, for fear of reprisal, only mumbled under their breath. Outspoken truths, while they can come back to haunt you, are always a welcomed rarity in pro wrestling.

Situations such as these sometimes caused me to sink as low as the con men who periodically surfaced. At times, I was provoked to fend for myself through means that were beneath the way I was accustomed to conducting business. But during the independent years, whenever I was left to wonder if remaining a part of the pro wrestling spectacle was worth tolerating the seedier side of the sport, I drew on the positive experiences from my many wonderful friends in the business.

Thankfully, I worked mostly for independent promoters who lived up to the terms of our agreements and more importantly, treated me with respect. They were entrepreneurs from different walks of life whose love of wrestling and the profits that could be garnered in its promotion led them to run well-organized and entertaining events.

It made sense for them to call upon me to emcee their shows. My familiar face and authoritative voice carried the feel of big time wrestling. I could lend an air of legitimacy to the small independents, which were springing up everywhere. Some of the more aggressive promoters even began producing bare bones TV shows ready-made for local cable access and the direct-to-video market. I welcomed the opportunity to remain active in the business with the hope that I'd soon be given another chance to re-establish myself on the national scene.

Jonathan Gold was perhaps the most creative of all. His tireless efforts to put together must see events are unsurpassed. Jon was the one who shined whenever the WWF gave him cards to promote with headliners who had lost their luster. While on paper the cards were often nothing special, Jon's offbeat promotional strategy made his events *seem* special. Jon's most memorable main event on the independent circuit featured The

Road Warriors tangling with Kevin Sullivan and Abdullah the Butcher. Who else would have advertised a match of such magnitude with a display ad picturing *me* in the area's major newspapers? Jon Gold did. And it worked!

"... and tonight, ladies and gentlemen, direct from the UNITED STATES TAG TEAM TOURNAMENT at the OMNI in ATLANTA, voted TAG TEAM of the Year, making their only NEW JERSEY-NEW YORK appearance...

THE ROAD WARRIORS!!

Tonight —— — — 8:00 P.M.

Dunn Sports Center
(Elizabeth High School)
Elizabeth, N.J.

Michael Cappetta **For further info:**

The Savoldis have been part of the wrestling scene for generations. Angelo, the patriarch of the Savoldi family, was a minor partner of Vince McMahon, Sr.'s Capitol Wrestling Corporation following his retirement from the ring. His son Mario often hired me to announce at his IWCCW shows throughout the Northeast, giving me my early experience doing ringside commentary as well as interviewing wrestlers.

Mitch Seinfeld, who I still affectionately refer to as "The Kid Promoter" was sixteen years old when he began to promote wrestling. He was a kid who easily held his own while negotiating booking fees with some of the biggest names in the business. Today, Mitch has turned to promoting of a different kind. He has appeared on The Home Shopping Network and QVC pitching an assortment of products. He has turned the simple pitch into an art form.

The "Unpredictable" Johnny Rodz, known in the Northeast as one of the best supporting wrestlers on countless McMahon, Sr. cards, booked me to announce for a series of televised events at the famed Gleason's Gym, located under The Brooklyn Bridge. A jeweler by trade, Rodz provided up and coming workers with their first taste of television, using me as the ringmaster to maintain order for the introductions of his unruly stable of young lions.

By the time my ESPN stint ended at the end of 1985, I had cultivated many ongoing associations with a network of independent promoters that lasted for my remaining years on the indie circuit and beyond. I feel fortunate for those relationships that have blossomed into personal friendships, which I cherish to this day.

My association with Pro Wrestling USA promoter Gary Juster allowed me to maintain a national presence. Beyond the Meadowlands events and the ESPN show, I began announcing for all of Juster's NWA and

AWA Northeastern house shows. I found Gary to be a multi-faceted individual who held a unique combination of insights into both the creative and business sides of wrestling. Growing up in Minneapolis, he developed a love of the wrestling spectacle as a fan of the AWA. After graduating from law school, he went to work in Washington, DC as a legislative aide to NJ Congressman, now US Senator, Robert Toricelli.

Contrary to the cigar-chomping stereotype of old time wrestling promoters, his refined manner gained him easy entree to the offices of TV executives and corporate sponsors where he sold them on the profitability of pro wrestling. Once inside, he was able to strike promotional deals, which, through his knowledge of wrestling and its fans, drew sizable crowds to Baltimore every month. He was as comfortable schmoozing station managers as he was joking with the wrestlers. Most importantly, his fair-minded dealing in both the boardrooms and the locker rooms gained him the respect of all.

Shortly after I began to appear on ESPN, Gary wanted to begin booking me into the Baltimore Arena, Pro Wrestling USA's most successful Northeastern venue. But to do so, he would have to fire the Baltimore announcer, an elderly gentleman whose position was endorsed by D. Chester O'Sullivan, the powerful athletic commissioner for the state of Maryland.

The veteran emcee was a dapper old guy. And he was spunky. But his over-exaggerated delivery and regular blunders became an embarrassment to the promotion. And Juster simply didn't have the heart to replace him.

Month after month Gary listened to the old man deliver an announcement that had been carefully outlined and explained beforehand. Each time a name was mispronounced or an important match stipulation was garbled, Juster cringed, shook his head and prepared himself for the harassing comments from his wrestling cohorts. Juster agonized over the thought of firing the veteran announcer. But when it became clear that the old fellow's blundering was hurting the promotion, there was no other option.

Gary explained his dilemma to me at an Atlantic City ESPN taping. As if he was ordering a doctor to disconnect his dear grandfather from his life support respirator, Juster mournfully laid out his plan for the transition. It was exciting news delivered in an ominous tone.

"Well, I've decided to bring you in to Baltimore next month," he lamented.

"Great. I've been waiting for you to say the word."

"But not to announce. Don't wear a tuxedo."

"What do you mean? Announce. That's what I do."

"I'm going to pull a couple of tickets for you. Bring a friend. I just want you to sit at ringside."

"Ringside. Okay. But why?"

"Because I just can't get rid of the old man that fast. I have to come up with a way that won't hurt his feelings. You know, some way that will make sense to him. Don't worry, I'll pay you for the night."

"That's fine with me. But what's the point of me sitting at ringside?"

"You don't have to sit there the whole night. I just want you to be at ringside when the old man introduces you. Then you come into the ring, shake the guy's hand and say something to the fans."

"Now wait. Let me see if I understand. You want me to be the replacement for your Baltimore announcer. But you don't want to hurt his feelings. And you think that by me taking over in front of a packed house is going to be a graceful transition?"

"No. No. At that point he won't know that you're going to replace him. You're just going to welcome the fans as the ESPN announcer and hand the mic back to him."

"Well, when are you going to tell him that he won't be coming back next month?"

"Why do you ask so many questions? I don't know that yet. I've got a month. I'll think of something."

By the melancholy look on Gary's face when I arrived at the Baltimore Arena, it was obvious that he was no closer to figuring out how he could fire the grandfatherly announcer without crushing the old man's spirit. Now *I* was feeling guilty as I snuck down to my ringside seat. At the appointed time, I was introduced, said hello to the crowd and then headed to the locker room to watch the rest of the show from backstage.

As the card continued, I sat with Rick Martel, who was readying himself for his AWA title defense. We reminisced about our days together with the WWF, laughing about the night that he and Tony Garea won the tag team straps from the Wild Samoans in Philadelphia. The finish was a double pin in which one man from each team simultaneously covered a member of the opposition with the referee making the three count in the middle of all four wrestlers. The winners would be whichever wrestlers the ref believed were legally in the ring. As soon as I delivered the suspense-filled announcement, an unbelieving Afa the Samoan reached up from his sitting position in the middle of the ring and yanked on my pants with such force that I was propelled buttocks first to the mat. The fans were in an uproar as I sat on the mat, face to face, with the three hundred pound salivating Samoan. When I realized the danger before me, my feet began to pedal in a bicycle motion, sliding myself backwards across the surface

Kamala vs. Martel. San Juan Jan,'89

of the canvas covered mat by the seat of my pants until I slid to the safety of the corner. I can still hear the TV commentator, Kal Rudman's shocked reaction as he shouted to the home viewing audience, "He's got Gary Cappetta! What's going on? Boy, Gary and Michael are both shook up!"

Sika & Afa, my Samoan buds.

Our lighthearted chuckling from reliving the ridiculous scene from five years earlier was starkly contrasted to Gary Juster's ominous expression as he paced the backstage corridors. The closer we came to the end of the card, the sooner he would be faced with firing his unsuspecting announcer. It wasn't until Bob Backlund's match that the good Lord delivered the solution.

Backlund was a former WWF world titleholder who never received the enthusiastic fan support that was necessary for the mega successful run that the baby face champions Sammartino and Morales before him had achieved. He was a tremendous technical wrestler, but no matter how hard Vince, Sr. tried to get him over, Backlund's lack of charisma and awkwardness made him unconvincing on interviews and the brunt of jokes by the more vocal fans. With his pale freckled skin, red hair and All-American boyish good looks, many thought he resembled Howdy

Doody. So the ringsiders reveled in mocking him by chanting "Howdy Doody" throughout his matches. Each time the chant echoed throughout the building, Backlund became visibly upset, which only encouraged his detractors to taunt him even more.

Regrettably (although not for Juster), the Baltimore ring announcer was not aware that the crowd's chant was meant to mock Backlund. So with his victory announcement, the elderly emcee, mistaking the crowd's jeering as supportive words of praise, sealed his own fate once and for all in Baltimore. The announcement that resounded throughout the arena went something like this. *Ladies and gentleman . . . the time of the match . . . eighteen minutes . . . forty-five seconds . . . and your winnah . . . the Howdy Doody of professional wrestling . . . Bob Backlund!* When the insulting announcement blared over the speakers throughout the backstage area, we could hear the echoing roar of Backlund's taunting detractors.

Backlund's white skin turned beet red. He glared at the announcer as the snickering fans rolled in the aisles with glee. If the announcer had been a younger man, Backlund would have ripped him apart. He stormed up the aisle with the unsuspecting announcer straggling a safe distance behind.

As Gary met the two at the locker room door, he profusely apologized to the fuming Backlund. Then in feigned anger, Juster sternly addressed the old ring announcer, reasoning that he had no choice but to let him go. As Backlund stomped into his dressing room and the forlorn announcer wandered out of the building, Juster's pretend look of horror turned into a twinkling grin of victory as he called over to me, "Cappetta, you're on next month."

F rom the start of Pro Wrestling USA in 1985, and throughout my next four years on the indie circuit, Gary Juster continued to book me on his shows. My performance fee ranged from the indie norm of $100 to the $350 that I was paid for NWA house shows. Baltimore was soon taken over by Jim Crockett's National Wrestling Alliance, while Gagne concentrated on his transplanted ESPN show, which was now based in Las Vegas. Before long, aside from appearing in Baltimore on a monthly basis, I became the NWA announcer in Washington, DC, beginning with The Great American Bash tour on July 3, 1986 and then started working in Boston the following year. In addition, I maintained a sporadic relationship with Verne Gagne's AWA which was limited to isolated Northeastern tours and their occasional pay-per-view events. With the NWA, the AWA and the independent work I was booking throughout New Jersey, New York and Pennsylvania, I was never busier. I was booking more big money shows than ever.

During my first two years with the NWA, the talent roster was filled with solid wrestlers on every level. From their incomparable champion Ric Flair on down, the nightly NWA lineups were without a weak link. The singles wrestlers, even from the undercard, boasted strong workers such as Eddie Gilbert, Black Bart, Manny Fernandez, Kevin Sullivan, Al Perez, The Barbarian, Mike Rotunda and Gorgeous Jimmy Garvin with his valet (and wife) Precious. Higher up on the card, Sting, Nikita Koloff, Ronnie Garvin, Barry Windham and Magnum TA. were constantly in contention for the world and US singles titles. The tag team division was dominated by the most accomplished teams in the history of the sport:: the Rock and Roll Express (Ricky Morton and Robert Gibson), the Midnight Express (Bobby Eaton and Stan Lane) with Jim Cornette, the Road Warriors, managed by Precious Paul Ellering and the Horsemen (Arn Anderson and Tully Blanchard) with James J. Dillon. The only two who were pushed without having solid ring skills were Lex Luger, for his sculpted physique and The American Dream, Dusty Rhodes, for his unequaled charisma and because . . . well, because as the boss, he booked himself.

Settling into my regular routine with Jim Crockett promotions, I soon encountered a stiff and bloodthirsty style of wrestling like I had never before witnessed. Growing up under the regional system, my only exposure was to the WWF, where the most daring events were cage matches, battle royals, lumberjack matches and strap matches; comparatively tame compared to what I was about to experience.

Working with NWA wrestlers was often as dangerous as standing in the middle of South Central Los Angeles during gang warfare. It was a style common in Southern rings that bordered on insanity. The NWA didn't *simulate* brutality, it *was* brutal. But even more peculiar to me was the nonchalant attitude that the boys exhibited toward their staged savagery. They carried the battle wounds that scarred their bodies as if they were medals of honor.

Of all the gimmick matches, the cage match is guaranteed to deliver blood and gore. It is booked to force a cowardly villain into a face to face fight following matches in which the heel repeatedly relies on outside assistance to escape the clutches of his baby face rival. A conclusive ending to the feud was assured when the archenemies were locked inside the fifteen-foot high chain linked cage. The steel structure is erected around the perimeter of the ring, with a single padlocked door cut into one side to prevent either guy from escaping.

While the ominous structure alone signals an absence of civility, the fans expect that in a cage match they will witness each guy trying to incapacitate his opponent by ramming his body into the metal beams and raking his face across the jagged surface of the fence. All in all that is brutal enough. But in the NWA, the cage match was taken to the next level.

During the Great American Bash Summer series in 1988, a simple cage match just didn't seem to promise sufficient punishment to settle an extra hot feud between Kevin Sullivan and "Gorgeous" Jimmy Garvin. Television viewers watched each week as Kevin began to win the attention of Garvin's "main squeeze", Precious, through a hypnotic spell that only the devilish Sullivan was capable of casting. The NWA took the cage match gimmick to the extreme, declaring the triple cage "Tower of Doom" as the one suitable remedy to determine, once and for all, who Precious really loved. Of all the gimmick matches that I've worked, this spectacle remains my favorite for the drama, the ingenuity and the display of man's basic instinct to survive.

The Tower of Doom consisted of three cages one upon the other with a platform and a trap door separating each of the stacked structures. Sullivan and Garvin each had four teammates for the battle over Precious. To start the match, two opposing team members entered the Tower from the top, which extended high into the ceiling rafters of the Baltimore Arena. Then every few minutes, on an alternating basis, another wrestler joined the fray, with Kevin and Jimmy going last. The men advanced down through the cages via the series of trap doors. The premise of the match was for all men to fight their way down to the bottom, where Precious held the key to allow the victors to escape.

When I arrived for the Baltimore Bash pay-per-view, Jim Crockett and Dusty Rhodes were standing behind an empty section of ringside seats. Their eyes were fixed on the three-tiered cage, which was suspended high over the ring.

Since the novelty match was scheduled in the middle of a commercial-free televised event, it was necessary for the towering structure to be lowered from high above the arena floor and then anchored to the ring posts in seconds. It was essential that the stacked cages descend from the rafters without hesitation to assure the smooth flow of the show.

As Rhodes and Crockett looked on, the road crew was testing the machinery that would slowly lower the steel contraption to the ring later that night on live TV. Just minutes before the arena doors were to open to the public they were plagued by an uncooperative generator, which repeatedly stalled. Instead of smoothly descending to the ring, the three cages stubbornly swung in mid air as Dusty stared at the structure as if it was the most beautiful woman in the world who was playing hard to get. Crockett didn't stare, he glared.

"Hey, big Dust. What's going on?" I chirped.

"Daddy, this is the most awesome sight on the face of the earth." His face sparkled, but Crockett's dead eyes were those of a man fearing the deluge of refunds that would be demanded by cable subscribers if the damn generator failed in the middle of the show.

I decided to be encouraging. "It'll work, Dust. I know it will. This is such an amazing concept."

"You've got that right, brotha," The Dream grinned. "It's called livin' life at the end of the lightenin' bolt. Welcome to the N W and A."

This was like great sex for Dusty. Crockett's eyes just got deader.

Since this was live

A bloody Dusty Rhodes with partner Nikita Koloff. Philadelphia, Mar'87

TV, regardless of the temperamental generator, the show started on time. It was a spectacle filled with gimmicks to settle the many feuds that had been building for months. When it was time for the stacked cages to make their grand entrance, the ominous structure miraculously descended upon the ring, glistening in the brightness of the television lights. What a marvel it was! As the spectacle began, it was clear that the boys were up for the event. Roman gladiators had nothing on the two bloodthirsty teams that battled their way down through the cages, as Precious stood blank-faced below.

The audience sat nervously at the edge of their seats to see who would win Precious' love. When Kevin Sullivan arrived at the bottom of the pit, he dumped Garvin out to the floor, locked himself inside the cage with Precious and began to stalk the distressed damsel on all fours. As a beast cornering his prey, the salivating Sullivan began to paw at Precious' blouse as she fended off his advances until Garvin could climb to the top of the three-tiered structure and repeat his steps all the way through the maze to make the save.

This is brilliant stuff. Drama of the highest order.

The violent scenarios that routinely bloodied the NWA rings were concocted by Dusty Rhodes and whoever else was feeling sadistically original at the time. They fought with loaded gloves, staged anything goes bunkhouse matches and swung high above the ring on a couple of suspended planks of wood in the dangerous tag team scaffold matches, in which the winner was the first to throw a free falling opponent twenty feet down to the mat. Night after night, I sat at ringside wincing and grimacing and loving every minute of each death defying thrill show.

I n April 1987, Jim Crockett, enjoying a successful run as the gritty alternative to McMahon's "powder puff" show, moved to expand his piece of the wrestling pie. He purchased the Universal Wrestling Federation from Bill Watts, adding depth to his talent roster and access to venues in Oklahoma and Louisiana, along with a minor string of TV outlets.

That same month, I announced at The Second Annual Jim Crockett, Sr. Memorial Tag Team Cup Tournament in Baltimore. My memory of this event remains vivid because of the remarkable strength of three individuals.

The first, who exemplified strength of heart, was no-nonsense wrestling heartthrob, Magnum TA. He had undergone extensive surgery and physical therapy after crashing his Porsche into a utility pole a year and a half earlier. This night, which marked his first public appearance since the tragic accident, saw Magnum, with the aide of a cane, courageously make his way to the ring to a thundering standing ovation.

The second, showing strength of spirit, was Mrs. Jim Crockett, Sr. Well into her 70's, Mrs. C. proved to be quite a feisty dame, despite Dusty and her son, Jim's concern for her health during our pre-show meeting. "Now take care of her. She's not feeling well. She's frail. She's not used to the TV cameras. She may need your help". But when she joined me in center ring for the presentation of the championship trophy to the winning team of Nikita Koloff and Dusty (Ya know, the booker . . . who did you expect would win?), she authoritatively snatched the mic and the spotlight with more authority than any heavyweight competitor with whom I had previously worked. There was little doubt that she was the matriarch of a show biz family.

The actions of the third, The Barbarian, displayed physical strength. But I was not all that impressed with the hulk's impressive power. Yes, he did punch a hole through the elevator control panel to express his upset that the Inner Harbor Days Inn bar was closing before he was ready to retire. But that's not why I remember the incident. Barbie's alcohol-induced outburst was more memorable by lending strength to the argument that the major promotions would be well served by having a substance abuse counselor on staff. But I'll save that topic for another time.

The Barbarian is one of the legit tough guys.

As you can see, I earned every penny of my biggest payoff to date . . . more than $900 plus expenses. Comparing that figure against what the independent stars were making, that was damn good money. Some would say it was out of line. But as you might guess, I wouldn't agree.

Other than Slaughter, who commanded $2500 per match, others who had followed me from the WWF such as the Samoans, the Iron Sheik and the Ugandan Giant Kamala were making $500 nightly. Ivan Putski, Wendi Richter and Abdullah the Butcher were pulling in $750. Even with the resurgence of the independents today, performance fees for comparable indie headliners have not changed. So for a supporting player like myself, whose name never sold a ticket, I was doing real well.

With so much money being offered to today's breed of wrestlers, I feel strongly that wrestling schools, besides teaching wrestling basics, should instruct their students on the business of wrestling. The Deal. The Con. The Counter Con. I touched on that topic earlier in this book and I will return to it later on.

When Jim Crockett sold his entire company to Ted Turner in November 1988, executives at Turner Broadcasting were eyeing me from afar.

They had seen my work on ESPN and the Baltimore Bash in July. In early December, Crockett, who had maintained control over the daily operation of the business for the transition, tracked me down at the school where I was teaching. Rose, the vice-principal's secretary, interrupted my class to deliver a message.

"Gary, this is an important message. This man, Jerry Crocker, says you must call him back immediately."

"But Rose, I don't know anyone named Jerry Crocker."

"Oh yes you do. He knows you."

"Rose, I'm in the middle of the imperfect subjunctive. This is a great lesson. I think this can wait until later."

"He's from the South. It's a long distance call."

"Is that what he told you?"

"Well, no. But he talks funny. I can tell from the way he spoke. Do you wrestle?"

"Wrestle? Rose what are you talking about?"

"He said this has something to do with wrestling."

I had always tried to keep my work in wrestling separate from my work in education. Many of the kids who watched my TV work were aware of my other life, but Rose didn't have a clue. But then again, Rose acted like she didn't have a clue about most things. She is a fun person to be with. That's why I really like her.

"Rose, are you sure the name's not Jim Crockett? I know a Jim Crockett."

"Does he sound funny too?"

As soon as I had a break in my classes, I went down to the pay phone outside of the school gymnasium to return Crockett's call. My mind was racing as to what could be so important that Crockett would summon me in the middle of a school day. When I got him on the phone, the call went something like this.

"Well heya there, Gary. I hope I didn't interrupt anything important."

"Not really, Jim. Just the imperfect subjunctive."

"The perfect what?"

"That's really not important now. What can I do for you?"

"Well, I was talkin' to Jim Herd. Ya know, he's the new head honcho of wrestling for Turner."

"No, I didn't know that. Don't think we've ever met."

"He knows who *you* are. And I was talkin' to him and suggestin' that we bring ya in for all of our special events."

In the wrestling business, whenever one of the bosses has good news for you, it's always due to his influence. Everyone wants to take credit for advancing your career and then point in every other direction when you're getting the ax. It's a way to secure loyalty. It's a cheap way to buy your allegiance.

"Jim, that's great news. Of course, I'm interested."

"Well, good. Let's make a deal. How much would ya want for *Starrcade*. It's comin' up later this month in Norfolk, ya know."

I was stumped. No one had ever asked me to name my price before. If I was a sophisticated negotiator, I never would have answered the question. First, I would have found out his ceiling. Or at the very least, I would have told him that I'd get back to him. But I didn't know any better. Based on what I was averaging for NWA house shows, between $250 and $350 per performance, I just spouted out the first figure that came into my mind and waited for him to tell me I was over the top.

"I'm not sure. How does $500 sound?"

"That sounds fair," he fired back immediately. A little too immediate for comfort so I added,

"That's $500 plus expenses."

"Sure, that goes without sayin'. I'll tell Herd it's a done deal and we'll Fedex air tickets to ya by the end of the week. See ya then." And he hung up. That quick. That easy. A little too quick. A little too easy.

While I was filled with excitement at having secured the major shows, I was suspicious because of how Crockett agreed without hesitation. It was as if I was missing something. Jimmy had always questioned Juster about my high house show fees. And he was never aware of the entire deal. Crockett would have had Sullivan cast a death spell on me if he knew that my pay was padded by an extra $100 each time by the commission. That was $100 over what he already thought was too much. So why had he agreed to double the amount that he didn't think I deserved to begin with? He had never paid this kind of money to a wrestling ring announcer before. I doubt *anyone* did!

Before long, I came to answer the question for myself. It was so obvious. If only I had realized that the reason that Crockett suddenly turned into Mr. Generosity was because Jimmy was no longer paying the bills. He was now playing with Ted Turner's money. If I knew that at the time, I would have asked for a thousand.

In addition to the pay-per-view deal I had struck with the NWA, later renamed World Championship Wrestling (WCW), I continued to work their live Northeastern events as well as scattered independent house shows. The last show that I worked for Verne Gagne's AWA, which was gasping its last breaths of life, was a pay-per-view in Chicago in December 1988. Superclash III, as it was called, was the worst pay-per-view event with which I have ever been associated.

Verne's concept for Superclash III was to combine his wrestlers with the talent from other struggling promotions, which had somehow managed to survive the WWF onslaught. It was a gallant idea. Perhaps the only idea that could have succeeded given the sorry state of the depleted AWA. And it wasn't a surprise when the Superclash pay-per-view failed miserably.

Of all of the acquaintances that I made that night, I was most struck by Kerry Von Erich, who headlined the show against Jerry "The King" Lawler in a dismal inter-promotional fiasco. Kerry was blessed with movie star good looks. His hunky body

Lawler vs. Von Erich topped the worst pay-per-view of my career.

would cause an intimidated Greek god to cover up. His wrestling was passable. But he was one of those guys in the business that I'd place in The Zone. Along with guys like Buzz Sawyer and the Iron Sheik, Kerry lived on another planet, a planet that NASA has not yet discovered.

It was nice enough that he brought his little daughter with him. But I was taken back when he brought the little girl (she was maybe ten years old) into the dressing room to mingle among the athletes in all states of undress. She stayed close to her daddy as the boys exchanged their who fucked whom stories. Not that she seemed to mind. My guess is that this was a regular occurrence for her in the Dallas locker rooms where the Von Erichs ruled. I never knew if Kerry was always high or if he just wasn't very bright. We sat across from each other as he suited up for his big match. I tried to hold a conversation with him, but gave up when his answers stopped matching my questions. Before I could switch to true or false questions to make it easier for him, he stood up to walk over to the sink and fell flat on his pretty face. The problem was that in the process of lacing up his wrestling boots, he unwittingly tied the laces around the steel-folding chair upon which he sat.

This was Verne's main eventer. It's amazing that Kerry found Chicago, never mind the building. But he had charisma, he had a hypnotic ring presence and the fans loved him. It wasn't his fault that his father Fritz, the patriarch of the Von Erich family of wrestlers had sired such a very sad bunch of boys. Five of his sons carried on the Von Erich name in wrestling.

Four died in the process. David died in his sleep while on tour in Japan in 1984 at age 25. Mike committed suicide in 1987, overdosing on the tranquilizer Placidyl. Chris committed suicide by a nine-millimeter pistol gunshot in 1991; he was 21. And in 1993, a little more than four years after our meeting, Kerry committed suicide by gunshot from a .44

Kevin, David, Fritz and Kerry Von Erich

caliber handgun, one day after being indicted on a cocaine possession charge at age 33. Tragic. Very tragic.

When a big show has a clinker of a main event, a strong undercard sometimes saves the night. But with The Gorgeous Ladies of Wrestling (GLOW) subjecting the audience to a Beverly Hills Lingerie Battle Royal, in which a dozen girls fought to strip each other down to their undergarments, there was just no hope. Only 1600 people showed up in Chicago to witness the event live. The pay-per-view buy rate was embarrassingly low. But one of the few who did spend the time and money to view Superclash was Jim Herd, the new executive charged by Turner to oversee WCW. And he wasn't pleased with my involvement.

I became aware of the controversy as Gary Juster and I were on our way to a WCW card in New Haven. I was always enthusiastic whenever I performed in Connecticut for two reasons. First, because it is where the WWF is headquartered. I loved playing in their backyard. It was like going up to the schoolyard bully and razzing him to his face. And second, because my old WWF bud, Pat Paterson, who had since become Vince's most trusted executive, was always sent to New Haven by Junior to spy on us. Pat's surreptitious visits with me at ringside became a highlight on the New Haven shows. So fortunately, I was in very good spirits when Gary questioned my appearance at Superclash.

"Ya know, I got a call from Jim Herd about the Superclash pay-per-view."

"Hey look, if he wants a refund, give him *Verne's* number."

"No. This is kind of serious. It seems he's pissed off that you worked the show. He thinks it doesn't look good for you to be announcing for our pay-per-views and theirs at the same time."

"Are you serious? That show was back in December. Ya mean he's been carrying this around for four months? If he's had a problem about it, then why didn't he call me himself?"

"I don't know. I'm just relaying the message. I'm not telling you what to do."

"Well Gar, it would be different if I turned down a WCW show to work for Verne. But that wasn't the case. I can't make a living from just working part time for WCW. Just tell him that the only way I'll be exclusive to WCW is if he pays me a retainer, whether or not he has work for me. If he wants me to sit home, that's no problem. But he's got to pay me. Otherwise, I'll announce for whomever wants to hire me."

"I understand your position. I'll tell him. But he's not going to like it."

Gary, always the diplomat. It was unfortunate that he found himself in the middle of such a trivial dispute. This was one of many times that Gary landed in an uncomfortable position because of me. He knew me well enough to predict what my response would be. Our friendship had grown, but he had an obligation to Turner Broadcasting. He had relocated to work full time in WCW's CNN Center offices in Atlanta. But while I valued our growing friendship, I had to stand on the principle of the issue. Most importantly, he showed his respect for my position without betraying his duty to Jim Herd.

I knew that Herd was just making noise. In February 1988, just two months after working the AWA pay-per-view, Herd sent word through Juster that the St. Louis ring announce position was mine if I was interested. St. Louis is Herd's hometown and the traditional home of the NWA. He wanted to spice up his hometown cards and saw my involvement as one way to add importance to the Kiel Auditorium events. So how angry could Herd have been? I knew from the start that he was testing me. Keeping me off the opposition's broadcasts was his attempt to keep me exclusive to WCW without having to pay for it. If I had caved in to his ploy, Herd would never have had an incentive to bring me in full time. So I simply sent my response through Gary and continued to book dates that were advantageous to both my career and my bank account, without giving another thought to Herd's disapproval.

The Kiel Auditorium shows were the first non-televised events to which I was flown on a regular basis. Because of the added expense of airfare and hotel, I agreed to a lower performance fee for the opportunity to work at the historic wrestling palace.

Sam Muchnick, the long time president of the NWA, had run the building for years. Sam was responsible for decades of great mat action as witnessed by overflowing crowds of appreciative St. Louis fans. And the key to his success was simple, though rare among promoters. He was an honest man. And he treated both the wrestlers and the fans with respect. Sam never shortchanged his workers on their payoffs and never failed to deliver what he promised to the fans. He was a model promoter who proved that a promotion could be run with integrity. A promotion in which everyone benefits. I had heard so much about the pro wrestling tradition in St. Louis that I looked forward to the opportunity to announce there.

In addition, there was an extra bonus in that the weekends became profitable whenever Juster booked a Sunday matinee within driving distance from St. Louis. I would work both shows, collect a double payday and fly home Sunday night.

The road trip of such a double booking between St. Louis and Carbondale, Illinois in late February 1989 presented my first glimpse into the guarded personal side of Ric Flair. During my first three and a half years with the NWA, while I had worked with Flair often, our relationship never extended beyond the ring ropes. His work was universally admired by industry insiders and appreciated by the fans. His money-drawing charisma and ability to make even his most inept opponents shine earned him the right to wear the NWA world title belt throughout Jim Crockett's most successful run. He consistently turned in flawless performances following all night marathons of partying in the fast lane. In interviews, he portrayed himself as a man's man, a playboy, a "jet flyin', kid stealin', wheeler dealer son of a gun". His locker room reputation was that he lived his gimmick. By teaming up for the trip to Carbondale with Juster and Flair, I'd now have an opportunity to judge for myself.

With a brutal winter storm sweeping through the Midwest, there was little chance that there'd be smooth sailing for my first road trip with Flair. High banks of melting snow had washed out many of the back roads of Southwestern Illinois. And any hope that Juster had for an 11:00 am departure to make the two o'clock matinee was dashed by Ric's characteristic lateness. At 11:20 he rushed through the Mariott lobby, running a comb through his still damp platinum hair. His coy smile signaled an insincere discomfort with delaying our departure. It was plain to see that he really regarded the inconvenience as your small price to pay for the privilege of traveling with The Nature Boy. I got the sense that Ric enjoyed being late. Liked being sought after. Wanted us to be waiting for him. And relished being chauffeured to his next performance. Whoo!

Once on the road, Ric began venting his frustration with the promotion's top brass. He complained about Crockett's silence as Dusty booked weak finishes to his title defenses or placed him in embarrassing scenarios. Flair saw the formulas as unfit for the world champ, especially when they were designed to make his perennial challenger, Rhodes, himself, look good.

About halfway between St. Louis and Carbondale, Flair asked Juster if he was hungry. That was Ric's way of saying, "I'm hungry, let's stop". Within minutes we found ourselves on the main street of a small Illinois farming community. It was the kind of a town where all the locals know each other, where a visitor is an uncommon occurrence.

We pulled up to a quaint café, where it seemed as if not much had changed for decades. As soon as we stepped inside, a chill could immediately be felt. Not only from the dampness of the unheated eatery, but also from the stares of the few elderly diners, with cloth coats draped over their shoulders and woolen scarves wrapped around their necks. Silently huddled over chicken pot pies and onion smothered beef patties, the locals warily inspected the fur trimmed cashmere dress coat that the bejeweled Flair sported.

When the matronly waitress delivered menus to our table, Ric immediately decided to play.

"Excuse me, ma'am. Can you tell me if you serve tuna?"

"Yes sir, we do. Would you like that on white or wheat?"

"Is it fresh?"

She stared at him with a puzzled look, not sure what to make of the question.

"Sir?"

"I said, can you tell me whether or not the tuna is fresh? You did say you have tuna, didn't you?"

"Well, of course we serve tuna. But how am I supposed to know if it's fresh?"

"Well, then, never mind. If you don't know, then I guess it's not and I'll just find something else on the menu."

As our disgusted waitress moved on to the next table, Flair, with the skill of a class clown who is expert in grating the nerves of his stuffy Latin teacher, added an audible sound of disgust which once again drew the attention of our fellow diners.

His repeated requests aimed at fraying our server's nerves continued throughout the meal. By the time we had finished eating, the waitress and Flair had resorted to shooting each other dirty looks. He was masterful in the way he could raise her ire without saying a word.

As we waited for the cashier to tally our check with pencil and paper, Flair stood before her staring at the cash register.

"Excuse me, ma'am. Why are you totaling our bill that way?"

"What way?"

"Why are you figuring it out on paper?"

"How do you want me to do it?"

"Well, what I mean is, why aren't you using the cash register?"

"Because I don't know how to use that machine. I haven't figured it out yet."

"If you want, I'll show you."

"No, that's all right. I'm doin' just fine."

Turning Juster's life upside down is fun for Flair. Here, Luger returns the favor.

Flair shook his head in disbelief. The waitress shook her head at his feigned arrogance. Juster and I shook our heads in embarrassed amazement. And as we made our way out of the chilly café, an hour behind schedule, everyone was shaking.

Flair's most devilish teasing was reserved for those, like our waitress, who he considered unhip. Which is probably why Juster, one of his most straight-laced cohorts in wrestling, has always been one of his favorite targets.

Time was flying by, as our journey seemed to have no end. For each of the numerous times that we veered off course, Ric alternately chided Juster for his driving and me for my inability to read a map. He did it in good fun. He was having a grand time without worrying about being late. It didn't matter that the box office couldn't open until Juster settled the advance monies. It wasn't important that I had to set up the show music before bell time. The champ was always the grand finale. He knew that he'd be on time for his part of the show, and that's all that seemed to matter.

At one point, realizing that we had crossed the same intersection an hour earlier, it was obvious that it was time to stop and ask for directions. Every so often we spotted a rustic farmhouse along the side of the road, but there was never any sign of life. Finally, Juster began pulling down driveway after driveway leading up to isolated farms. Each time my knock at the door was met with silence.

Watching from the heated comfort of the Lincoln's cushy back seat, Ric took pleasure from my unsuccessful attempt to find anyone home. As I trudged through the snow, trying to dodge nuggets of pelting hail, knocking on vacant farmhouse doors, Flair seemed comforted by my discomfort.

"I can't believe that no one is home," he quipped. "Did you ring the doorbell?"

"They don't have doorbells," I defended my efforts. "I think everyone must be in church."

"In church? Everyone?" Flair scoffed in disbelief, as if this most logical notion could in any way be true.

As we continued down the road, Gary spotted the flashing red lights of a state police car, which had followed a vehicle down a short path, into the woods. The instant we pulled behind the patrol car, the trooper bolted out of his vehicle, one hand resting upon his holster, the other flailing a pointed finger in the air as he screamed, "Move! Get back! I said pull your vehicle back onto the road NOW!"

"Well, I wonder what his problem is?" Juster muttered.

"Did you hear what I said? MOVE YOUR CAR NOW!"

"Just roll down your window and tell him what you want," chimed Flair. "He'll understand."

The agitated officer approached the car, his hand still resting on his weapon as Juster, following Flair's advice, began to open the window.

"Excuse me, officer. All I want is directions to get me back on the county road. We're running a little late and . . ."

"*I don't give a damn what you want. You pull this vehicle back onto the shoulder of the road until I'm finished. If you don't follow my instructions NOW, you will be charged with obstructing the duties of a police officer.*"

It must have been the legal sound of the officer's threat that connected with Juster's lawyerly sensibilities, because he immediately backed the car out of the path and onto the shoulder of the dirt road.

An indignant Flair scoffed, "He can't talk to you like that. He doesn't know you're a lawyer."

As luck would have it, when Juster swung the Lincoln back onto the muddy shoulder, the tires of our car began to sink. "Oh no!" Flair lamented. "Who's gonna tow us out of here? I told you not to move the car. What are we gonna do now?"

Somehow, by the grace of God, we managed to find our way to Carbondale, leaving just enough time to get the show started as planned. While Flair acted annoyed with the muck that had gathered on his leather Gucci's from the two of us giving our car the needed boost to get us back on our way, this trip had provided him with a great time.

As I got to know Ric better with the passing of years, I came to marvel at his ability to have the best of times under the worst circumstances. He can be more playful than a cantankerous child, always with a devilish glimmer in his eye. Whether he's strip dancing on the bar top of a local gin mill or dancing up and down the aisle of a tour bus in Europe, he's always up for a party. But once he steps into the ring, there has never been anyone more professional. Few more skillful. Flair, with the cunning of a kid and the professionalism of an admired corporate executive, has always been one of my favorite wrestling buddies.

Part Three

THE TURNER YEARS

1989 – 1995

Chapter Eleven
"The Grudge Match"

Nothing angers me more than when people refer to major and minor sports. There are only major and minor athletes, depending on who cares, who tries, and never mind the sport.

Frank Deford, Sports Columnist

Enter now and win the WCW Intercontinental Travel Sweepstakes. Receive an all expense paid trip to every region of the United States, Canada, Europe and the Bahamas. Fly on the airline of your choice between destinations of more than three hundred miles where a car will be furnished for transportation to intermediary locales. Stay in your favorite hotel at every stop. Airfare, ground transportation, lodging, meals and all incidental travel expenses are included in your grand prize. You will attend a WCW wrestling event every night along the way and will appear on the WCW television network every week. Grand Prize value of The WCW Intercontinental Travel Sweepstakes is valued at over $100,000 per year.

My monthly trips to St. Louis, regular pay-per-view appearances and intermittent work for the Turner organization throughout the Northeast allowed me the opportunity to demonstrate my announcing abilities to the bosses in Atlanta. At the same time, they came to appreciate my work ethic. These early assignments served as an audition for the position that they were about to offer. My dream was about to come true. Before the summer ended, I was out of the classroom and out on the road full time for WCW!

I felt like I was the recipient of the grand prize. As if WCW had invited me to explore the world at their expense. I set out on the joy ride of a lifetime, departing to announce in city after city for the next six years.

The assurance of steady work and guaranteed money by one of the country's two major booking offices was quite a departure from the tiresome ordeal of bouncing back and forth between unreliable hit-and-run promoters. Although I had managed to keep my name alive in the national wrestling magazines and newspapers, it was always temporary. I was never sure if the next appearance would be my last. But for ring announcers, that's the norm. We are almost always nameless part-timers. Gaining full time employment in the field was unthinkable. While even the lead announcer for the WWF had daily office responsibilities far beyond his limited ring work, my only responsibility was to announce.

So the deal that I struck with Turner in 1989 broke new ground in the industry. For the first time, the TV announcer would be making the rounds to *all* of the house shows. After four years of living the unstable life as a gypsy announcer, I was excited about my new home.

I anticipated that Ted Turner and the influence of Turner Broadcasting would easily overthrow Vince McMahon and the WWF. There was no doubt that Turner was equipped to humble his rival wrestling kingpin. Since pro wrestling had always been a weekly staple on TBS, the Turner sales department and programmers had identified the target audience. Turner's media conglomerate also had access to endless resources to give them the competitive edge in the battle for the new generation of younger and more affluent fans who, thanks to the WWF, now saw wrestling as fashionable. In addition, Turner had a powerful public relations machine in place and owned an assortment of media outlets with which to cross-promote his new wrestling product.

His holdings were staggering. In 1976, Turner bought the Atlanta Braves. One year later, he purchased the Atlanta Hawks. In 1979 CNN, Turner's all news network, went on the air. In 1986 he acquired MGM/UA which included the MGM studio, the fabled MGM lot in Culver City and most significant to his cable stations, a library of 3500 MGM films, plus 1450 films from the old Warner and RKO studios. The deal garnered such classics as *Gone With The Wind, The Maltese Falcon, The Wizard of Oz* and *Citizen Kane*. Also in 1986, Turner introduced The Good Will Games, his version of the Olympics. He launched TNT on cable in October of 1988, and the next month he finalized the deal to gain control of The National Wrestling Alliance, later renamed World Championship Wrestling.[1]

Ted Turner's vision is legendary and his astounding successes speak for themselves. With his hunger for being

---

[2] In 1991 Turner Broadcasting changed the name of its promotion from the National Wrestling Alliance (NWA) to World Championship Wrestling (WCW). For the purpose of clarity, the author will refer to Turner Broadcasting's promotion as World Championship Wrestling throughout.

number one, compounded by his personal dislike for Vince McMahon, Jr., I expected this contest to be lopsided from the start. When the final bell sounded, I thought that Turner would be declared victorious. Like when Andre the Giant pulverized a terrified Frankie Williams in seconds. I expected a full throttle attack on McMahon's WWF with Ted heading the charge and quoting his favorite motto: "Lead, follow or get out of the way."

By reputation, Ted had been known for running his empire hands on. He nurtured each new addition to his corporate kingdom with care, as if it was another family business. While he sometimes overpaid for properties, once at the helm, he personally monitored each new acquisition with cost conscious frugality. His in-house management style always seemed to bring about superior results from an efficient, dedicated family of workers. But shortly after arriving in Atlanta to finalize the details of my agreement, I soon began to see that WCW was considered the black sheep of the Turner family. The embarrassed organization would not be welcoming us to our new home with open arms.

This photo is a rare public acknowledgement of Ted Turner's link with WCW.

During the early years that WCW came under TBS' control, the corporate administrators offered little support and, in fact, withheld the company's vast resources from the wrestling division. WCW was considered below the organization that prided itself on the prestige of CNN. The supervision of WCW's daily operation was left to executives who seemed determined to engineer its early death. The feisty spirit of Ted Turner was missing. There was no evidence of the aggressive competitor whom biographers claim always fought hardest when he was doubted most.

Early on, I discovered that an inadequate staff, entirely unfamiliar with the intricacies of the wrestling business plagued WCW. Many recruited from outside of the organization had secured their positions as a payback for past favors. Those who were transferred from other departments within TBS were often incompetents who were quickly shuffled over to the wrestling division at the first opportunity.

His staff saw Ted Turner's half-hearted endorsement of WCW as nothing more than a public formality. He failed to send a clear message to his subordinates that WCW was to receive the full cooperation from its TBS siblings and share in the unlimited resources of the Turner Empire. Without Ted's support, we were unequipped to enter the ring every night to battle the overwhelming onslaught of the WWF. We felt like frustrated lightweights competing in the heavyweight division. When we staggered back to our corner, bloody and beaten, we found that the Turner executives had retreated to the safety of CNN Center's Executive Tower. The neglect that we suffered at the hands of our own parent company was humiliating.

It wasn't surprising that McMahon, a polished entrepreneur with a solid wrestling heritage, was more

Vince McMahon, Jr.

innovative, slicker and marketed his wrestling product to perfection. But it was incomprehensible that Turner allowed himself to be out-maneuvered in his own arena, television. Vinnie wisely concluded that the earlier he could gain the allegiance of a younger generation of fans, the longer he would profit from their loyalty. The magnet McMahon used to draw the kiddy crowd to the WWF was the boob tube. He was just getting started when he enlisted the highest rated independent stations of the most populated cities in the country to air his TV shows. He made sure they ran on weekend mornings when he could be assured of a predominantly adolescent viewership. He created a cast of wrestling cartoon characters, which became entangled in easily understood story lines with underlying good versus evil themes. It was *Looney Tunes* come to life.

McMahon then carried his legions of little fanatics through the week by selling the WWF merchandising rights to countless manufacturers. Now kids started their day with Hulk Hogan vitamins, grappled with their Roddy Piper wrestling buddy before dinner and took Miss Elizabeth to bed each night. It became as important to know what was going on in the WWF as it was to see the hottest new movie on its premiere weekend. As kids boarded yellow school buses every Monday morning, the latest WWF gossip became the trendy topic. And the monthly payoff came when kids dragged moms and dads to arenas across America.

At the height of business in the mid-'80's, the WWF criss-crossed North America with three separate casts of characters, running three shows a night. Wherever WCW held live events we were forever overwhelmed by a WWF tidal wave. The WWF wrestlers swept through every city just before we'd hit town, taking the public's monthly allowance for family entertainment with them. McMahon seemed to know our itinerary better than anyone. In fact his full court press recurred with such frequency that there was widespread paranoia within the company. Some even suspected that a former WWF assistant arena booker, recently hired by WCW, was still on Vince's payroll.

McMahon had the most desirable venues locked into non-compete contracts, which forced WCW to play secondary sites all over the country. In cities with deep-rooted sports traditions, the public identifies primary buildings with major happenings. If an event doesn't take place at Madison Square Garden, then it can't be special. Crossing the San Francisco Bay to see wrestling at Oakland's Kaiser Convention Center is unthinkable when, for years, The Cow Palace had been the mecca of northern California mat action. Who would go anywhere but the old Boston Garden for an important match?

In places that offered newer suburban facilities, we were faced with the reverse dilemma. In the nation's capitol, people feel safe taking their families to the US Air Arena, not to the DC Armory. Those in the suburbs of Detroit waited for wrestling to come to The Palace in Auburn Hills and avoid Cobo Hall in the downtown area at all costs.

It seemed that Turner could do nothing right. Our primary television program, *WCW World Wide Wrestling*, often aired in the middle of the night on the most obscure outlets in the market. We regularly took our live shows to crime-ridden neighborhoods where even the most daring suburbanites refused to attend. We were plagued by a constant turnover of uncreative bookers providing a continual shift in our uninteresting story lines. When I saw how easily McMahon's organization out-maneuvered our unprepared office staff, I wondered if Ted Turner even knew that he owned a wrestling company.

Two of our problems - poor television time slots and roadblocks to desirable arenas - could have been resolved with Turner's influence and money. But all of his wealth couldn't buy the talent of a gifted booker. An expert wrestling booker must combine the vision of a screenwriter, the keen eye of a casting agent, the communication skills and patience of a director, and the managerial proficiency of a producer.

The core responsibility of a promotion's booker is to hire a cast of gifted wrestlers with a vision as to how their talents can best fit into the intriguing stories that he has scripted. If he stages the production in a way that will grab the audience's attention, then they will be hooked into regularly viewing the program. It follows that television ratings will rise, pay-per-view buy rates will increase and house show attendance will swell. In the process, increased revenues from advertising rates, box office receipts and merchandise sales will result.

Like a championship tag team, a successful wrestling promotion requires dedicated teamwork from everyone. While everything flows from the booker's vision and the direction that he sets for the company, the cooperation of his team is essential. Each wrestler has to be believable in his role. The production crew has to effectively capture the action for television. The arena booker has to negotiate the most advantageous deals for the primary buildings in each city. The public relations department has to shrewdly promote the event. And ultimately, the show must be convincingly and professionally executed.

Vince's success in creating new characters by repackaging raw talent and marketing them to his core audience is unparalleled. Over and over, he has shown his ability to propel undiscovered and overlooked performers to super stardom. A prime example of how McMahon took advantage of what has always been one of Turner's fundamental shortcomings is when he snatched away WCW's underutilized and underestimated Mark Calaway to create The Undertaker.

I met Mark during the second week of January in 1990, when WCW started a six-city Midwestern tour. It began with a TV taping in Saginaw, Michigan, followed by house shows in Ohio, Indiana and West Virginia. The first night we shot three editions of *World Wide Wrestling* before a rowdy crowd which had rallied to welcome their hometown heroes, the Steiner Brothers.

During this time, WCW was showcasing singles wrestlers Ric Flair, Sting, Lex Luger, Brian Pillman, Tom Zenk, Cactus Jack, "Mad Dog" Buzz Sawyer, Kevin Sullivan and Mike Rotunda. The impressive talent roster of tag teams included The Road Warriors, The Skyscrapers (Sid Vicious and Dan Spivey), Jim Cornette with the Midnight Express (Bobby Eaton and Stan Lane), The Fabulous Freebirds (Michael Hayes and Jimmy Garvin), The Rock and Roll Express (Ricky Morton and Robert Gibson), The Dynamic Dudes (Shane Douglas and Johnny Ace), The Anderson Brothers (Ole and Arn), Teddy Long with Doom (Ron Simmons and Butch Reed) and The Samoan Swat Team.

After closing the TV show, I made my way back to the dressing room. The wrestlers and referee who had worked the final event were happily chattering about the way their match had been received. I opened my locker and peeled the perspiration soaked tuxedo from my overheated body. As I began to scrub the show makeup from my face, the guys made their way to the showers. Suddenly, I was startled by a deep bass voice from the other side of the poorly lit room.

"Where are ya goin' from here?"

Following the low-pitched southern drawl, my eyes fell upon a massive silhouette, which was propped up in the shadowy corner. I gradually moved into the shadows in an attempt to recognize the faceless voice.

"What did you say?" I cautiously inquired.

"I said, 'where ya headin' from here'?"

As I closed in on the corner, my eyes focused on a newcomer who had debuted earlier in the evening. I introduced him as "Mean Mark" at 6'9", 328 pounds. Unlike most of the wrestlers, there was no need to exaggerate his immense size. His pale, expressionless face, framed by a shock of long reddish hair, only added to the striking appearance of the giant rookie.

"So, where are ya headin'?"

"I'm going on to Toledo tonight. And you?"

Shaking his head, he shrugged his broad shoulders. "I don't know. I was looking for a ride back to Detroit."

At the start of this tour, most of the talent flew from Atlanta to Detroit, drove up to Saginaw and planned on making their way back to the Motor City before taking off for Ohio the following morning. My plan was to drive through the night.

"Well, I've got to pass by the city. I don't mind swinging through to drop you off."

"No. No need to go out of your way . . . but . . . uh . . . would you mind if I hooked up with you? I'd rather not hang out with the boys anyway."

I looked toward him for an explanation, but he just blankly stared back. Despite this odd remark, in fact maybe because of it, I took the newcomer aboard.

Through Flint, bypassing Detroit and on to the Ohio border, we glided along the frost-covered freeway in icy, strained silence. Mark remained motionless as he stared into outer space. My attempt at small talk was met with short whispered responses. As we wandered through the stillness of the night, so did my mind. I wondered about Mark's strange behavior. I was uneasy about his unusual comment back in the dressing room. Why had he refused to ride with the boys? What could be so terrible that he'd risk being stranded in Saginaw? Considering the possibilities made me more uncomfortable than before.

In WCW he was Mean Mark.

The next morning, having rebounded from his somber mood, Mark agreed to continue following my timetable. To begin with, we'd leave the hotel early so I could set up the show music, test the sound system and solve any problems before the doors opened. Then, my plan was to drive on to Hammond after the show in order to avoid the next morning's traffic. It came as no surprise that my itinerary, which ran contrary to the wrestlers', suited Mark's needs as well as my own.

When the Toledo show was over, we set out westward across Ohio's span of Interstate 90. It usually took a while for me to settle down after the excitement of a house show. So, like after every other event, I babbled on aimlessly. But unfazed by my leftover energy, Mark once again sank back into silence. It was like the bitter Midwestern winds had frozen him as stiff as a corpse in the passenger seat.

Fearing that the lifelessness of my co-pilot would put me to sleep behind the wheel, I devised a plan to escape what I dreaded would be four more hours of numbing solitude. At the first sign of an all night convenience store, I picked up a couple of six packs, cranked up the country music, and rolled down my window. By the time we sailed across the Indiana State line, the mixture of beer and fresh air, along with the twang of Willie Nelson tunes blaring from the tinny car speakers, gradually brought Mark back to life. Watching his gradual awakening was like witnessing the slow comeback leading to the finish of an Undertaker victory, the character Mark would one day portray.

Vince McMahon transformed Mark into The Undertaker

Now refreshed, he told me about his recent wrestling debut and filled me in on life growing up in Texas. Then he started to ask questions about my work with WCW. I gave him an idea of what to expect, whom to watch out for and whom he could trust.

It was after 3 am when we crossed the bridge leading into East Chicago, Indiana. By the time we made our way through the fumes and smoke which billowed from the stacks of the oil refineries huddled below, Mark had turned into an entertaining travel partner. I began to detect an odd pattern to his mood swings. I noticed that when we were a safe distance from the boys, he relaxed and his good-natured humor resurfaced. But as soon as we approached the locker room, he tensed up and settled into a stiff, somber funk. I couldn't help but wonder about his peculiar behavior.

Late the next afternoon, we found a little mom and pop cafe in Hammond's old downtown area. It was a favorite hangout where the locals came to swap the latest town gossip. Running on little sleep, we amused ourselves with pointless nonsense. I speculated that the overweight waitresses could whip most of the guys on the tour. Mark named the rodents and which of their body parts went into the making of my meatloaf. We had become so weary from the strains of the road that we began to act like dizzy school kids.

By now, after so many consecutive shows, I was on automatic pilot. Since we had been running many of the same matches all over the country, there were no surprises: the same spots, the same finishes and the same crowd reaction to it all. When the matches became predictable, my performance at ringside became second nature and my attention was drawn to details that had eluded me before. It's like watching a movie for the second and third time, when your critical eye stops focusing on the actor who is delivering his lines and begins to notice the reactions of the other players. You begin to analyze the intricacies of the performance beyond its initial impact.

As I watched Mark's performance for the third night, his inexperience in working the crowd was evident. His facial expressions alternated between a sneering look of disdain and no expression at all. Trying to put over the "Mean Mark" character would be any rookie's nightmare. A character who appears out of nowhere and acts with no apparent motives gives fans little reason to care about him. He was as handicapped as a nameless masked wrestler from parts unknown. The best Mark could do, being harnessed by the apathetic character that he was given to portray, was to learn as much as possible from working before live audiences until a booker who recognized his potential would some day come along. For now, he'd have to make the best of WCW's uninspired booking. Mark had to resign himself to accept the limitations of the "Mean Mark" character. He had to understand that as long as he worked for WCW, even though he was a naturally talented athlete, his appeal and money making potential would be severely limited.

And back in 1990, there was no doubt that Mark demonstrated enormous athletic potential. The big man's agility and extraordinary sense of balance are God-given talents. He would apply an arm bar, mount the top turnbuckle and poise himself on the top rope. He'd then drag his opponent from one turnbuckle to the next, balancing himself like a tightrope walker high above the mat. Then he'd come crashing down on his victim's twisted arm to the shrieks of the stunned ringsiders. Mark performed aerial feats that one might expect from a flying lightweight. To witness this three hundred pounder fly across the ring with sure-footed confidence was nothing short of amazing. Given a little direction and the right gimmick, Mark could one day become a headliner.

Except for a short stint as the second Skyscraper with his partner, Sid Vicious, WCW used him as a preliminary player who demolished undercard wrestlers on TV, only to be destroyed by the established stars at paying events. Mark did not hit his stride until the WWF's makeover department exploited his intimidating size and pale, expressionless face to repackage him in the role as The Undertaker.

The 290 mile trip from Hammond to Cincinnati was a roller coaster ride of emotional highs and lows. Something amazing happens when two complete strangers are locked up together for hours at a time. Initially, you test each other to establish common ground before feeling safe enough to share your more personal thoughts and feelings. If a level of comfort is never reached, then the communication remains superficial. But by the time we motored on to Cincinnati, Mark and I were beyond that. We found plenty to talk about after hours of being "couped" up together.

Maneuvering around Route 465, which encircled Indianapolis, we once again joked about the folks who had crowded into the lunchtime grill earlier in the day. Mark leaned back, folded his arms and heaved a deep sigh. Quietly staring at me for several minutes, he finally broke the silence.

"What if I told you that there's someone on the tour who I knew a couple of years ago? Someone I met when I was breakin' into the business."

"Who are you talking about?"

"One of the boys. We have an old score to settle."

It would have been sensible to change the subject. But I didn't.

"Is that what's bothering you?"

"No, not exactly."

"Well, what did he say to you?"

"He didn't say anything. He doesn't remember me."

"So why don't you talk to him?"

"'Cause when I do, I'm goin' to beat the shit out of him."

"Why? Who are you talking about?"

"Buzz Sawyer. How well do ya know that perverted asshole?"

"Well . . . he's trouble . . . I stay away from him."

"Our paths crossed down in Texas and I'm goin' to be sure he's never gonna forget me."

"I don't know what happened between the two of you, but I've heard a lot of bizarre stories about him. Nothin' much would surprise me."

His voice took on a hauntingly dark and somber tone.

"It was about two years ago that I decided to get into the business. I needed the money and when I saw what the wrestlers were doing on TV, I knew it'd be easy for me to catch on. Physically, I felt I could do it, but I was a mark and didn't know how to break in. Then I heard about a training school and decided to go down to the gym and check it out. There were about twelve of us who showed up. Buzz was the trainer."

Mark Calaway's attempt to look intimidating falls short next to WCW's menacing manager, Paul E. Dangerously. Mark went on to portray one of the most marketable stars ever in the WWF. Paul founded ECW, which became the 3rd most popular promotion in the US.

As he began to unload, there was no stopping him.

"The only problem was that I didn't have the money to pay for it."

"How much did Buzz want?"

"A couple of grand. It may not sound like big money now, but when ya don't have steady work, and there's nothin' in the bank, a couple of grand is like a couple of million."

"So what happened?"

"I thought it was a good enough deal. It sounded easy. Sawyer had been around a lot of years. I figured he was legit. So I went to my brother for a loan."

It was clear that this part of the story was the most painful of all. As Mark's voice began to tremble, he slowly continued.

"Now my brother's not a rich guy. He didn't have a whole lot of extra money, ya know, raisin' a family and all. But he believed in me. He went to the bank for the cash to pay for my wrestling school.

"So, I paid Sawyer and he started training me and the others who came up with two thou. We only had a couple of lessons and this one-day, ole Buzz didn't show. So we just worked out and figured he got held up for some reason. But when he didn't show the next time, I had a feeling that we were fucked. When I checked around town to find out what the story was with this guy, I come to learn that he had skipped town. Not bad. The motherfucker was on his way to California with twenty grand."

He was both solemn and seething at the same time. I didn't know what to say, at first. I didn't know how much more he wanted to tell me.

"Then you were out two grand of your brother's money? You never got it back?

"You're goddam right. I had to go to my brother and tell him that I lost his money. But I made two promises. One to him and one to myself. I promised him that I'd do whatever it took to pay him back. But it was goin' to take time. There wasn't much I could do to make that kind of money fast. It took me almost a year, bouncing at a local bar, to get enough cash together to make things right with my brother."

"And what was the other promise?"

"I promised myself that one day I'd track Sawyer down and make that motherfucker pay for what he did to me."

Considering the possible consequences of Mark's plan for revenge, we *both* sank back into silence.

Stories about Buzz Sawyer's antics had been circulating within the business for years. Sawyer, still only 31, had entered the pro ranks in 1979. He was just 5'9", but the bearded firebrand weighed 250 solid pounds and was as tough as they come. Except for a tiny tail that hung from the back of his head, he was mostly bald. He was Florida's high school athlete of the year and as a pro, was a three-time tag team champion. But somewhere along the way, Buzz became a heavy user of drugs and their effects had taken their toll. He developed an unpredictable temperament. He became crude, abrasive and careless in his treatment of others.

When I was around him, I avoided making eye contact. Otherwise, I stayed away. Everyone knew that the drugs he consumed ruled his life. Beyond his anti-social tendencies, Buzz had lost all ability to reason when under the influence. He drew his share of money in the Southeast, which was the reason he got a position with WCW. Those who he was tied to in the past now influenced WCW's booking. It's the politics of wrestling. It's loyalty. But with an individual like Sawyer, it's dangerous. To get out on the mat and trust your physical well being to someone so wired, so careless, so unstable was hazardous duty. He was a public relations time bomb.

Perhaps the best illustration of Mad Dog's insanity is depicted in a story that has become a classic in locker rooms over the years. Sawyer had been mixing alcohol and drugs at a late night hangout, when he became involved in a heated argument with another barroom bruiser. When words couldn't settle their differences, they started to shove each other around the bar. After they were booted out onto the sidewalk, they continued to cuss each other out.

As Buzz was in the midst of spewing his home grown brand of profanity, the other guy suddenly pulled out a gun, jammed it in Mad Dog's mouth and cocked the trigger. The gunman warned Buzz that if he said just one more word, he'd blow his head off. The hateful scowl on Sawyer's face transformed into a mile wide grin and he burst out in wild laughter. The deranged response unnerved his foe. Buzz snatched away the gun and savagely stomped his enemy into the pavement. If a crowd of onlookers had not restrained Sawyer, the damage could have been far more serious than the broken bones he left behind.

This was the sort of maniac that Mark was planning to tangle with. And knowing the lay of the land, I had good reason to expect that the blowoff would come this night at the Cincinnati Gardens.

It is a dinosaur of a structure. At the time of its opening in 1949, the Cincinnati Gardens was the seventh largest indoor arena in the U.S. with a seating capacity of 11,000. Built on 22 acres on Cincinnati's north side, The Gardens, with no interior pillars or columns obstructing sight lines, was modeled after the popular and historic Maple Leaf Gardens in Toronto. The Sheik, Handsome Johnny Barend,

Roddy Piper, Hulk Hogan, and hundreds of other big time wrestlers have entertained ardent Cincinnati crowds for decades.

The Gardens contains only two small dressing rooms for the wrestlers to use - two tiny team rooms, each isolated on opposite sides of the arena floor. It is unlike today's more modern facilities, where separate exit ramps from the ring funnel into a series of connected dressing rooms allowing the wrestlers plenty of private space to come and go as they please. The Cincinnati Gardens was different. The heels are housed on one side of the building, the baby faces on the other with no contact between them backstage. So Mark would be confined for hours tonight with Buzz. They would share the close quarters of an undersized team room reserved for all of the heels, and I was nervous.

Earlier in the day, I pleaded with him to work out his differences quietly. On the way to the arena, I tried to persuade him that violence was only going to make things worse. But he wasn't in the mood to listen. As we pulled up to The Gardens' parking lot, I feared that the stage was set for the inescapable showdown.

It had been a while since the last time WCW had been to town. The Cincinnati fans were always enthusiastic supporters of our rougher style of wrestling. The WWF had saturated the market with more show than action. The crowd's enthusiasm through the first half of the card had my blood pumping. At intermission, most of the heels were still milling around the crowded locker room. Mark and Buzz were far apart, each talking with a separate group of guys. But by the time I returned to the dressing room at the end of the night, they were the only two guys remaining.

Mark was waiting at one end of the dressing room, his gear packed and ready for our departure. Buzz, sweat still streaming down his face, having just wrestled in the last match, was at the other end. Standing in the center, I began changing from tuxedo to street clothes faster than ever before. Buzz had just begun to unlace one of his boots when he looked across at Mark. He wiped his brow with a towel he had picked up from a hotel along the way and tried to jog his misplaced memory. But his brain was not cooperating. He began working on his other boot when suddenly, he looked past me again and squinted.

"Don't I know you from somewhere?"

173

With beads of perspiration splattered across his grinning jowls, Buzz waited for the answer. Silence was the only response.

"You know, you look familiar. Sure I don't I know you?" he repeated.

By this time, Sawyer was impatiently poking his forefinger in the air.

In one sweeping motion, Mark lifted his immense frame and kicked a steel-folding chair against the far wall. He was an imposing presence as he slowly swaggered toward Sawyer. As he passed by, Mark ignored my look of warning. His concentration was focused on Buzz. It seemed like hours before Mark arrived at the other end of the small room. But in the time he took to confront his demon, more messages were sent than any amount of words could express. It was the stalking of The Undertaker two years too soon.

At the other side of the room, he reached for a chair, slowly spun it around backward and settled down nose to nose with the Mad Dog.

"You *should* remember me, motherfucker." Mark's gritty whisper hissed through his clenched teeth.

Mad Dog briefly cocked his head to one side. That maniacal grin reappeared before he exploded in reckless laughter. When Sawyer rose to his feet, Mark rose with him. They paused for a moment and then settled back down in their chairs.

"Is it coming back to you, you worthless piece of shit?"

Buzz' only response came in a series of jerky nods and a wider grin than before. As their uneasy reunion continued in hushed tension, I backed out of the foul smelling locker room. After warning a security guard who was stationed at the door that there might be problem, I searched in vain for our road agent. The only ones left in the building were the members of our roadies who were hustling to load the ring into the truck for the long trip that lay ahead.

When I returned to the locker room, Mark and Buzz were still sitting face to face. Buzz' non-stop chattering would have made the slickest back peddling politician proud. Mark just stared at him in utter disdain.

I pretended to be unaware of how dangerous the situation could become and casually called out, "Time to get going, Mark. Charleston's about 200 miles from here. And with the weather and the mountains, it'll take a lot longer than you think."

After a moment's hesitation, Mark slowly rose from his seat, never letting Sawyer out of his sight. Buzz never stopped babbling. Ignoring his outstretched hand, Mark slowly backed away from his foe.

"Hey, look, we'll discuss this." Sawyer's final appeal went unanswered.

We made our way through the few loitering fans and disappeared into the darkness of the cold winter night.

"I'm goin' to break that asshole's legs. His legs and his arms. All of them."

I had never seen Mark so agitated. As we joined the late night traffic on Cincinnati's ice covered streets, I tried to calm him down.

"You handled it well. Just let it go. Don't let him get to you."

"No man, it's not over." He twisted and turned in his seat. His mind was racing. "No. It won't be like that." The cold monotone of his voice communicated his serious determination

I'm goin' to wait 'til the time is right. I'll catch him alone. Away from everyone. Ole Buzz is not goin' to know what hit him. It'll be quick. That no good bastard's gotta learn that he can't play with people's lives."

"Look," I said, "don't let him fuck things up for you again. What do you think'll happen if you hurt him? Look who's running the office. Ole Anderson. Who do you think brought him in? Anderson, right? Can't you see? He'll get rid of you so fast, that you won't even know what's happening. Don't let that jerk-off get."

Mark's final response had the stone-cold delivery that could have passed for another Undertaker audition. "He's not gonna get away with it."

In a way that we couldn't predict at the time, Mark was right. Sawyer didn't get away with it. Throughout his wrestling career, he preyed on the weak. In the end, it wasn't Mark but his own weakness that caused his demise. On February 7, 1992 "Mad Dog" Buzz Sawyer was found in his apartment in Sacramento, California reportedly dead from a drug overdose. His life was snuffed out by the demons that haunted his later years, the same demons that victimized so many around him. And in his controlled restraint, The Undertaker, a future WWF World Heavyweight Champion, was able to bury the hatchet.

Chapter Twelve
"The Boot Camp Match"

. . . the only way to survive in the circus was to build a private world on one's own. Circus people, I realized, are like tigers: they have a tendency to devour their own. Those who survive do so by living in a tiny cage and only coming out when they have to perform. . . . the only way they survived in the circus was by minding only their own business and nobody else's. They survived by reaching some mysterious vigilante nirvana, where they trusted no one else and worried only about themselves.

Bruce Feiler, "UNDER THE BIG TOP, A SEASON WITH THE CIRCUS"

The tours that I most enjoyed began and ended in a hub city where we returned after performing in surrounding towns following a series of one night stands. If Chicago was the starting point, the tour might run Milwaukee, Hammond, Indianapolis, Dayton, Ft. Wayne and then

President Jimmy Carter and Miss Lillian, his mom, were huge fans of Mr. Wrestling II

return to Chicago. We would then fly to Atlanta and work Macon, Savannah, Charleston, Columbia, Greensboro, Roanoke, Charlotte, Asheville and drive back to Atlanta. Ordinarily, the cities were less than 300 miles apart. Averaging a four-hour drive, four hours at the show and eight hours at the hotel, I had plenty of spare time to uncover interesting people and places across America.

Between Albany and Columbus, I took Route 19 to swing by Plains, Georgia, population 716. This sleepy Sumter County community capitalizes on the name of its favorite son, former president, Jimmy Carter. Jimmy, along with his late mother, Lillian, was a wrestling fanatic. While The Jimmy Carter National Historic Site, The Lillian G. Carter Nursing Center and The Carter Worm Farm on Moon Street exploit the family name, no one is as shamelessly enterprising as is the president's cousin, Hugh. I found him with a few other old timers lounging in front of the antiquated Carter General Store where he peddles photos, books, post cards, buttons, mugs, shirts, place mats, pencils and plates all with the toothy grin of our former president prominently displayed. You'd be hard pressed to find a store that sells more purposeless, outdated goods.

Driving from San Francisco to Fort Ord, I discovered Gilroy, California, where The Gilroy Garlic Festival Association down on Monterey Street promotes their pungent smelling township as The Garlic Capital of the World. I was particularly pleased with this find. Being a garlic lover, I felt a kinship with the crowds of curiosity seekers lining up to buy the house specialty, decorative wreaths of . . . what else but garlic.

The John and Mabel Ringling Estate was another offbeat place to visit. In Sarasota, Florida just off Interstate 75, between St. Petersburg's Bayfront Center and Fort Myers' Civic Center stood the Ringling mansion and museum. As a carnival and circus buff, I was fascinated with the history of America's most famous circus impresario. To touch Bruno Zacchini's Sure Repeating Cannon . . . what a thrill!

As a child I waited for the Ringling Brothers ringmaster's pronouncement that it was time for the grand finale. Anxiously squirming in my seat, I watched spellbound as the long fuse of the huge cannon, flaming in freeze frame motion, reached the gigantic and menacing barrel, setting off a thunderous explosion which rocked the building amidst billows of smoke. And Bruno, the human cannonball, would suddenly be propelled through the air from one end of the old Madison Square Garden to the oversized net at the other.

As I nostalgically admired the circus memorabilia of yesteryear, it occurred to me that just like the majestic ringmasters of old, I too was now overseeing the proceedings from center ring. I too was taking spectators through an evening of grand entrances, mischief and heroism. Whether it was an entrance marked by the pomp and circumstance of Ric Flair or the excitement generated by the introduction of Sting; whether it was the deceitful mischief of Steve Austin or the daring athletics of Chris Benoit and Beautiful Bobby Eaton or the daredevil feats of Cactus Jack; many of the same elements of our nightly shows have entertained circus crowds for centuries. Each night, as I looked out on the sea of innocent faces that gathered around ringside, eager to catch the first glimpse of their heroes, looking on with concern and then awe and then smiles, I saw myself thirty years earlier. Now, instead of Bruno Zacchini, it was Ric Flair or Sting or Hulk Hogan wowing them in the grand finale.

But my childlike enthusiasm was tempered by the hardships of constant travel. Some days I announced two shows, a matinee and an evening performance. On others, I flew to the Atlanta studio to voice over TV shows in the morning and announced across the country that night. My grueling schedule kept me on the road 200 days a year which resulted in spending less and less time with family and friends back home. The wrestlers, referees, managers and road crews became my second family. We spent holidays and birthdays together. We shared problems. We looked out for each other. We understood one another's needs like no one outside of the business could.

While I enjoyed the freedom of traveling alone, the most memorable trips, were those that I made with the boys, like those with Flair and The Undertaker that I recounted earlier in this book. Inasmuch as their living expenses, hotel, food, gym fees and recreation gobbled up 25 to 40 per cent of their yearly income, it was no surprise that some of the boys were eager to travel with me, as I often extended my corporate perks to pick up the tab in restaurants and shared hotel rooms with them.

One of the more colorful characters who periodically traveled with me was Abdullah the Butcher. For years, I've been expecting this durable performer, to make his final lap around the career track. But he just keeps on going. Abby's ring persona is that of a bloodthirsty savage. Unlike Mark Calaway, who can back up his Undertaker character with ample athletic ability, Abby is all show. While he has displayed some knowledge of the martial arts and at times delivered the flying elbow with grace, he is best known as the brawling cannibal from Northeast Africa's Sudan.

At six feet, 430 pounds, cloaked in loose-fitting drawstring pants cinched high on the enormous girth above his mid-section, sporting curly toed footwear and draped with flowing headgear, Abby is a frightful sight to behold. For 43 years, he has incited riots in arenas around the globe. He storms the ring, recklessly throwing his headpiece aside to expose a bald head, much too small in proportion to the immense size of his body. His forehead and the top of his skull are creased with deep scar tissue-filled parallel grooves – the result of years gashing himself with razors for the dramatic effect that a bloodstained warrior evokes. Scarred with faded layers of dead skin, the top of his engraved cranium, far from the beauty of a fine African wood carving, is as wrinkled as a dried raisin.

When Abby wrestles, the fans can be assured of a brawl. His repertoire consists of jabbing, stabbing, stomping, eye-gouging, head butting and a nice enough flying elbow. When the Butcher works, the action is guaranteed to spill outside of the ring, up the aisles and often into the ringside seats. He incites as much as he excites and is well aware of the mat world motto: "red turns to green". Simply put, the fans' expectation that a match will turn into a bloodbath draws dollars at the box office. As long as he's willing to slice his own flesh, promoters pay what he demands. Well aware that his name on the card is like money in the bank, Abdullah has earned as much as $10,000 a week in Japan and $1,000 per performance from smaller US promotions between Asian tours.

Abby and Bruiser Brody often turned "red" to "green" at the box office.

When in character, he maintains his maniacal mystique by never speaking English. Instead, he utters a crude, indistinguishable gibberish. When out of character, he's a soft spoken, mild mannered, well-tailored gentleman, whose fine silk suits are custom made in Japan.

From humble beginnings in Canada, Abby has always been resourceful. In his earlier days, he worked as a janitor and then formed his own janitorial service in Windsor Ontario. To make extra money, he pretended to be a poverty-stricken soul, going door-to-door, to beg for used furniture and assorted goods. He then sold the items at a healthy profit until the local authorities caught on to the con.

The con, or what we refer to in wrestling as "the work", is to knowingly misrepresent the truth, to lie, to deceive or mislead someone. Most often it takes the form of a harmless prank, an inside joke. For Abby it's a way of life. Abdullah "worked" everyone.

I found myself the object of one of Abby's cons while touring the Carolinas. He asked to ride with me, claiming that he was unable to fit his rotund 400 pound bulk behind a steering wheel. This was just a softball con to distract me from the way he would work me later in the day. I remembered how early in my career, 605-pound Haystacks Calhoun drove himself throughout the northeastern states with little problem. And I knew that back home, Abby freely motored around suburban Atlanta in his luxury vehicle. But he was a character, a shrewd character, and I wanted to see what I might learn from someone who had successfully survived this tough business for so long.

Our tour ran from late April and into the early part of May in 1990. It spanned Baltimore; Greensboro; Camp Lejeune in Jacksonville, North Carolina; Rainsville, Alabama; Greenwood, South Carolina and Fort Bragg in Fayetteville, North Carolina.

You can store spare change in the deep crevices of Abby's scarred forehead.

By the time we were on our way to Camp Lejeune, I found that Abdullah spent most of his day sleeping while I drove. He'd be in the middle of a story about his life before wrestling and suddenly I'd hear him snoring. He'd tell me how Jim Barnett, the promoter who ran Australia, years earlier, regularly underpaid the boys who were in debt, based upon information from their "confidential" financial statements that he obtained from the president of the Aussie bank entrusted by the guys to wire money home to their families. And then Abby suddenly he snorted back into slumber. He'd tell me how he provided monetary support for his mother in Canada each month and then wheezed and snoozed for another forty miles.

We didn't arrived at the Hampton Inn until late in the afternoon. When I went to register at the front desk, Abdullah didn't move from the car.

"Hey Abby, what are ya waiting for? Aren't you goin' to check in?"

He simply waved me on, rolled his head back and closed his eyes. Upon my return, I questioned him further.

"How come you're not getting a room?"

"No problem, Gary, I'll take care of that later."

"How do you know they'll have a room later?"

"Don't worry. I've been here many times before."

"Well, ya know, we're not goin' to bunk together."

"No problem. I'll take care of it after the show."

We worked Camp Lejeune before a tanked crowd of hooting and hollering servicemen. It was customary at all of the military base shows for beer to overwhelmingly outsell WCW souvenirs. Invariably, the military police had a tough time restraining the unruly soldiers from jumping into the ring. After everyone safely survived the rowdy event, we were on our way back to the hotel.

"Gary, how about stopping for something to eat? I'm hungry."

"All right, Abby. There's a restaurant across from The Hampton. Is that okay? I think it's a Chili's or an Applebee's or a Ruby Tuesday's."

"Sure, sure. That would be fine."

"You know, we've got an early flight in the morning. Tomorrow's the TV shoot in Alabama. The next night is TV in Greenwood. I don't want to stay out too late."

"No problem. We'll eat and get back to the hotel."

I pulled into the packed parking lot of Applebee's Neighborhood Grill. We made our way through the crowd, some who were gnawing on their sirloins had just witnessed Abby gnawing on the forehead of his opponent. Some withdrew from the enormous giant. Others weren't so timid.

"Hey, he don't need no appetizer. He just ate."

"Give him one of everything on the menu. That'll hold him for a little while."

Abby always handled himself well in these situations, mostly by ignoring the taunting troubleseekers.

A half-hour passed before our dinners came. The faster I ate, with one eye on the hotel across the street, the slower Abby sipped his drink. I finished my meal and waited as Abby poked at his double order of apple pie a la mode.

Just when it seemed safe to ask for the bill, Ric Flair and his nightly entourage made a grand entrance. Applebee's erupted with "Whoo, it's the Nature Boy!" He spotted us on the far side of the restaurant and made his way over to our table. Abby's face lit up like a rotten pumpkin. The carved smile was still intact, but it looked dark and sinister. Something smelled and I couldn't figure out why.

"Have a seat, Ric. Do you want something to drink?"

Asking Flair if he wants something to drink is like asking the Pope if he's Catholic. Notice that Abby didn't say, "I'll buy you a drink". Abby never did that.

Throughout the next hour they talked about the business: past, current and into the next century. At fifteen-minute intervals I interrupted. "You know, we've got a six o'clock flight in the morning." They complained about the way our office was being run. "I need to get some sleep if I'm going to be worth anything at TV". Vince is kicking our asses. When is Turner going to wake up?

Killer Cruz, Little Tokyo and The Karate Kid prove that while Abby's shoes may be tough to fill, his pants aren't.

Finally I said, "Look, I'll walk across to the hotel. Abby, here are the keys. When you're finished, you can bring the car over."

"Oh, no. No problem. Do you want to go? We can leave if that's what you want."

Abby lifted his 400 pounds from the table, leaving Flair with the drink bill. As we got into the car, Abby casually glanced at me.

"How about we find a nice place for a nightcap?"

I couldn't believe what I was hearing. What was going on? Why was he doing this?

"Look Abby, have you taken too many bumps? You slept all damned day while I drove. If I don't get some sleep tonight, I'm not going to last through the next two nights of TV."

"Well . . . then . . . just drive down this road. We'll find a nice place and you can drop me off."

"And how are you going to get back?"

"I'll call a cab."

"Are you crazy? You're going to find a cab in the middle of the night in Jacksonville, North Carolina?"

"Don't worry. Just drive down this road."

No, Abdullah wasn't crazy. I was the lunatic for putting up with him.

We drove down Marine Boulevard for a few miles until Abby finally pointed to the side of the road.

"Here. Pull in here. See that sign? This is a nice place."

Abdullah's idea of a nice place was a dilapidated concrete building with plywood-covered windows next to the longest strip of testosterone-inspired businesses anywhere. There were pawnshops, used car lots, gun and ammo dealerships, auto-parts shops, gin mills and X-rated bookstores. And in the middle of it all was Jughead's Tavern.

"All right, Abby. Here you go. See you in the morning."

"Wait a minute. Won't you come in for just one drink?"

"No!"

"But what if I don't like it here?"

"No!!"

"I have to take a look."

"Abby, either stay or come back with me now. I'm through riding around this God forsaken shit hole."

"Look, just come in for one minute. If it doesn't look like the kind of place I want, then we'll go back to the hotel."

"No!!!"

"If I go in there, and someone causes me trouble, then what will I do? All alone . . . no car . . ."

I took one step inside and went no further. There was a handful of scruffy local toughs engrossed in a Hells Angels pool tournament, a few wobbly marines barely balanced on their bar stools and dozens of young, under-dressed, overly-perfumed, tattooed adolescent girls milling throughout.

When Abdullah reached the bar, he looked over his shoulder and realized I was missing. He peered through the smoke and pulsating lights just in time to notice my quick exit. By the time I got to the car, Abby was rapidly waddling right behind.

"Aren't you going to stay?" he huffed.

"What do you think? Our flight leaves in five hours. How can you think this dive is a 'nice place'? And those degenerates . . . even you're a hell of a lot more normal-looking than any of them."

"All right. All right. Listen to me. Here's what you do. My wrestling gear and the rest of my things are in the trunk. If I get lucky, I won't be at the hotel in the morning. Just bring my things to the airport. Don't worry. I'll be fine. But are you sure that you don't want to stay for just one drink?"

I wasn't sure what "getting lucky" meant. Was he looking to score some coke? Or was he looking to get laid? Either would have been expected from some of the boys. But from Abdullah? And while I don't know if either was accomplished at Jughead's, I have since realized what his primary goal was on that evening.

Abby is so immersed in the culture of the con that he assumes everyone operates in the same way. He thinks that "the work" is everybody's way of life. To prevent himself from being a sucker in a world of con men, he has become excessively paranoid. It is an existence of constant distrust. With the belief that everyone is scheming to cheat him, he takes the necessary preventative measures to protect himself. And that means to strike first. And that is how Abdullah operates.

He suspiciously guards every penny, fearful that crooks are waiting at every turn to swindle him. With all of the money he has made over four decades in this business, Abby is determined to retire with the payoff from his first job tucked away for safekeeping.

There were times when he entrusted me with bankrolls of up to $10,000 in cash, wrapped tightly by an elastic band and stuffed into a sock, to safeguard for him while he wrestled. Granted, I wouldn't leave enormous amounts of money in an unguarded dressing room either. But, why was Abby carrying $10,000 on the road with him at all? I never found out the answer to that question, but it does explain the wad that protruded from my tuxedo pants pocket whenever Abdullah wrestled. Just in case you had noticed. But let's get back to the story at hand.

The object of his charade in North Carolina was simple. He weaseled someone into driving him between towns so he could sleep all day. Then he conned them to stay out all night so he didn't have to pay for a hotel room. Remember that this is the guy who was pulling in ten grand a week in Japan. But this is what happened every time he found a gullible mark; someone he could con; someone like me.

But the payoff of this story about con men and marks has a uniquely innocent ending.

M onths later I was on an overbooked flight from Knoxville to Atlanta which was filled with WCW wrestlers. Among those on board were Abdullah, Kevin Sullivan, Nancy, his wife at the time and Kevin's two children. Abby was stuffed into his coach seat and overflowing onto Kevin's young son, skinny little Ben. Although it was a short flight, Abby saw Ben as easy prey and he couldn't resist. Out came a deck of playing cards and the con man started shuffling. Ben's eyes were drawn to Abdullah's hands, fluttering with lightning-like speed. As the mesmerized youngster came under the spell of the Las Vegas shuffle, Abby closed in on his mark.

"Do you know how to play rummy?" He was like a mountain lion cornering a mouse.

"Sure. Let's play."

"Are you any good?"

"Yeah, I always beat my sister."

"Then what do you want to play for?"

"What do you mean?"

"Well, if you usually win, then you shouldn't mind if we play for something."

"Like what?"

"How much money do you have in your pocket?"

Ben pulled out eight one-dollar bills, laid them on the tray table and the game began. As Abdullah won each hand, he took a dollar and stuffed it in his shirt pocket. After they had completed five hands, the score was clear from the frustration on the youngster's face. When he saw the last of his allowance disappear into the big man's pocket, Ben was visibly upset.

"You cheated! You cheated!"

"I cheated? No, I didn't. I won."

"No, you cheated. I don't know how you did it, but you cheated."

"Do you want to play again?"

By now, Ben was choking back tears. "I can't play any more. I don't have any money left."

"Well, that's a nice gold watch you're wearing. If you think you can beat me, put it up. We'll play once more. This time, for the watch."

The youngster stared at Abby for a few seconds. Abdullah softly smiled back. He pleadingly raised his eyebrows, which turned the scarred slits on his forehead into proverbial swerves. Ben found no way to back down from the challenge

185

and the game continued. Before the second hand swept around once, the watch was added to Abdullah's winnings. Unable to control the emotion of the moment, Ben jumped up, squeezed passed Abby, kicking him in the process and ran to the bathroom.

Abdullah reached into his pocket, fished out the money and the watch and passed it on to Kevin's daughter.

"Here, these belong to your brother. Put them in your pocketbook, but don't tell him I gave them back until you get home."

Upon returning to his seat, Ben crossed his arms and silently pouted for the remainder of the flight. Abby's eyes occasionally wandered in his direction, but Ben defiantly looked away.

At the end of the flight Kevin, Abby and I patiently waited for the front cabin passengers to deplane while Ben squeezed ahead to the front of the line. As we approached the airport terminal, we could hear a commotion in the distance. The closer we got, the louder the screams. When we finally entered the waiting area, an outraged crowd had circled around young, tear-filled Ben who was pulling on the coat of two airport security guards, jumping up and down yelling, "There, there he is! See that big fat black man! Arrest him! He stole my watch and all of my money!"

I remembered the rib Abdullah had pulled on me in the Carolina's, as I joined the crowds shuffling through the airport. Looking back at Abby, pleading his innocence to the skeptical security guards in the face of the screaming youngster, I knew how Ben felt. Thanks, kid!

One ironic update about Abdullah the Butcher . . . today, at the age of 64, Abbie is still actively working the US indie circuit as well as in Japan where he captured The Big Japan Death Match Championship in Fukuoka on January 10, 1999. And as fate would have it, Abdullah, The King of the Ribs, has finally invested a small chunk of his wrestling fortune to provide for himself when he finally hangs up his curly toed boots . . . it's a restaurant in the Atlanta area appropriately named . . . Abdullah the Butcher's House of Ribs and Chinese Food. It's gotta make ya smile!

By and large, pro wrestlers are a great group of guys. Most lead relatively normal home lives with devoted wives and children. The one factor that most tests the wrestlers is the strain of never-ending road trips. While the schedules in other sports are limited to shorter seasons, a wrestler's work never ends. And even with a limited season, major league pro athletes have the luxury half the time of sleeping in their own beds for home games. While the basketball season runs 89 games and hockey players square off 82 times a year, a touring wrestler plays as many as 200 one-nighters in countless towns and cities all over the world, year round.

With the built-in pressures of such an unsettled lifestyle, it's surprising that most of my wrestling colleagues are such well-adjusted individuals.

Sting is one of the most down-to-earth of all. While the Stinger has always been one of WCW's top moneymakers, he never pulled rank on me or displayed an elitist attitude. He was a pleasure to work with, always ready to lend a hand and willing to listen.

Beautiful Bobby Eaton tops the list in humility and reliability. While he is best known as the silent partner of The Midnight Express tag team, he is undoubtedly one of the most flawless workers still active in the business. Since his effectiveness on interviews has been handicapped by a thick Alabama drawl, his former manager, Jim Cornette, handled all of the mic work. The violence that he portrays in the ring is the antithesis of what he can stomach in real life.

The Midnight Express: Stan Lane, Jim Cornette and Bobby Eaton

Eaton and I gained heightened respect for each another the night we were equally repulsed by the actions of Cornette. During one of his Altoona, Pennsylvania tag team matches, Bobby and his partner, Stan Lane, were continually gaining the upper hand over their opponents due to Jimmy's constant illegal interference. Cornette was trumpeting his evil deeds in the face of the enraged fans at ringside. He pranced around the ring with his trademark tennis racket, fully in character as a spoiled mama's boy.

As the match continued, with the Midnight Express flagrantly ignoring the rules, the frenzied fans were on their feet.

One by one, they started to approach the protective fence that surrounded the ring. The attention of the security guards, local volunteers who took none of this seriously, was focused on the action instead of on the provoked fans. Suddenly, an elderly spectator, who must have been in his 70's

A flat swat stings. Frame first is deadly.

began berating Eaton and Lane for their unsportsmanlike conduct and gave Cornette a piece of his mind as well. The old-timer stepped up on the lower rung of the fence and managed to lift one leg over the top of the railing. Cornette, still gleefully prancing around ringside, spotted grandpa and called to the guards who just laughed at the sight of the frail guy teetering on top of the fence. Before I could make my way around to the other side of the ring, Cornette rushed over to the old man, hauled back his tennis racket and nailed the guy squarely on the bridge of his nose with the wood frame. It was like smashing a tomato with a hammer. Blood spurt everywhere.

As the angry Altoona crowd surged toward ringside, Bobby and I looked at each other in stunned disbelief. It was rare that any of our performers crossed the line between simulated violence and real life brutality.

The security guards, finally realizing the threat of a full-blown riot, dragged the gory faced old-timer up the aisle kicking and screaming all the way.

As the match continued, the stunned audience, reluctantly realized that the incident they had just witnessed was real. The illusion of what was portrayed in the match had been ruined. And although the fans quietly returned to their seats, I knew from experience that we had not yet escaped their wrath.

188

They were boiling beneath the surface and the slightest offense would set them off once again. The wrestlers quickly began to go home (conclude the match), but danger still filled the air.

To my disbelief, the old man, still bleeding profusely, re-entered from the other side of the arena and charged back down the aisle toward the ring. He got back in Cornette's face, threatening and screaming for Jimmy to be arrested. As I stepped between the two, the guards lifted the old man up and once again removed him from ringside.

As soon as the match ended, Cornette and his team hopped in their car and scurried out of town. The next night, Jimmy tried to justify slugging the old guy. After all, who knew if he had a concealed weapon? And besides, if Cornette had run away, it would have undermined the role that he plays. His character never retreated when his wrestlers were nearby to protect him.

I guess I was supposed to pat Cornette on the back for upholding the authenticity of the business. But I couldn't. And I have enormous respect for Jimmy's knowledge of and love for wrestling. He has been one of the game's most effective managers. But he got carried away that night. Corney was now rationalizing his actions, expecting everyone in wrestling to shake his hand for standing up for the business. I wouldn't. Jimmy overreacted in the heat of the moment. The old guy could have been taken down in a less violent manner. After all, the guy was in his 70's!

There is no better example of a true gentleman than The Enforcer, Arn Anderson. Aside from his effectiveness in the ring as well as his behind-the-mic artistry, Arn has long been the guy to rally the troops when morale is low. His common sense and cut-to-the-quick sense of humor lend a dose of reality when egos get out of control. Later in this book, we'll see how Arn's intense loyalty to his friends lured him into a bloody altercation with Sid Vicious in Bournemouth, England during one of our early European tours.

189

Ricky "The Dragon" Steamboat will go down in the record books as one of the sport's most competent ring operatives. He is appreciated by fellow wrestlers for his sincerity and generosity. Unlike stars of equal repute, Ricky readily accepted the input of his opponents. Although he was able to get away with calling his own matches in a way to put himself in the best possible light, Ricky was never above following his opponents' lead for the good of the match. He places such a high priority on family life, that one of his early WCW contracts provided that his wife, Bonnie and son, Richie accompany him on the road. I think that speaks volumes.

Ricky Steamboat, an incredible athlete and a true gentleman.

My friendship with "Stone Cold" Steve Austin began when he entered World Championship Wrestling as "Stunning" Steve Austin in 1991. Steve was so good at putting over his wrestling persona, that at first, I wasn't sure how much of the arrogance he displayed in the ring was his natural way. Upon his arrival to WCW, it was tough to strike up a conversation with him, since when he wasn't working, he kept to himself. At the time, he sported shoulder-length golden locks, wore sequined studded robes and smirked at the taunting ringside fans. His ring work was always excellent. He had learned his craft well. But until I was able to get beyond his character, I cautiously kept my distance.

The very attractive Vivacious Veronica won the job of accompanying Steve to the ring. Not because she was an experienced valet. Not because she showed the potential for becoming as effective as Sensational Sherri, Miss Elizabeth, Precious or other top flight female managers who had preceded her. No, Veronica began sharing the spotlight with Austin shortly after she began sharing the nightlight of one of Turner's corporate executives. I'm still not sure whether she was a slick operative or a very troubled young lady or both. In either case, Veronica's most effective managing took place *outside* of the ring. She managed to cast a spell over the otherwise levelheaded married exec, turning his professional and personal life inside out. I felt powerless as I watched him foolishly risk his position within the Turner organization, as well as his marriage, by coupling her with one of the most promising new talents that Turner had acquired to date. Casting decisions are almost always the domain of the booker. Corporate execs rarely have a hand in recommending unknown talent. And Veronica is a perfect example why this is, and should be the case.

Needless to say, Austin was not happy about his inherited valet, especially since his wife at the time, Jeannie (former wife of Austin's first wrestling instructor, and World Class Wrestling regular "Gentleman" Chris Adams) had played the part so well in the past. His disappointment bordered on anger, since when he signed with WCW, Steve expected that his pleasant, petite British bride would accompany him on the road.

So Steve was faced with the challenge of convincing the WCW bookers that his valet should be Jeannie and not Veronica. And he played it perfectly. It was as if he had taken the solution to his dilemma from The Gary Michael Cappetta Book of Getting the Boss' Attention that I used when Iron Mike Sharpe knocked me out at the Philadelphia Spectrum. Austin's solution was actually quite simple. And very effective. He just didn't work with her. Yes, she

Jeannie, "Stunning" Steve's wife at the time, was his natural choice to accompany him on the road and to the ring. In no time, Veronica was out and "Lady Blossom". was in.

accompanied him to the ring. And of course, the broadcasters billed her as his doting girlfriend. But there was nothing in Steve's demeanor to support what they were saying. He simply did nothing. He ignored her. He undermined her attempts to pamper him in public, as was her job. Austin treated her like a nonentity. Some nights, when she lovingly reached out to help him disrobe, he'd turn his back on her and undressed himself without the simplest acknowledgement that she even existed. He, in effect, made her look silly in light of how the WCW publicity machine portrayed her. I learned early in my career that the fans couldn't be fooled by what does not ring true. And it didn't take long for the bookers to see the effects of Austin's ploy. Eventually, they realized that the success of their newest performer, and more importantly, their latest investment, was in jeopardy. That's when they decided to pull the plug on the vivacious vixen.

By the time she realized that her short-lived television career was in jeopardy, Veronica's personal relationship with her victimized beau had spun out of control. And as the pressure to replace her began to mount, Veronica became even more demanding of her exploited sponsor. When he finally came to me for advice about how to escape her hold on him, my usually conservative colleague was down for the count. He confessed that when she cried that the loss of her WCW income would make her unable to support herself, he began to pay her household bills. She was worried that losing her position with WCW would force her to return to her abusive lover, an independent wrestler from Tennessee, who she said was in the habit of beating her. As her chances of continuing to team with Austin lessened, Veronica began to call the married exec's home and her demands, though demurely stated, became unbearably outrageous.

Then she began showing up at our live events when she wasn't booked to plead her case through teary eyes. I marveled at her unique ability to completely transform herself into the model of the minute. Each time gorgeous, but each different from the last. In Charlotte she was as beautiful as the cover girl of Vogue. In Cleveland she transformed herself into the Max Factor model in a Seventeen Magazine ad. And in Boston, where she was quickly escorted to a side dressing room when she arrived at the Gardens sobbing, demanding an audience with management, she looked like Psychology Today's "other woman" pin-up. After pitching a screaming and crying fit, she must have realized that the casting couch could be a very precarious place to conduct business.

None of her theatrics worked with the bookers. Within weeks, Vivacious Veronica was out and Lady Blossom (Jeannie) was in. With time she was gone from the scene, back to her boyfriend in Tennessee, and everyone was happy except Veronica and the guy whom she had tormented for months.

But before Jeannie joined her husband on the road, Austin asked me if we could team up on a trip between Corpus Christi and Houston. While it should have been a simple three and a half-hour drive, I never reached the Crown Plaza in Houston until sunrise.

After I finally chipped away at "Stone Cold's" rigid, self-protective facade I found that he was really an easy going, unpretentious kind of guy. From our first trip through Texas, it was as if we had teamed up on the road many times before. Conversation with Steve came easy, even though "getting to know you" chitchat with some of the boys often had been uncomfortable and guarded. Those were the guys who had learned the hard way not to be too honest, too soon. But Austin trusted me from the beginning with the basics of his background and I responded with mine. While we cruised through the sleepy towns of Sinton, Refugio and Beeville, I shared some of my experiences in the wrestling business, which led to a topic that caused Austin to come to life once again.

"Did ya always announce for a living?" he queried.

"Nope, I was a high school teacher for the first fifteen years that I announced for Vince and then for Verne and then for Crockett."

"A teacher? Hell, I would have been your worse nightmare."

"Oh yeah? Why's that?

"Cuz I hated school. By the time I got to college, I spent half of my time playing football and the other half frustrating the hell out of my teachers. I just did enough to get by. All of the teachers thought I was a dumb jock so I acted that way. I just sat in the back of the class, kept to myself and nobody bothered me. I thought it was a bunch of bullshit. They expected me to be dumb and I gave them what they expected. I did just enough to stay on the team."

Austin told me that since his real name, Steve Williams, was the given name of veteran tough guy wrestler Dr. Death, he chose Steve Austin as his stage name. His choice was based on *The Six Million Dollar Man* character that he enjoyed, as played by Lee Majors in the 1970's TV series.

As we approached the Victoria / Edna area, Austin

Austin is one of the many wrestlers who became a superstar in the WWF after being turned away by WCW.

asked me to turn right off of the state road. Without a convenience store or a restaurant in sight, I questioned why he wanted to drive through the desolate streets of this closed down town in the dead of the night. His answer was a simple, "Cuz I said so!" followed by a sly chuckle. As it turns out, years later, when Austin rose to super stardom in the WWF, *Cuz Stone Cold Said So!* became the signature phrase that captured the attention of millions of wrestling fans around the world.

We slowly rolled into the darkness of a hauntingly hushed town. As we crept crossed the main downtown road, a phone booth, lit by a solitary street light overhead, stood before us. Austin suddenly perked up.

"This is it! Pull over. I'll be right back."

When he rejoined me ten minutes later, Austin seemed revitalized.

"What was that all about?"

"Just wanted to call ahead to my brother."

"Your brother?"

"Yeah, and I wanted to touch base with my family."

"You've got to be kidding! It's the middle of the night!"

"Naw, we don't mind."

When we approached the city limits of Houston I asked Austin for the name of the hotel where he was staying.

"I'm not staying in a hotel tonight. We gotta find a strip club just outside of the city."

"You're staying at a strip club?"

"Naw, that's where I'm meeting up with my kid brother."

"Okay, where is it?"

"I've got an address right here." He dug deep into his pocket, fishing out the shredded scrap of a hotel receipt with

Fantasia, or Xcalibur, or some other such establishment scrawled haphazardly across its face. "It shouldn't be tough to find."

What should have been and what turned out to be were two entirely different things. We cruised the streets of Houston for hours in search of the place.

As two o'clock turned into three o'clock, with no strip club in sight, Austin felt a twinge of guilt.

"Just let me off on the side of the road. I'll ask around. I'll find it."

"Naw. I don't think that's a good idea."

"Why not? It can't be too far from here."

"Because I'm not letting you loose in the most depraved district of Houston in the middle of the night. Plus, if you don't show up for your match in Beaumont, I'm the one whose gotta break the news to your redneck neighbors. So let's keep looking."

"Now don't get smart with me, Cappetta. I wouldn't be pushin' to find the place except my brother's gonna be waiting for me."

"What's gonna happen if we find it and he's not around?"

"I'll have his ass, that's what's gonna happen! But if he said he'd be there, he'll be there. Don't worry."

It was four o'clock when we finally found the porno palace. We rolled into the deserted parking lot with no brother in sight.

"Damn, I'm gonna whip my brother's skinny little ass," my dumfounded buddy moaned. His desperate eyes peered through the darkness of the deserted blacktop parking lot.

"It's okay, Steve. Why don't ya just come back to the Crowne Plaza with me and we can . . . . ."

Before I could finish my sentence, he slapped me across the chest with an abrupt backhand. Without another word, he bound out of the car and disappeared into the darkness. A minute later, Austin reappeared alternately pushing and hugging his long lost brother through the early morning mist. And yes, his kid brother was as skinny as a rail.

"Would ya believe it? I found him hugging one of those damn flower pots around the side of the building! Sleepin' like a damn baby!"

Sleepily gazing through the morning mist at the tacky, cement-chipped, Roman columns, which towered on either side of the sleazy club's grand entrance, I was touched.

195

Chapter Thirteen
"Highway Horseplay"

Athletes have more contempt for authority, authority of any kind, than at any other time in sports history. On the field of play, off the field, it doesn't matter. It seems that every day another incident in the sports pages makes you want to throw the whole newspaper across the room, just because you'll never get the chance to roll the paper up and smack some of these ballplayers across the head with it.

Mike Lupica,
"Mad As Hell, How Sports Got Away from the Fans And How We Get It Back"

Since one of my favorite bargain hunting regions of the country is the upper Midwest, I was excited in November of 1992 to have been assigned a tour that would take me to Joplin, St. Joseph and Springfield, Missouri as well as Topeka, Kansas. With Christmas only a month away, I was ready to scour the heartland in search of last minute buys.

Everybody on the tour arrived in Kansas City together on a flight the day after a show in Macon, Georgia. Some of the guys made their way down to the baggage claim area, while others headed for the rental car counters. WCW was still paying for rental cars when three wrestlers shared the vehicle. If a wrestler leased a car without submitting two other names on his company travel voucher, he was stuck paying the bill himself.

After everyone teamed up to start the weeklong tour, the last three guys remaining were Marc "Buff" Bagwell, Ron Simmons (Faarooq) and Too Cold Scorpio (Flash Funk). From opposite sides of the baggage carousel I could see that Ron was fuming as he and Scorpio stormed away from Bagwell and headed in my direction.

"Hey, Cappetta," scowled Simmons with a "you'd better not piss me off" tone of voice. "Who are you riding with?"

"I'm not riding with anyone. I never ride with anyone." Ron knew the answer before he asked the question.

My intentionally direct response caught him by surprise. I had become accustomed to the games often played by some of the wrestlers. To stand back and watch how they used their notoriety and bulk to get what they wanted was amazing. I knew that the All American from Florida State was far from a bully. The boys respected Ron. He was one who didn't have to prove himself to anyone. But he was also someone that you didn't want to provoke. That was never an issue for us. But by the time he realized that his intimidating approach wasn't necessary to get my help, it was too late. He now had his pride to protect. He continued to peer down at me not because

This threatening look that Ron fired my way when we worked together in the ring was the same intimidating glare he used at the Kansas City airport.

he believed this to be the way to gain a favor, but because he had to.

"Why, what's the problem?" The 6'2", 250 pounder knew I was playing dumb, but we continued the game anyway.

"That fuckin' pretty boy over there was supposed to share the car with us, but he went and made other plans. And he didn't even tell us. Shiiiiit, he shouldn't have his wife on the road with him anyway."

"You mean he took the company car for him and his wife?

"You got that right. And I just know he'll sign our names to the voucher. Now what are we supposed to do?

I just looked up at him and shrugged as Scorpio watched with delight. He knew Simmons and I were working each other and waited to see who would come out on top.

"If you guys need a ride, I'll help you out. But there are a couple of things we have to agree on."

Ron spotted the opening and quickly shot back. "Great, how about if you go get the car and we'll bring your gear outside for you." He knew I wasn't finished yet.

"I'm not so sure you're going to want to travel with me."

"That's all right. We'll put up with you"

"It's not *me* I'm worried about. It's *you*. Look, we travel on my timetable. I need to get to the buildings two hours before the shows start. I can't wait around for you. I've got a sound check and music to set up before doors open. And I'm not going to be your chauffeur." I was sounding real strong until I got to my final condition. "And we'll have to stop a few times to shop."

Simmons' eyes narrowed to a bewildered stare.

"Did you say *shop*?"

"Yeah, shop. I have to shop. It's almost Christmas."

"Oh, jeez, Cappetta!" Shaking his head in disbelief he turned to Too Cold, "Ya think we can survive the week with Cap-pet-ta?"

"I don't know", chuckled Scorpio. "Cappetta drives a *haaard* bargain."

Ron turned back to me. "Get outta here. We'll meet ya on the sidewalk."

I wasn't kidding. Some of my most enjoyable times were spent wandering through unique gift and novelty shops. I found the most unusual crystal ornaments at Christmas on the River in Savannah, Georgia and pine cone candles dipped in scented wax in Odessa, Texas and the only place in the world where you can find the finest German blended tobacco products is at the Peter Heinrich Smoke Shop in Cologne, Germany. I'd find unique Christmas presents for family and friends all over the world. It was a year round pastime earning me the nickname among some of the boys of "Mr. Christmas".

When I arrived at the Avis shuttle bus I found Bagwell and his wife at the time, Tanya, already on board, waiting to be taken to "their" company car. Marc and Tanya were a picture perfect couple. Marc's life centered on keeping his beefy body perfectly sculpted through rigorous workouts at the gym, a strict dietary regimen, and the use of steroids, which he insisted were physician prescribed. Tanya's long blonde hair softly flowed down the back of her petite, shapely swimsuit calendar figure. On this occasion, she acted uncharacteristically friendly. Perhaps she was pleased that Marc had cashed in frequent flyer credits to bring her along for the week. I, too, thought it was remarkable since Delta SkyMiles were more often reserved to fly in special girlfriends by the few boys who had them. That was the advantage of screwing a flight attendant. It kept your frequent flyer miles intact.

Marc's physique and innocent good looks brought in a yearly income of $65,000 that Tanya carefully controlled. His brawn and her brains had afforded the young couple a more comfortable life than most of their former Sprayberry High School classmates.

Tanya babbled about what they had planned for the week. But when Marc mentioned that he and Tanya were staying at the Super 8, the boys' preferred hotel in the Kansas City area, I had a feeling that this couple's storybook marriage was headed for an unhappy ending. As I pulled out of the Avis lot in my Corolla and the Bagwells followed in their Lincoln, Marc was about to encounter a rocky road ahead.

We headed straight down Route 71 toward Joplin, our first destination. I drove, Ron rode shot gun and Scorpio relaxed in the back. After an hour and a half of grunting about Bagwell, Simmons shot a glance my way. "Cappetta, you must be getting hungry."

More games straight out of Ric Flair's playbook. Why couldn't he just suggest that we stop for lunch because he was hungry? Simple. Direct. Honest.

"No. I'm fine." I didn't take my eyes off of the road.

"Well, ya know, if ya don't stop now, ya won't have time to eat lunch later."

"Lunch? I don't eat lunch." I eagerly awaited his response.

"What? You don't eat lunch? There something wrong with you?"

Bagwell has taken on a harder edge in today's WCW.

I burst out laughing and took the Nevada, Missouri exit. Luckily, I spotted May's Flower & Gift Center at the junction of Highway 54 and Business Route 71, a quaint shop around the corner from a local restaurant. They ate, I bought ceramic Christmas village buildings, and everyone was happy.

By the second day we had given up the games and worked out a suitable arrangement. I shopped in the morning while the guys slept in. We drove through the afternoon and worked the show at night. Then they dropped me off at the hotel, took the car for a few hours of freedom and then left the keys for me when they got back.

With passing each day, Scorpio found himself more barricaded into a corner of the Corolla's back seat. I had already filled the trunk of the car with gifts, making it necessary to wedge my books and calendars from the Joplin, Missouri For-all Bible Center and the pile of village buildings from May's Gift Center and assorted other Christmas presents around Scorpio.

The Bagwells' week had not gone well. After only two days, Tanya had flown back to Atlanta in a rage. It didn't take her long to learn of her husband's custom of entertaining the local arena rats at the Super 8 on our previous swings through Kansas City. When the phone in the Bagwell's room rang all night long, Tanya was not amused. You can imagine her fury when instead of taking "no answer" for an answer, Bagwell's persistent admirers started pounding on his door in the middle of the night.

Marc had broken a fundamental rule. When you bring your wife on tour, never stay at the same hotel where you've broken your wedding vows so many times before. This was not the first time that Bagwell's indiscretions had caused him embarrassment. But that's an entirely different story.

After repeated tours of the Midwest, I came to appreciate Middle America's hospitality. So while the houses that week were only fair, the fans were receptive, the shopping was good and our travel arrangements worked out for the best.

I t was early on a cold, drizzly Sunday morning when we left our Kansas City hotel for the last time. En route to Springfield, Missouri for our final show of the tour, an afternoon matinee, the boys were still gloating over Bagwell's misfortune at the Super 8.

"Every dog's gonna have his day. Ya know what I mean?" Ron crowed.

"That's right", added a supportive Scorpio. "She showed him who's boss. Didn't she Gary?"

While they delighted in the news of Tanya's sudden departure, they seethed each time they crammed themselves into the crowded Corolla as Marc sailed by in his empty Lincoln. It was bad enough that Marc had finessed the Lincoln from them to begin with. But what made matters worse was that after Tanya returned to Georgia, Marc never had the courtesy of offering them the comfort of the Lincoln, even though he had signed their names to the WCW expense voucher. And then there was the added irony of Scorpio and Bagwell wrestling as tag team partners every night of the week!

The Christmas packages, which were heaped on the back seat, began to obstruct my rear view. Too Cold began using them as pillows, falling soundly asleep as I single-mindedly headed toward Springfield. Simmons' snoring drowned out the sound of Scorpio's funky music, which boomed from the car's tape player. As the guys slept, I steadily drove ahead.

In Appleton City the rain turned to tiny ice pellets and our vehicle began to sway. Seconds later the wheels locked. The car spun out of control. I frantically pumped the brake pedal, but it was too late. We twirled across the multi-lane highway accelerating toward the median. The Missouri countryside whirled past the icy windshield in a blur. I felt the same light-headed sensation that Domenic DeNucci's helpless opponents must have felt, locked in for the ride as he applied his dreaded airplane spin. Sliding sideways back across the lines of traffic, I held on to the wheel in horror, as the car skidded toward the shoulder, spinning all the while. When we finally slid to a stop, we were facing on-coming traffic teetering at the edge of an embankment. A number of cars had been propelled by the same icy patch of road. They spun out in our direction coming to a stop just a few feet away on all sides.

Having to team with Bagwell throughout the Midwest was the toughest part of Scorpio's week.

With the engine stalled, I sat for a few seconds in eerie silence with both arms wrapped around my head. Suddenly, Ron began to gasp for breath. Nervously turning to him, I was amazed that he remained slumped over in peaceful slumber. As Ron continued to snore, Too Cold, whose sleep was disturbed by our sudden stop, groggily sat up in the back seat. Realizing that our car was hanging over an incline on the side of the highway, the confused Scorpio whispered, "Gary, are you all right?"

I squeezed Ron's arm in dismay only to be casually waved off. His odd display of nonchalance was more unnerving

201

to me than my ride of terror. Finally, he squinted from across the console, jerked the gearshift to park and calmly mumbled, "See if it starts." I obeyed. It started. They went back to sleep and we proceeded to Springfield where teaming with Marc Bagwell against Steve Austin and Brian Pillman turned out to be the most disturbing event that Scorpio endured all day.

F ollowing WCW's 1993 Battlebowl pay-per-view in Pensacola, Florida, I decided to drive five and a half hours through the night back to Atlanta. If I could catch an early morning flight from the Eastern time zone, I'd pick up an extra hour which would allow me enough time to stand up as godfather for my Cousin Paul's son's baptism the following morning. From our childhood days of attending the matches together, Paul and I had remained close. It was important to me.

When I mentioned my plan to Cactus Jack, his face lit up and he asked if he could join me. It was always an experience to have Cactus, one of my most bizarre wrestling friends, along for the ride. At three hundred pounds, with long, unkempt hair and beard, he wore the tooth missing from his mischievous smile around his neck. The war torn Cactus Jack quickly became one of my favorite co-pilots.

I didn't understand why he wanted to endure a 350-mile overnight excursion, knowing that the company would fly him home the next day. Leaving at 11:00 p.m., we wouldn't arrive in Atlanta until dawn. His answer was simple. "I want to be home when my family wakes up."

Cactus is close to his children and devoted to his beautiful wife, Nicole, a top-flight model, whose figure had adorned the sides of New York City buses when they met. Remembering the fun Cactus and I had when we played toy trucks with his son, Dewey, Cactus' decision made absolute sense to me.

Speeding up Interstate 85 through Montgomery, Alabama, with Auburn straight ahead, I began to burden Cactus with my house hunting horror stories. I told him how it bothered me that whenever I showed interest in a house, the first thing that the sellers made clear was that the swing set was not for sale. I found it puzzling that they could have jeopardized the sale for a rusted metal structure. While this baffled me, Cactus understood completely. He spared no superlatives in singing the praises of Dewey's playground heaven. Sometimes excitedly, sometimes with great emotion, Cactus described every attachment, every sliding board and every up-grade of his prized possession. Wrestling fans knew him as a maniacal lunatic who prided himself on his suicidal style of wrestling. To me, he was just a sentimental mush.

Our conversation took more turns than the interstate as we rolled across the Georgia State line heading for La Grange. Cactus was forever asking me what I thought about the way WCW was handling his career. He feared that they weren't taking the Cactus Jack character seriously. And he was right. Consequently, Cactus dedicated himself to getting noticed with a repertoire of insane, self-destructive moves on concrete floors in arenas from coast to coast.

Finally his time had come, as Ric Flair, the current booker, began to set the stage for his long awaited feud with the WCW heavyweight champion, Big Van Vader. Cactus was enthusiastic when he was told that Vader would power bomb his 300-pound body, headfirst on the unprotected concrete floor at Atlanta's Center Stage before the TV cameras. To add to the believability and ultimate success of the incident, he urged the brutal Vader, to hold nothing back. And Vader, as usual, didn't. When the bookers followed up the concussion causing brawl with a series of foolish, ill-conceived videos portraying Cactus as an amnesia victim ministering to the homeless, he was disheartened and knew the time was right to move on.

After leaving WCW, Cactus embarked on a leather goods mail order business. He then went on to shock the Philadelphia based Extreme Championship Wrestling (ECW) fans in a series with Terry Funk where he was battered with broken beer bottles and flaming branding irons. Today, he is one of Vince's top WWF draws who has been known by various names including Mankind, Dude Love, Cactus Jack and Mick Foley, his birth name.

When Art Barr joined WCW as The Juicer, we promptly teamed up to scale the Appalachian Mountains en route to the Charleston, West Virginia Civic Center. Possessing the adventuresome spirit of a child, Art was a people-loving rascal. We traded story for story contrasting his upbringing in the Pacific Northwest with mine in urban New Jersey. I learned more about what to do when confronted with snakes in the wilderness than I hope I ever need to know.

He told me how his polished ring performance grew from his early training and exposure to the business, having been reared in a wrestling family. His father Sandy and brother Jesse wrestled in Portland, Oregon, where they ran a local promotion. He relied on his close friend Rowdy Roddy Piper to help him with his business decisions, as well as with the politics of the industry.

As we sped through the mountains, we tossed around various bits of business to add to The Juicer's repertoire. Sparked by a few of my suggestions, Art tried over and over to call Piper back home. He told me that Roddy was responsible for The Juicer, wrestling's personification of the movie character Beetlejuice, and was reluctant to add anything to the gimmick without asking Piper's opinion. It was clear that he idolized Piper.

Art was a great guy. He was as fun loving as the kids who sat at ringside.

When WCW was in need of presenting a gimmick that appealed to children in an attempt to combat the WWF's stronghold on the kiddie demographics, Art was hired. The Juicer was gaining momentum with his adoring young fans. He wrestled in baggy clothes, white face and powdered hair that puffed into the air when he was pounded by his opponent. I believe that Art Barr's success as The Juicer was based on the way he easily related to the open innocence of his own sons. His favorite stories always centered on his children. Art proudly described how he never directly responded to their questions, but instead taught them to come up with their own answers with the help of riddles and games. There is no doubt that Art was a good father to his kids.

WCW's favorite children's act was abruptly cut short when news reached Turner Broadcasting that Art had been charged with having forced sex with a nineteen year old fan following a wrestling show in an empty Pendleton, Oregon arena. While Art acknowledged the 1989 incident, he insisted that the encounter was consensual. Wanting to get on with his life, he pleaded to a lesser charge of first degree sexual abuse and entered a community service program. Art told me that Jim Herd called him into his office and promised to stand by him. But the media pressure that the Turner organization was experiencing became too great to continue with his youth oriented character.

When he left WCW, Art began wrestling in Mexico and later in Japan, calling himself, strangely enough, Love Machine. As a heel, Art blended the Latin American style and that of the Orient with his knowledge of his home grown brand of wrestling. The marriage of his near flawlessly timed technical ability, along with the ring psychology that he had perfected over the years, finally brought him praise throughout the industry. At twenty-eight, Art Barr was now earning $3,500 per week wrestling in Mexico. In a perfect world, his triumphant rebound and spectacular transformation should have guaranteed him a long, lucrative career. But in the imperfect world of pro wrestling, this story did not have a happy ending.

As I reflect on our time together, it is difficult to accept his premature death just when it appeared that he had finally escaped the ghosts of his past. His career and ultimately, his life itself had been haunted by sexual indiscretion. Art Barr died just days after giving his most acclaimed performance to date. His mother found his lifeless body on November 23, 1994 at his home in bed with his five year old son, Dexter, sound asleep at his side. While the coroner's report was less than conclusive, it was reported that a mixture of prescription drugs and alcohol was present in his bloodstream.

While Piper guided him around the politics of wrestling, Art was unable to escape the seduction of wrestling's free and easy lifestyle. Wrestling was Art's life and life did not treat him kindly.

Chapter Fourteen
"Falls Count Anywhere In The World"
Part 1

People do things for athletes they don't do for others. To you and me, people say 'no', make us suffer the consequences of our behavior. Not athletes. Until they retire, 'no' isn't a word they hear much. The outcome? Values are modified, sometimes misplaced entirely. Even good guys, humble guys, are vulnerable to change.

Add this to the mix: the fear of losing everything with one injury, the sleaze coming at them from every direction, the inflated expectations. It can spin almost any man's head around; it just isn't a 'normal' way to live.

Mike Trope with Steve Delsohn, "Necessary Roughness"

T he most exhilarating experiences of my two-decade tenure in pro wrestling occurred during the international tours for World Championship Wrestling. These also were the times when I found myself squarely in the center of the most horrifying, most unfortunate and most publicized events of my career and have become the source of gossip and rumors ever since. Let me take you back to these infamous incidents and to some equally interesting, though less celebrated. Let me explain how and why our international tours turned into behind the scenes free-for-alls. It is time to end the speculation once and for all. It is time to hear the truth about what really happened.

M y first international excursion for WCW came in early May of 1990. It was a short spin through three Canadian locales that served to underscore how the World Wrestling Federation's unrelenting reign of terror fueled the paranoia within the Turner organization. Away from the turf that McMahon controlled, I mistakenly expected Canada to be free from the long, ominous shadow of the WWF. But by the second night of our short stint, I realized there was no escaping the WWF influence.

After our successful debut at the University of New Brunswick, Fredricton, I looked forward to playing St. John and

Halifax, where advance ticket sales were ahead of expectations. After my obligatory Christmas shopping spree in a commercial district of St. John on the second afternoon of our stay, I returned to the Hilton Hotel where I had arranged to meet our road agent, Sandy Scott, for a short drive to the Lord Beaverbrook Rink. As we approached the ice arena, police cars surrounded the building. Hundreds of people, none of them smiling, milled outside the rink's main entrance. When I inquired why the fans were locked out, I was told that the workers hadn't finished setting up for the show.

Assuming that the ring crew had arrived late, I entered a side entrance of the building, paying little attention to the shouts of the mob huddled close by. I had taken no more than six steps inside the building when my eyes began to burn, my throat closed and I started to gag from the fumes that filled the air.

Rushing outside to clear my lungs, I found Sandy, a St. John police officer and an elderly workman in the middle of an animated conversation. The man, who had worked at the ice rink for years, insisted that nothing like this ever happened before.

"What's going on?" I asked between hacking coughs. "What is that foul smell?"

"An ammonia leak," the old man excitedly explained. "Ammonia from the underground refrigeration system. Someone must have forgotten to tighten the valve of the underground pipes. Must have happened this morning. Everything was workin' fine when I left last night".

Someone forgot to tighten the valve that would release toxic ammonia fumes into the air? It had never happened before? The workman's words kept bouncing about my brain as Sandy and I drove back to the hotel from the cancelled show. He lamented the lost revenue. I thought sabotage. Could McMahon be responsible for fouling the Canadian air that we breathed? There seemed to be no escape.

Although we returned to Brantford, Toronto and Niagara Falls the next month without incident, we were always on guard against the threat of Vinnie's underhanded tactics. Whether or not he actually sabotaged our efforts in St. John, his constant shadowing of us on the road and openly provoking Ted Turner on his Monday night broadcast, proved to be a potent psychological weapon.

Later the same year, when we traveled to the Paradise Islands in the Bahamas, it wasn't necessary for McMahon to do anything to undermine our shows. Our visit to the subtropical retreat would self-destruct without any help from Junior.

Sadly, Gordon passed away on July 27, 2000. He set the standard for announcers in our game. His professionalism is unrivaled and I'm proud to say, that he was a true friend.

The island event was sandwiched between events in Ft. Pierce and Sunrise, Florida during the last weekend of September. It was planned as a quick detour to bring wrestling back to a native population which grew up on Florida Championship Wrestling hosted by my good friend, "The Dean" Gordon Solie. His familiarity with the customs and the politics of the island was instrumental in WCW gaining entrée to the politically corrupt resort.

Promoting an event in the Bahamas was a tricky proposition. It was like gaining access to a private clubhouse where admittance was granted only to those willing to pay the price and only through a "trusted" sponsor. That's a nice way of saying that there would be payoffs to the politically connected through an intermediary who had proven himself loyal to the paradise's political powerbrokers.

Our go-between was a pleasant fellow by the name of Charlie. Everyone on the island seemed to know Charlie. As soon as we entered the airport terminal, all of the tourists were directed to the customs checkpoint. Charlie, with one arm warmly wrapped around the chief customs inspector, parted the line, a la Moses, leading us through throngs of travelers who were impatiently undergoing inspection. As he strolled arm in arm with the chief, Charlie waved to every uniformed official in sight.

We were whisked off to a resort hotel, courtesy of Charlie's bus driving buddy, where thanks to Charlie's close relationship with hotel management, we were quickly shown to our pre-assigned rooms. Charlie seemed to have such a large following on the island, that booking him on top against Hulk Hogan for the Nassau show or against anyone for that matter, surely would have guaranteed a sellout.

In a flash, the boys gained control of the sun deck, the adjacent tiki bar and the attention of the bikini clad beauties at poolside. The music was cranked up, the Bahama Mamas were flowing and the party was on. Me? I was hungry. And since food wasn't on anyone else's mind, I set out to find a nearby restaurant by myself.

As I walked along a tropical path a young bicyclist began to trail closely behind. He slowly passed by, then circled around to rejoin me. I was beginning to feel stalked by the unknown predator. But he never uttered a sound. So I kept my pace steady and my focus on a restaurant that I spotted in the distance.

The third time that he circled around me, he cycled in even closer to gain eye contact.

"Hey, mon. You like to bike? You want to rent a bike?"

I was a little startled by the question.

"No thanks, I'm not interested."

He circled back once again, this time advancing still closer than before.

"You sure, mon?"

By now, he had moved in a little too close for comfort.

"Yeah, I'm sure," I repeated sternly.

"Okay. No problem, mon. Then how about some semolina?" he blurted.

His question whizzed by me. And it didn't make sense.

"What did you say? Some what?"

"Some semolina, mon. I've got some fine semolina. You'd like."

I glanced at him one last time trying to understand why a stranger would want to sell me pasta. This was a little too strange and made absolutely no sense. Such a weird thing to say. So, deciding that he was suffering from some rare, tropical, sun-induced brain cell disorder, I picked up my pace and continued on to the restaurant.

When I returned to the hotel, I was still confused about the cyclist's sales pitch for pasta. Someone with an ounce of street smarts would have realized that I was being lured into an illegal transaction. But I was oblivious to the culture of the seedy side of the island. I made the mistake of asking the first familiar face in the lobby, someone who was very familiar with seedy, "Fabulous Freebird", Michael Hayes. No one else was better qualified to clear up my confusion. And no one would have been more amused and amazed.

After recounting my pasta-peddling story to Michael, he hesitated, then cocked his head to one side. After a few seconds, his perplexed expression gradually broadened into a sly, ear to ear grin. That was when he realized how naïve I actually was. It took a few seconds more for him to consider what my contact with the islander could have meant to him. That's when his facial expression turned to one of outrage. Then he exploded.

"Fabulous Freebird" Michael PS Hayes was astounded by my naivete of the real world.

"Say what? Are you putting me on, man?"

"Putting you on? I'm not putting you on. How could I make up such a stupid story?"

"No. Don't tell me. No. Yer kidding. Ya gotta be kidding."

"Kidding? Kidding about what? This idiot tried to sell me pasta! You know, semolina."

"Sem . o . leee . na?" He spat the word out as if it was dog food. "*He's* not the idiot, *you* are!" I couldn't figure out why Michael was yelling at me. "Moron, he didn't say semolina. He was sayin' sinsemilla."

"What does that mean?" I was impressed that Michael was well versed in the language of the islands.

"Dude, he was trying to sell ya some *weed*."

"Weed? Ya mean like marijuana? Naw. Ya think so?"

"Do I think so? I can't believe that got by you."

"Well, it doesn't make any difference. I don't touch the stuff anyway."

"You? Who's talkin' 'bout *you*? What about *me*?"

I searched for a reason why my ignorance should have made a difference to Hayes. He just seemed so devastated.

"Michael, it doesn't matter."

"What do ya mean it doesn't matter?" His graveled voice somehow got more gravelly.

"Because if I knew what he was selling and I knew you wanted some, there would be no way to get it back to the States anyway. So it really doesn't matter."

Michael shook his head and gave me a hopeless look of disbelief.

"Now I know you gotta be kidding."

"Why's that?"

Hayes fired back with machine gun precision, "Cuz ya dumb shit, there wouldn't be any weed left by the time we got outta here in the morning! Man, you are a moron!"

"Oh. I didn't think of that."

We left the hotel with plenty of time for the short ride to the Nassau Stadium. After a couple of turns, it was as if we had entered another world. Hidden away, just beyond the beauty of the vacation paradise, was a cluster of dilapidated shacks. The contrast between the lush tourist side of the island and its impoverished residential section nearby was astounding. It was as if our hotel and the extravagant casinos on either side were part of a Warner Brothers soundstage where entire beachfronts are nothing more than painted scenes on thin plywood facades. Hidden behind those rich, ornamental flats was life in all its squalor. It was that striking. From prosperity to poverty in a matter of minutes. And in the center of this poverty-stricken neighborhood sat Charlie's Place.

Charlie's Place was a tiny, rundown cafe right out of a low budget Humphrey Bogart movie. It was nothing more than a wooden shack, with broken boards nailed haphazardly along its front exterior. Inside, a few tables and chairs were scattered about. The squeaky ceiling fan that grinded slowly overhead failed to nudge the hot, heavy air that stubbornly settled all around. Stools butted up to a slimy countertop. Hand-written signs, sloppily printed on yellowed paper plates decorated the walls of Charlie's muggy smokehouse, identifying the specials of the day. These dishes must have been favorites of Charlie's patrons, since they appeared not to have changed in years. Charlie's greasy spoon served as the outer front lobby of the Nassau Stadium, his show palace, which could be seen just beyond the café's back door.

It was a shell of a structure, ringed with broken beer bottles jutting out from atop the surrounding stone walls. Positioned in the center of the dusty dirt pit sat the ring, barely illuminated by a few sputtering bulbs that swayed overhead from a threadbare wire. The souvenir stand, nothing more than a thatched hut, had no lights at all. Worn wooden bleachers lined the walls behind cramped sections of ringside seats. There was only one small dressing room to house all of the boys, which was nothing more than a dirt floored cell resembling a subterranean bomb shelter. Above my head a protective netting of chicken wire sagged over the path that led to the ring, and then suspended over the ring itself.

At show time, a squad of security guards, armed with wooden clubs, led me through the throngs of islanders who mobbed both sides of the wire-covered aisle. As the sun set beyond the ominous walls of the stadium, the faces of the natives slowly began to disappear into darkness. Periodically, a guard sprinted to the top of the bleachers to beat back the gatecrashers who had scaled the walls in the blackness of the night.

As I stood in the center of the ring I tried to distance myself from the threat of this dangerous scene without the aid of "pasta". Performing on automatic pilot, I looked into the swaying trees beyond the walls . . . drifting away in thought . . . escaping to a safer place . . . remembering a humorous story that I had heard years before about this stadium.

It was a story about a how an indie promoter sought revenge on the Bahamians who had figured out a way to enjoy the show without paying. Those islanders who were not bold enough or foolish enough to scale the stadium walls. Those who waited for the sun to set before shimmying up the tree trunks until they reached the highest branches, where they settled into makeshift skyboxes to enjoy the show beside the island's exotic parrots.

For every event that these eavesdroppers enjoyed, the promoter became more resentful, until he devised a plan that was designed to shake the freeloaders from their perches. On the afternoon of his next monthly show, he sent his workers up into the trees equipped with hacksaws. Their mission was to cut grooves half way through all of the upper branches. They were inconspicuous incisions, slight enough to be invisible, but deep enough to crack under the pressure of the slightest weight.

That night, when the sun went down and the show was under way, the promoter sat back and patiently waited until he heard rustling in the trees. The stunned shrieks of the natives, as they plunged to the ground from high atop their perches, provoked in him howls of joy.

"It was a riot. I watched the whites of their eyes and these big toothy grins inch higher and higher into the trees. They thought they were gonna get over on me again. But no damn way! It was funnier than hell to hear them screaming, then hitting the ground, boom . . boom . . boom . . . Damn, we laughed our asses off!"

I was jolted back to our Nassau Stadium show where at the end of the night, no one was laughing. The event miraculously ended without incident. Aside from ducking a few flying objects that burst through frayed strands of chicken wire, I somehow escaped another risk-filled situation without incident. But the night did not end without a bit of island intrigue.

Charlie, as it turned out, had a little bit of the blood of Blackbeard, one of his slippery ancestors, an early island privateer, who like Charlie, was licensed by the government to plunder and ransack enemy merchant ships. In this case, Charlie was the pirate; we were the unsuspecting merchants.

After the show, when it was time to settle accounts, we went up front to Charlie's Place where he produced only a portion of the night's receipts.

The very squeaky, proper and humorless comptroller from Turner's accounting department was not very happy. She paced back and forth, her powder blue linen suit becoming increasingly damp and clingy. Charlie periodically emerged from his box office with a carton filled with raffle type tickets, shrugging his shoulders, innocently smiling and chirping, "No problem. This is everything."

While Turner's testy accountant repeatedly insisted on a recount, I knew that more likely than not, additional dollars would somehow disappear each time Charlie recounted as proper compensation for the extra time and inconvenience that her mistrust was costing him.

My buddy Gordon, who had acted as the good company man by gaining WCW entrée to this paradise retreat, sank into a sullen funk at Charlie's sudden betrayal. Well aware of the politics of the Turner organization, Gordon expected to take the fall for the evening's disastrous debacle. Regardless of the unfairness of corporate finger pointing, when things go bad, that is what always happened.

My take on it was a little different. The reality is that on a nightly basis, WCW was even more treacherous than Charlie. The only difference was that the cash entrusted to Charlie disappeared all at once, while WCW had been pirating money from their fans all along with no show talent and a substandard product. The only difference was who was screwing whom.

No other experiences were more exciting for me than World Championship Wrestling's European tours. Our broadcasts were seen around the world. From Madrid to Maui, from Panama City to Paris, WCW programming was as much of a weekly tradition overseas as it was in Greensboro, North Carolina. But reading the vast list of markets where our show aired, and actually meeting the fans in those countries, who had watched us on television for years, was entirely different.

Luckily, WCW never actually promoted our live events across the Atlantic. We were therefore spared many of the front office glitches that plagued us in the States. But as you might expect, everything that did go wrong was due either to the suits in Atlanta undermining the best efforts of our European hosts or to the embarrassing behavior of a few out of control wrestlers.

The promoters for our first trip to the United Kingdom were Alan Lacey and Brian Kraus, partners in Bravo Productions. They paid a $400,000 guarantee for five shows in addition to spending $15,000 to bring P.N. News (Paul Neu), Johnny B. Badd (Marc Mero) and announcer, Jim Ross to England a month in advance for promotional appearances. In addition to the hefty price they paid, the arrangement called for Bravo to book venues, publicize the events, sell tickets, underwrite hotel stays, pay per diem food allowances, contract tour buses, as well as offer on site support personnel at each of the buildings.

Our first trek to the United Kingdom in December of 1991 was called the Roar Power Tour. We played only three cities - three shows in London, and one each in Sheffield and Dublin. An extra day was added up front for press interviews.

I was free for the first two days in London to explore the city of Big Ben, the Thames and the hallowed halls of Harrods where you can buy anything imaginable. What better place for "Mr. Christmas" to spend his birthday than London decked out for the holiday season? I gleefully roamed the bustling streets, elbow to elbow with the gift buying Brits courtesy of Bravo Productions.

Our shows during this London debut were held at the old Olympia. Each night the arena was set up with the lighting grids and entrance ramp of a full-blown television special.

A match of local interest was added to our London shows. The legendary Giant Haystacks was brought in to wrestle an unknown English kid. It was a classic David and Goliath match, where the bigger man dominates most of the bout, but the youngster manages a comeback leading the fans to believe that the Giant could indeed be defeated, and this very well could be the night.

Haystacks, a mountain of a man, had earned his reputation over many years in rings throughout Europe. At six feet, eleven inches, weighing in excess of 630 pounds (45 stone) at his heaviest, his long-standing feud with, Big Daddy another British goliath, was legendary. By the time I met him, Giant Haystacks had been wrestling for 24 years. In his prime, Haystacks counted Paul McCartney and McCartney's son among his fans at the local Sussex shows. McCartney was so impressed with the big man that he asked Haystacks to appear in his 1984 film, *Give My Regards To Broad Street*.

In 1996, Haystacks wrestled in the states for WCW as The Loch Ness Monster. One of the most recognized British grapplers of all time, Giant Haystacks died in 1998 after a two-year bout with cancer.

His opponent during the London leg of the Roar Power series was a young, well-groomed, gentleman. I took an immediate liking to him for the respect that he showed toward the wrestling business. I wasn't entirely familiar with his background at the time, but from the little that he told me, I sensed that he was a dedicated, hard working youngster. It was clear from the beginning that he was well schooled in the scientific style of wrestling, where holds and counter holds are executed with precision and reason. He started his career at the age of sixteen. He became a traveling journeyman who wrestled in Africa and Europe. He paid his dues in the tough world of carnival wrestling and ultimately began working for independent promotions in England. But what struck me from the start was that a guy with such a gritty and rugged upbringing could remain so genteel.

WCW road agent, Grizzly Smith and event coordinator, Wayne Coulter saw the same solid qualities in him. In the future he would be brought to Atlanta for a tryout, impress the booking committee and go on to make a name for himself worldwide in WCW and then in the WWF. His name was Steve Regal, as in Lord Steven Regal.

Although our European debut was brief, many of the boys just couldn't adapt to the togetherness that comes with group touring.   Unlike their schedule in the States, where the wrestlers travel by rental car with their buddies, lodge wherever they please (or could afford) and eat at their favorite spots; when we toured Europe, everybody was required to conform to a set itinerary. This was a drill that was foreign to them. And it didn't take long for the personal animosities that independent travel had tempered to escalate from verbal attacks to hostility and eventually to brutality.

The average traveling performer of other entertainment forms would scoff at the wrestlers who complained about life on the road. Unlike traveling with a circus or touring as a musical act, many of the wrestlers, making top money, just didn't appreciate how well they were treated.

Customarily, being part of a traveling unit of circus performers or rockers requires everybody to travel together, to room in the same place and often to eat together. It is a self-contained community that roams from place to place with the neighborhood squabbles that are a natural part of communal living resolved quickly and forgotten, knowing that "the family" will be moving on with you or without you.

It took only one 161-mile bus trip for the wrestlers to begin turning on one another. The first guy to shatter the brotherhood's brittle bond was Curtis Hughes

Under the rules of independent travel in the States, whether or not it was the right thing to do, we were able to overlook Hughes' self-destructing abuse of drugs. But it was impossible to ignore the consequences of his addiction while in Europe, where everyone was forced to spend long periods of time together on tour buses. Although his mood swings caused most to stay clear of him, Curtis managed to offend the entire troupe from a distance. His crime, his social violation: he farted. No, Curtis just didn't fart, he farted repeatedly, and continuously as he slept slumped in his seat on the bus. And the foul odor, this repulsive stench that pervaded the stagnant air from the time we left London until reaching Sheffield was nauseating.

At first, Kevin Nash and Grizzly Smith alternately shook Hughes into consciousness and asked him to control himself. In response, Curtis taunted them with more farts.   Lex Luger sneered in disgust, but aware of his limitations, knew better than to take on the big man. The Freebirds unlatched the overhead hatch to inhale as much of the frigid English atmosphere as possible before our shivering bus driver ordered them away from the portal. But the farts never stopped.

Ultimately, I was convinced that Curtis began feigning sleep to gas up the bus just for the fun of it. But laughing gas it wasn't. By the time we were half way to Sheffield, it was a toss up as to whether Nash, Arn Anderson or referee Nick Patrick would be responsible for lighting a match under the big man's butt for the vengeful fun of watching him blow up. And coming to blows was about to happen when Grizzly dragged Curtis to the back of the bus, like a misbehaving juvenile delinquent on an ill-fated class trip. And this Friday the 13th only got worse.

By the time we got to Sheffield, the weather had turned as foul as our tempers. There was fear that our commercial flight to Dublin the next day would never get off the ground. While this wasn't

I always believed that Curtis' gross behavior was the anti-social act of a guy who felt like he didn't belong.

of immediate concern, the news only served to stir the uneasiness of the more squeamish flyers in the group; an anxiety that swelled to near fisticuffs that night when it was discovered that we had a thief on board.

During the intermission of our Sheffield debut, I learned that a watch and a couple hundred dollars were missing from the lockers of a few of the wrestlers. All eyes darted to P.N. News since many of the boys believed that he had been the culprit in past petty heists. While the mystery was never solved, the Steiner Brothers were convinced that News was guilty and decided to get back at him the next day at the airport.

The weather predictions proved accurate as our commercial flight from Sheffield to Dublin was grounded by a dangerously slick runway. Our beleaguered British hosts, who by now not only avoided the wrestlers, but each other as well, found a private air carrier willing to fly us from Manchester to Dublin.

So it was back on the bus to the Manchester airport for forty more miles of farts and fits and fights. Everyone stayed clear of Curtis. P.N., still pleading innocent to the charges from the night before, sat alone.

With the bulk of the commercial flights cancelled the Manchester airport was swarming with disgruntled travelers trying to get home for the holiday. But English disgruntled is very different from American disgruntled. In America, we would be pounding the ticketing counters and threatening the defenseless agents. The reserved Brits just sat at the boarding gates and silently simmered. You'd never know they were peeved because it was a reserved kind of peeved. Nothing much seemed to shake them. That is until the WCW wrestlers descended upon the boarding gate. The troupe always caused a stir by their overbearing appearance and loudness alone. They were accomplished disturbers of the peace.

Soon after settling in, Curtis and P.N. fell asleep on opposite sides of the crowded concourse. I became lost in my book of cryptograms, my way of escaping the rigors of the road.

Suddenly, it sounded as if the roof was about to blow off the building. An eruption of snoring and wheezing and gasping, the intensity of which was no match even for the whirling gusts of arctic air that whipped around the terminal, rocked the noisy concourse to its foundation. The bustling of the busy airport settled to a disquieting silence as passengers peered about in search of the source of the beastly sounds.

Over the top of my puzzle book, my eyes settled on the 350-pound heaving hump of Curtis Hughes. His immense frame overflowed onto the adjoining seats of an impeccably attired businessman on one side and a demure grandmother on the other. His dark shades had slipped down the nose of his contorted face as he instinctively began scratching his crotch. Repulsed passengers peered at the grossly offensive sight of Curtis' restless ritual. Tourists from other gates began wandering over to find out the source of the hideous sounds that he spat through his vibrating lips. As luck would have it, they were not the only ones disturbed by Hughes' outbursts. P.N. News was shaken from his snooze in the midst of the commotion. And that's when the storm hit.

When News woke up he looked down at two naked feet. When he realized they were *his* feet, he shook his head to be sure he was awake, and then began to panic. It seems that in the midst of his deep sleep, the Steiners had carefully stripped his feet bare. You would expect a road wise traveler to have packed an extra pair of shoes. But not P.N. He was missing the only footwear that he had brought with him to Europe.

The shoeless, sockless News stood in the middle of the busy boarding gate as the boys taunted him with wisecracks and catcalls. He shot back with a string of vulgarities that would have made the gangsta rappers after which he patterned his wrestling persona cover their ears. If News expected the culprit to come forward with his missing moccasins, he was sorely mistaken. When nobody did, he began to pitch a fit. His cussing and fussing, pouting then shouting only added to the amusement of the boys who were roaring at the sight of P.N.'s hissy fit.

Embarrassed before our British host promoters and what seemed like the rest of England, road agent Grizz tried to quell the family squabble. Several minutes passed before he was able to calm the 400-pounder down. For the next half-hour, Grizz did his best to break through the boys' wall of silence. When his best wasn't good enough, News began to threaten the Steiner Brothers who thought this was funnier than a Jim Carey film festival. Grizz, who demonstrated the patience of a saint, took P.N. shoe shopping.

A while later I decided to remove myself from the scene in search of a quieter and safer haven. As I wandered over to the next boarding gate, my attention was drawn to a

Unlike Curtis, who was feared for his tough guy reputation, PN News paid a price for not being one of "the boys".

commotion at the far end of the concourse. Two bobbies marched in lock step with the distressed businessman who had most suffered the effects of the erupting Curtis. He was the unfortunate chap who had been sitting aside Hughes when the big man exploded.

Not wanting to be roped into *that* scene, I made an about face to wander in the opposite direction only to find Grizz and a tearful P.N., returning from their expedition to a few of the airport clothing boutiques, none of which carried the extra wide size that

News required in footwear. I tried not to look down at P.N.'s bare feet as an exasperated Grizz spotted the bobbies behind me.

When our private jet was finally ready for boarding, Scott Steiner slipped into the ladies room, reached into a recessed ceiling tile and retrieved P.N.'s moccasins.

The private aircraft was nothing more than a puddle jumper used to transport corporate execs. As the pilot assessed the weighty cargo that boarded the plane before him, he began to have second thoughts. Twenty athletes with an average weight of 250 pounds would tax the plane to its limits. After we found our assigned seats, the pilot decided to distribute the weight of his passengers evenly throughout the aircraft. When Freebird Michael Hayes was told that he and his wife had to sit apart for the safety of the flight, another donnybrook ensued. He was so vehement that the separation for the one-hour flight would be a hardship, that he threatened to punch event coordinator Coulter in the face. It was one nightmare after another until finally we arrived back home two days later.

Our subsequent tours of Europe made headlines. Not for the success of our shows. Or for the arrival of celebrity American athletes. But for the brutality that the boys heaped upon each other.

CHAPTER FIFTEEN
"Falls Count Anywhere In The World"
Part 2

In a way, after so many months of touring the U.S., another round of hotels and airplanes and concert halls must have felt more normal than being home. After a while, as a veteran tour manager once said, you get so you have to look out the window and check the language of the street signs to know which country you're in. The shows themselves become sort of a maze, the band winding from one to another until they finally work their way out and return to homes they barely recall. It's no life for someone who doesn't love it. And it's no life for anyone who isn't traveling with friends.

Dave Marsh, "Glory Days, Bruce Springsteen in the 1980s"

Shortly after returning home, word reached Atlanta that Brian Kraus and Alan Lacey's partnership could not withstand our unsuccessful mini tour of the UK. They lost their partnership and a half million-dollars, which broke the back of Bravo Promotions. A full year and a half passed before WCW found a promoter daring enough to invest in our tried, but unproven product.

Barry Clayman is one of the premiere European promoters of touring musical acts as shown by his successful Rolling Stones and Michael Jackson tours. About the time he became interested in promoting WCW, Barry Clayman Concerts was infinitely better equipped to handle the unique challenges that rockers and wrestlers presented. And by the time WCW returned to the UK in March of 1993, we too were better prepared to offer talent that could draw fans to the arenas.

After several unsuccessful attempts to create wrestling stars able to draw money, WCW began to raid McMahon's stable of established stars. With the earlier addition to our roster of "Ravishing" Rick Rude and the most recent acquisition, a real coup for the European market, "The British Bulldog", Davey Boy Smith, we now offered familiar headliners that the fans of the UK had come to know on the strength of their popularity with the WWF. The money that World Championship Wrestling spent to acquire the services of The Bulldog was worthwhile from the return received on its investment in Europe alone. By the time we reached England for what was billed as *The Real Event Tour*, Smith and Rude's faces were splattered across nationally circulated magazines and every major newspaper in the cities where we played.

"He stands 6ft. 3 inches, weighs in at 253lbs, moves like a snake in the ring before trundling across to devastate his tremulous opponents. Ravishing Rick Rude, champion wrestler and glistening monster of meat and muscle has them all at his feet, begging for mercy from his vice-like grip."
The Evening Herald, Dublin, March 17, 1993.

The British Bulldog's established strongman routine against Rick Rude's arrogant sex pistol persona thrilled the throngs in every arena we played. *The Real Event* drew 9,204 for a gate of $195,000 at London's Wembley Arena, sold out the 9,200 seat NEC Arena in Birmingham and played to 8,000 fans at the G-Mex Centre in Manchester. Aberdeen, Scotland and Belfast, Northern Ireland each drew 4,000 strong before winding down the tour at The Pointe in Dublin on St. Patrick's day. In addition to the large gates, merchandise sales were at an all time WCW high of $6 per person totaling $55,000 for our one show in London alone.

The co-feature of Sting and Vader led the undercard wrestlers featuring Cactus Jack, Johnny B. Badd (Marc Mero), Ron Simmons (Faarooq), Dustin Rhodes, Van Hammer (Major Stash), Paul Orndorff, Michael Hayes, Maxx Payne, Scotty Flamingo (Raven) and Vinnie Vegas (Kevin Nash).

The difference between this trip and the torturous tour of 1991 could not have been more striking. With the success of our shows, thanks to the drawing power of Smith and Rude, everyone comported themselves more professionally. There was a sense of duty to their performances and a feeling of accomplishment in thrilling the crowds that came out to see us each night. The absence of the negativity stirred up by Hughes, News and the Steiners also played a big part in the camaraderie that we enjoyed.

Contrary to the petty quarrels that marked the previous tour, Kevin Nash and former NWA champion Harley Race, Vader's manager at the time, emerged as natural leaders whose influence kept everyone at ease. Between Nash's humor and

Race's even-tempered handling of the boys, the tour turned out to be the most enjoyable of all.

The professionalism of the Barry Clayman Concert staff was unlike anything we had ever experienced. The shows ran like clockwork. The second that our pre show music ended each night, I headed for the ring to warm up the crowd knowing that the BCC staff was in position and ready to roll. Malcolm and Simon, the roadies assigned to me by BCC, were always nearby to keep the show moving smoothly. I performed with confidence knowing that if anything went wrong my two-man crew, my safety net, was nearby to back me up.

The manner in which Phil Bowdrey, BCC's tour manager, catered to the boys was first rate every mile of the trip. At home, we were accustomed to eating at greasy spoons like Denny's and The Waffle House. Courtesy of BCC, a private catering service accompanied us on the road serving all of the broiled chicken and steamed rice and veggies that the guys prized in maintaining their body building diets. Once in a while we were treated to down home cooking with dishes like bangers and mash topping my list of favorites. The tour buses were fully stocked every night with sandwiches and drinks a plenty.

In order to allow the road crew time to transport the ring to Ireland by ferry, we were given a day off in Aberdeen, on the coast of Scotland. Journeying along the North Sea shore with Nash, Cactus, Marc Mero, Bagwell and Sting was akin to the fellowship of a

We had a cohesive crew touring the shores of the North Sea in Aberdeen, Scotland. I'm pictured with Mike Weber, Bill Dundee, Cactus Jack, Maxx Payne and Van Hammer (WCW's Major Stash).

family reunion. There was so much harmony among the wrestlers that we even opted to eat dinner together at an

Aberdeen restaurant on our down day. Can you imagine that happening with Curtis, P.N. and the Steiners on board?

We experienced only one minor glitch during the six-city tour. The day before our arrival in Belfast, terrorist members of the IRA bombed a police car on a city street in broad daylight. This only added to our concern for the safety of The British Bulldog whose top billing in the politically volatile city was risky from the start. The decision to travel to Dublin immediately after the Kings Hall show, instead of remaining in Belfast for the night, allowed us to escape without incident. But even this potentially dangerous scenario could not damper the intense feelings of friendship that our success each night sustained. The trip was so successful that Barry Clayman booked us for a more extensive tour later that same year.

Our itinerary for *The Halloween Havoc '93 Tour* the next Fall included five venues for Barry Clayman Concerts (Cardiff, Blackburn, Bournemouth, Birmingham and London) and seven dates in Germany for Hermjo Klein's Sunrise Concerts (Russelheim, Essen, Munich, Halle, Cologne, Hamburg and Bayreuth.)

The transatlantic trip followed a hectic weekend. It is essential to track the stressful pace of the days leading up to our arrival in Blackburn, England in order to understand the circumstances that contributed to the incident which made headlines in tabloids across Europe.

On Friday we traveled to Phoenix for a house show and then continued on to New Orleans on Saturday to prepare for the tour's namesake pay-per-view, *Halloween Havoc*. The show aired live on Sunday evening, and the next morning we flew from New Orleans to Atlanta to catch a 7:20 p.m. flight which arrived in London at 8:25 a.m., the morning of our first UK show in Cardiff. And the nonstop pace was not to end when we arrived in Europe.

As was customary when we flew overseas, the business class cabin was transformed into WCW's private party room. Overtired never enters the guys' vocabulary when alcohol is flowing and free. The crew for this trip was beefed up considerably compared to our previous European excursions. In addition to Davey Boy Smith, Rick Rude, Sting, Johnny B. Badd (Marc Mero), Arn Anderson and Dustin Rhodes, all of whom were onboard six months earlier, several wrestlers joined us for the first time. Led by "Nature Boy" Ric Flair, Ricky "The Dragon"

Steamboat, Sid Vicious and Vader, Steve Austin, Marc "Buff" Bagwell, Too Cold Scorpio, Flyin' Brian Pillman, The Nasty Boys and Maxx Payne were all making their first European appearances on a WCW card. Bill Dundee (Sir William) doubled as both road agent and valet of Lord Steven Regal, who was making his triumphant return to the United Kingdom from humble journeyman to sniveling royalty, all in the span of two years.

Fortunately, we were once again spared the antics of Curtis Hughes and P.N. News who were gone from the company, while the Steiners were left behind to work minor venues in the States.

The Delta flight attendants somehow kept up

I was thrilled to play Royal Albert Hall in London along side one of my favorites, Too Cold Scorpio. Note the historic show poster from a wrestling card which took place in the legendary venue.

with the drink requests of the guys who restlessly roamed about the cabin. The wrestlers good-naturedly kibitzed in the aisles, raising the eyebrows of our fellow passengers who were unlucky enough to have booked one of the few non-WCW seats in the front cabin. Confining the wrestlers to such a small area for such a long time with such a large amount of free alcohol is begging for trouble. It wasn't a matter of *what* could happen. The question was *how long* it would take. I slumped low in my seat, buried my nose in my cryptogram book and braced myself for the mayhem to come.

At first, all remained calm. Perhaps it was the upscale menu that distracted the boys. The dinner choices of "poached prawns and pan-fried turbot in a wine sauce" or "steak a la Bordelaise enhanced by an herbed wine sauce" must have been enough to stump my burger and brew buddies for a while. But while peace prevailed, it was temporary. I just knew it. *Something* was bound to interfere with the gourmet dinner that

Delta was about to deliver. And true to form, my devilish buds didn't let me down.

Enjoying the peace that my puzzles provided, I suddenly heard loud laughter. No, it wasn't laughter. It was more like cackling. And the odd thing about it was the high pitch of the unrestrained snicker. It sounded like a giddy little girl overdosed on laughing gas.

I peeked across the aisle from behind the safety of my cryptograms already wincing at what might be happening. The source of the riotous roar was a very petite, very pretty flight attendant, uncontrollably quivering, both hands covering her mouth, eyes bulging in disbelief. I followed her line of sight to Bill Dundee who was seated smack in the middle of the business class section. He was sitting up, though leaning forward. With one hand gripping a plastic cocktail cup, he remained immobile, eyes closed, mouth opened. What appeared to be a pile of whipped cream was perfectly balanced on the top of his head. Carefully positioned in the center of the white fluffy foam, sat a maraschino cherry. Flight attendants were drawn from every corner of the aircraft to witness this bizarre scene. And without a doubt, it was a very amusing spectacle.

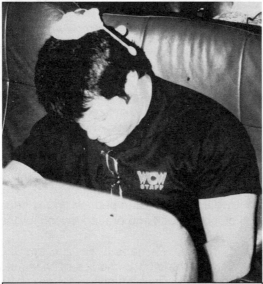

Bill Dundee was the life of the party.
Unfortunately, he doesn't remember it.

Bill broke one of the basic rules of wrestling etiquette: Never leave your drink unguarded, for even a split second. Once distracted, it was rumored that one of the Nasty Boys slipped a fizzy in Dundee's drink. When he passed out, they spritzed his head with shaving cream and added the cherry as a finishing touch.

Yes, it was a funny sight. But it was one of those jokes that could have turned fatal if Dundee was medicated or had a violent allergic reaction to the drug that was slipped into his drink. This time, the mischief proved harmless. But guys like the Nastys, who love to pull pranks for the sake of a belly laugh, either never consider the consequences of their actions or don't care or both.

On Tuesday morning, the buses were waiting at Gatwick Airport for the 150-mile trek to Cardiff, Wales. The first event of the *Halloween Havoc '93* tour would be held that same evening. We arrived at the Cardiff Marriott at noon, which allowed us just enough time to eat, take a short nap and be ready to board the bus once again at five for the short trip to The International Arena. After a fairly successful Cardiff show we were whisked off once again for a late night 160-mile journey to Blackburn, the site of the next night's event.

Although everyone was understandably exhausted, spirits were high and spirits were flowing throughout the motor coach that served as our home on wheels for the next week. Most of the seats in the bus were of the standard variety, facing forward. In some of the sections, pairs of seats faced each other and were separated by drop down tables with built in drink holders. The rear quarter of the coach was separated from the rest of the seats by a bathroom. Equipped with a drop down bed, this back section of the specially built tour bus usually served as private quarters for the show's headliner. On this particular night, I shared the cubicle with Arn Anderson, tour manager Phil Bowdrey and overflowing coolers of beer and soda.

As guys continually wandered back to the makeshift bar, we chatted about the upcoming stops and the number of tickets already sold. Arn, one of the most respected guys in the business, expressed his appreciation to Phil for the way that BCC took care of us. It was a relaxing conversation at the end of a non-stop five-day trek.

We arrived at The Moat House Hotel in Blackburn after midnight. The receptionist on duty was pleased to report that the lounge remained open as a courtesy to their American guests. The temptation was too great for several of the wrestlers to resist. So they moved the festivities from the bus to the bar and the boozing began once again. The rest of us dragged our sleep-deprived bodies off to our rooms to recuperate from the short naps, transatlantic antics and late night road trips of the preceding days. There was nothing that I desired more than a full night's sleep.

It was one o'clock when I finally plopped into bed for what I thought would be a sound, peaceful sleep. But the sounds that stirred me from slumber were far from peaceful. Shouting and pounding jolted me back into consciousness. My first thought was that the boys were just roughhousing up and down the hall. I then realized that the racket was taking place just outside my door. Seconds later, I heard thunderous thumps, or whacks against either the walls or the doors or both. I couldn't be sure. The pictures and mirrors that hung in my room vibrated from the power of each impact. I quickly became convinced that *this* wrestling was for real.

Alarmed, I moved closer to the door. Without a security peephole to see what was happening on the other side, I impulsively reached for the doorknob. Between the smacking sounds, which continued without pause, I heard the intense, persistent shrieks of a determined, but desperate voice. It was the voice of Sid Vicious.

"*Arn, I've had enough.*" A few seconds of silence, then a whack. *Arn, it's got to end.* A little more agitated. Another whack. *Arn, let's settle this right now.*" I heard the door across the hall burst open, a smack of flesh and the struggling of two bodies bouncing off walls. Heavy, heaving grunts and groans.

During this scene of sounds I nervously backed away from the door. Then I couldn't move. I should have. I should have picked up the phone to call for help. But I didn't. I couldn't. I was frozen in fear.

By the time I regained my composure, the commotion subsided into quiet murmurs of concern and shock at the bloody aftermath of the fight. Sid was removed from the scene as the boys huddled around Arn in the crimson-splattered hall. WCW's head of security, Doug Dellinger and Vader inspected the lacerations that covered the face and upper body of their bewildered and bloody friend. Arn looked up at Vader repeating over and over again, *Leon, you know me. I don't carry a knife. You know me, brother. I never carry a knife.*

By now, the Blackburn police and emergency squad members had joined the crowd. Both wrestlers were taken to the hospital and we were left to sort out exactly what had transpired.

Blame it on too little sleep and too much alcohol. If not in Blackburn, it could have been London or Munich or Hamburg. Or Birmingham, England *or* Alabama. Given the circumstances, it was bound to happen. The only surprise was that it didn't happen sooner.

TELLY WRESTLING STARS IN 2am HOTEL KNIFE BRAWL
Grappling pals pull them apart

Enforcer ... bar brawl   *Sid ... stab wounds*

Within hours, news of the fight was splattered across the British tabloids. Embarrassed WCW officials arrived in Europe to answer media inquiries. The wrestlers were upset that the "family's" feud was now public.

The bad blood began to boil in the hotel bar when the conversation turned to the politics and the pecking order within WCW. Arn defended his best buddy and booker, Ric Flair, when Vicious accused Flair of unfairly promoting his pals instead of the wrestlers who could draw money. Sid sees himself as a draw. And he knows Anderson and Flair are pals. They are really more like brothers. He was well aware of the bond and the loyalty that for years had existed between the two veterans.

Arn aimed for Sid's sore spot, with disparaging remarks about his limited wrestling ability and overrated reputation. When voices were raised and threats were traded Dellinger sent both wrestlers to their rooms for the night. Arn's room was across from mine. Sid's room was on the opposite side of the hotel. Arn did as he was told. Sid stopped at his room, picked up a chair and then carried it over to our corridor.

He was like a man possessed. Like a wounded animal that found itself trapped. Wounded by Arn's words, trapped by their inescapable truth. Sid returned for revenge. This was no longer the result of lips loosened by alcohol and hurt feelings. This was a premeditated attack. Arn, whose barbs can be biting, hit the bull's-eye with his verbal assault. Sid, incapable of countering, retaliated the only way he knew how. Once Arn was lured into the hall, Sid was armed for the ambush.

The battering of Sid's chair against Arn's door explained the power-packed thumps that had vibrated the walls of my room. When the repeated pounding and taunts continued, Arn grabbed the only weapon he had with which to protect himself, a pair of scissors from his grooming kit. When he opened the door, Vicious cracked him over the head with the chair. The two then wrestled for control of the shears, stabbing each other as they bounced off the walls.

This rare photo shows the strong loyalty that Arn and Ric share. As Flair tosses a fan out of The St. Louis Arena, Anderson is in the background ready to come to the aid his buddy.

If you had scored the fight from the gashes, which scarred both men's bodies, Sid would be declared the winner. But judging from the sentiments expressed by the wrestlers it was no contest. Arn was the crowd favorite. You'd have to know these two guys to understand why.

Sid and Arn come from places as far apart as can be. Each views the wrestling business from an entirely opposite perspective. The ease with which Sid came by his success has caused him to show little appreciation for his position. For Arn, on the other hand, it's a matter of pride. He has worked long and hard to rise to the top of his game. The respect that he shows for his craft has been formed from overcoming challenges that Sid has never faced.

Sid is blessed with the genetics of Superman and the luck of an Irishman, but is shackled by the ignorance and the arrogance of a street tuff hoodlum. He has been known to sit out bookings to play softball for his hometown team. He thinks nothing of walking out on a promotion without regard to contracts. Forget contracts. What about doing what's right? What about professionalism? He has repeated these stunts time and again believing that he will always be hired back. And he usually is. Despite the fact that beyond his "monster look", he is only a mediocre worker, Sid repeatedly has been rewarded with headlining positions by the promoters he screws. That has been his experience.

Arn, on the other hand, is of average stature and has made his mark in the wrestling world not on appearance, but by perfecting his ring work. His consistently solid performances, along with a reputation as a team player, make up for the "monster look" that he does not and never can possess. His interview skills are second to none. He has agreed to take pay cuts instead of losing his position, yet never shortchanges the promoters or his co-workers or the fans.

When a prima donna the likes of Sid contentiously accuses a dedicated loyalist the likes of Arn of maintaining his position because of

When Sid is on one knee he's almost as tall as me!

patronage, there's bound to be a fight. It was not surprising that the WCW and WWF wrestlers who know both men were overwhelmingly in Arn's corner.

The immediate reaction of the boys on tour was one of sadness. There was an outpouring of concern for Arn's health as well as uneasiness as to how the fight and all of the press coverage that followed might effect his position with the company. As was often the case, some of the guys found humor in what had happened. Maybe it was their way of coping. Perhaps it's a callousness developed from being exposed to so much lunacy day in and day out. It took only hours for Marc Mero and Marc Bagwell to commemorate the incident with a Mohammed Ali style poem as delivered by Mero in his best Little Richard impersonation.

When I'm in the shower, I'm afraid to wash my hair,
I might open my eyes and Psycho Sid will be standing there.

Bodyslams!

Some people think I'm crazy, maybe a little touched,
But showers remind me of Sid Vicious too much.

When I opened the door, he hit me with a chair,
I said "Sid Vicious, you know that isn't fair.
So I got a pair of scissors, and stabbed him in the gut,
You should have seen Sid Vicious bleed from that cut.

He staggered and stumbled, and down the hall he fell,
How can you rule the world, when you can't even rule the hotel?

The buzz around the locker rooms lasted for months. The buzz by ringside observers continues to this day. Arn and Sid's hotel grudge match has been talked about almost as much as an eerie incident that happened in March of 1994. It was on a tour of Germany. It was in Munich when Cactus Jack lost his . . . uh . . . well you'd better let me set the stage for yet another horrific happening in which I unwittingly became a major player.

The relationship between WCW and the promoters of our German tours was much more complicated than the Barry Clayman Concerts alliance. Barry Clayman's sole interest was filling the arenas. The German deal involved not only of Hermjo Klein, the live event promoter, but also DSF, the German Sports Network, which was the exclusive outlet for WCW wrestling throughout Germany. Unlike most of WCW's international clients, DSF aggressively marketed our wrestling program. It hired on air commentators to voice over the play by play announcements in German, thereby creating its own TV celebrities. It even published a German language edition of the *WCW Magazine*.

The all-Germany tour, *Battle Stars '94*, was billed as a tournament for the previously non-existent and never again heard of European Championship Cup. We were in Germany for two full weeks, playing Ludwigshafen, Cologne, Halle, Dresden, Kassel, Rostock, Munich, Hof, Frankfurt, Wuerzburg and Hamburg, the site of the tournament finals. It was such an extensive tour that every German citizen, regardless of where he lived, was within travel distance of least one of our shows. Hermjo set up a tour route designed to minimize long, tiresome treks between the eleven cities that spanned the entire country.

The itinerary was finalized, the buildings were booked and media buys were made. And that's when the suits at the

232

CNN Center in Atlanta came up with a brilliant idea: to air the final night of the tour "live" on TBS. The broadcast would be part of the *Clash Of Champions*, an early series of Turner Broadcasting TV specials. This spectacular was to be beamed via satellite around the globe. The only condition of their proposal was that the marquee match had to be the final bout of the European Cup Tournament and would have to originate from Hamburg, the German Sports Network's home base. The only problem with this scenario was that Hamburg was not originally scheduled to be the last city on the original tour itinerary. But that was Hermjo's problem. This plan was too good for the two TV companies to pass up.

The theory behind this brainstorm was that there would be enormous interest generated by the international flavor of the program. The ratings would zoom to historic proportions, surpassing all previous wrestling shows, including anything that the WWF had presented. We were going to stick it to McMahon! Finally! No doubt about it!

When Dr. Dieter Krap of the German sports channel learned of Turner's plan to broadcast a live American special from his country, he was ecstatic. DSF pledged all of its resources to ensure the success of the tour and the TV special.

As soon as TBS released the air date to Hermjo, he moved quickly to rework the tour schedule so that the tournament final would take place in Hamburg. But when Hermjo began to call the arenas to switch dates, he found conflict after conflict, making it impossible to stick with his original intention of short trips between cities. His inability to secure available nights that fell into a logical progression for travel considerations became secondary to pleasing the top brass at TBS.

Promotions and media buys had to be changed in each city. It was a nightmare to reorganize. But all of the additional work would pay off for the prestige of hosting a live American TV special! Hermjo could boast to his arena managers and media outlets that he was the promoter who could produce not only sellouts, but also draw international attention to them. He would score points with all of his concert outlets. Hermjo's position would be strengthened on all fronts once he was known as the guy who could deliver.

Krap salivated at the thought of delivering a ratings giant to Germany's premiere sports network.

And for WCW . . . we would once and for all, out-Vince the in-Vince-able Vince. All parties involved would be elevated. Everyone would have so much to gain. That is, unless the Turner execs reneged on their end of the deal. Unless they changed their mind. Unless they nixed airing the live special from Germany. Which, as it turned out, was exactly what they did.

When Hermjo went back to the buildings to rebook his original dates, they were unavailable, resulting in a travel itinerary that would make sense only if we were a troupe of touring vampires. Every night along the way was a sleepless one. After working each show, we were herded on the bus and traveled through the night, arriving at the next city in the wee hours of the morning. We walked half asleep. We ate half asleep. We worked half asleep. And we paid dearly for the excruciating schedule with more discord and more injuries than we had ever experienced before.

The Battle Stars '94 tour bus served as our hotel, our restaurant and our game room throughout the endless tour. This is the "A" bus, the "baby face" bus.

The challenge of our agonizing itinerary was compounded for me by the strain of ongoing contract negotiations. There were early signs that the Turner execs wanted to rework my six-figure deal, which was to expire on April 30th. They said it was a matter of finances. They wanted me to move to Atlanta to work at their CNN Center headquarters to justify the price tag. With the recent purchase of a house in New Jersey, moving was out of the question. So seeing the beginning of the end of my WCW experience, I embarked on this tour in a funk. It was the first time that I dreaded the thought of performing in Europe.

My daily travel journal from the beleaguered *Battlestars* tour offers a raw perspective of the personalities, the politics and the competitiveness within WCW at the time. These spontaneous observations, interspersed throughout the following passages, provide an uncensored, unfiltered insight into the discord between the company and its talent.

<u>3-7-94 - Frankfurt, Germany</u>

Feet dragging each inch of the way, whisked across the Atlantic with no will to perform. It is two months after moving boxes piled high in every room of the empty dream house that I now call home. The improbability of delivering inspired performances at a time when the politically perverse predators at Techwood and Marietta play power ping-pong in the negotiation of an extension to a contract that has been quite lucrative looms overhead . . .

On the bus back to Frankfurt after the Ludwigshafen show . . . surrounded by separate conversations, all for distinct motives. In front Flair and Steinberg comparing notes, seeking info to gain an edge in their respective arenas of power . . . Flair – booker, anti Dusty Rhodes. Steinberg – director of marketing research and merchandising. Steinberg: "I did the research. I had a market sampling of men, women, teens and kids hooked up to dials as they watched our shows - 1 for lowest approval to 10 for most approval . . ., but Dusty wouldn't listen. Flair: "In the past, and I'm not mentioning any names, I told them. They wouldn't listen either. Across from me Steamboat and Frank Anderson talk about the proper psychology of a match. I wish Anderson would listen to Ricky. In back Max, Scorpio & Nick talking about what they heard from others about fucking little fraus.

<u>3-8-94 – Breakfast in Frankfurt</u>

With Cactus & Frank Anderson . . . Frank talking about not ending a Greco Roman match when he could have won early to make it more interesting – his coach threatened to kick him off the team and Frank said, 'You wouldn't do that. You need me.' Frank says he was paid 30K for wearing a brand name on tights, 3K for sponsor on jacket.

Many of the problems that we encountered on this trip were due to the addition of unskilled, yet self-important personnel who were placed in key positions. While they played important roles both behind the scenes and in the ring, their incompetence and unwillingness to learn caused bad blood in the shadows and spilled blood in the ring.

Frank Anderson was one of the early acquisitions of WCW's new executive vice-president, Eric Bischoff. Eric bent over backwards for Anderson, a legit Swedish wrestling champion. He may have been a gifted competitor in the amateur ranks, but his ascent to the pros was a classic example of The Peter Principle: he rose to his level of incompetence as evidenced by his bland, unconvincing style of wrestling. The problem was that Eric bought into the Swede's misguided notion that his background legitimatized WCW in the minds of European fans. And the price that was paid was more costly than Frank's fat contract. The resentment among the boys resulting from the sweet deal that Frank was given, at a time when some of our best talent was being cut, was by far more costly to the company.

3-9-94 - Cologne, Germany
　　　　Uninspired performances. . . . Pee Wee tears knee ligament . . . Flair, Vader, Sting discussing what the office wants for the finish of the tournament — Vader beats Sting . . . Greeted crowd in German — thought they booed . . . Later (found out) they said goooood!

Another addition to the tour was Don Sandefeur, WCW's latest arena booker. He acted as tour manager for this trip. And "acted" is an accurate depiction. To survive in the corporate world, he went along with whomever was in power at the time in order to preserve his position. He never made an independent decision. Not the perfect profile for a guy responsible for making judgment calls at every stop of the tour. He was lost, far from the familiarity of the political games that he played in Atlanta.

3-11-94 — Travel from Cologne to Halle — Scheduled departure is 10am
　　　　Sandefeur changed departure time to 9:30am but didn't tell me . . . . 8:30am wakeup knock on door by bell hop instructing me to have bags outside door in half hour. . . . . I rush down to the lobby at 9:55am. — Vader at reception desk. I walk out front door of hotel where Sandefeur is pacing and grumbling. — He gives me grief. "If Vader didn't have credit card problems and if the hotel didn't have to call back to Phoenix for verification of his balance, then Cappetta, you would have been stranded." — I asked Sandefeur how I was supposed to know about the change in schedule. - He said he called my room this morning at 9:15 — I asked what good that did if I was sleeping and never heard the phone ring — He was a blank . . . We get on the bus — He turns to me and starts up again. "You would have been stranded here." . . . I fire back, "What is that supposed to mean?" Don mumbles. "You heard what I said." He repeats himself, then looks away with a nervous laugh . . . I'm stuck on "B" bus, the "heel" bus.

The trip from Cologne to Halle takes 7 ½ hours including a bus rest at old German checkpoint — . . . As we approach the town, Vader gets up, walks to the back of the bus, then returns to the front and sits across from Sandefeur . . .

"Don, I just polled the boys and because it's so late, we want to go right to the building."

"We have to go to the hotel first."

"Well, Don, by the time we get to the hotel we'll only have time to bring our bags up, turn around and go back to the building."

"We're going to the hotel first."

"But, why?"

"We have to pick up the keys."

"They can hold the keys until after the show."

"Doug and Ric will be looking for us."

"They're big boys. They're competent to take care of themselves. You can call back to the hotel from the building."

"The building in Halle doesn't have a phone."

"You don't know that."

"I remember from when I was here the last time."

"Look Don, I'm being a gentleman. All of the boys agree. We should go to the building first."

SILENCE

"We can get to the building and stretch, then eat."

"No food will be served until quarter of six."

"Don, we're performers. We just traveled seven hours. This is how we get injured. You don't care. You don't know what it's like. It's just because you say so. That's it. It's just what you want to do."

SILENCE

"Don, who are you, anyway? What's your job? Listen to reason before I tell the driver to go straight to the building. You're not my boss. I don't care what you say."

"You're not telling the driver anything."

Vader's battle with Sandefeur was a classic management vs. talent power play. This picture is from more cordial times. Vader is showing me how to make the "Vader Time" sign after letting me play with his Super Bowl ring. It was huge!

"I'm going to get this straightened out. You haven't heard the last of this."

Vader sits directly behind Don, puts his headset back on and sings Whitney Houston's "The Bodyguard. Everyone stares out the window in silence.

I suffer through the "Silence of the Lambs" and "Full Metal Jacket" videos. Don seems to enjoy both movies.

The bus pulls up to The Maritime Hotel. As Regal passes Sandefeur he says, "I didn't want to go to the building first."

One half hour later in the Halle locker room with Scorpio, Steamboat and Austin.

Flair, Vader, Sandefeur gather in the middle of the room. Vader recounts his disagreement with Don and then says to Flair, "What is his job? If he's my boss, no one told me. He's just here to see if the money is right or if there's an insurance problem or if we need cash advances. Right? Can he fire me?"

Flair remains silent throughout Vader's entire rant. Then he says, "Look, Leon, he's second in command to Bob Dhue. He's my boss too. I'm only in charge of the wrestlers and what goes on in the ring."

"But all the boys agreed."

Don interjects, "That's not what they told me."

Vader:shoots him a dirty look. "Now you're calling me a liar? Is that what you're saying? We need time to warm up. You think this is a game. We could get injured without prep time. If you don't believe me, come in the ring for fifteen minutes and I'll show you."

As Vader storms out of the room, Sandefeur mumbles, "Well Regal and Orndorff said they wanted to go to the hotel first."

I'm not sure how we did it, but we had managed to make it half way through the tour. Some found traveling in rental cars, away from the troupe, a way to survive the rigors of touring. Others became lost in the videos that played over and over on the bus. It had been grim up to this point and foul mood lingered as we entered East Germany.

<u>3-12-94 - Bus leaves for Dresden, Germany at 4pm</u>

East Germany — dark, dank, dreary — The streets are lined with empty buildings, broken windows. — The fans are very disciplined. — No one runs up to rails. — All wear somber colored clothes. — Few of the fans speak any English. — The crowd is quiet except for the matches' high spots. — Experience has shown that pent up emotions can turn dangerous. — As soon as Vader wins his match, a fan moves toward him. The young security guards pick up the excited kid and toss him back onto his seat. The high point of the day was enjoying the two meatloaf sandwiches that the cook prepared for me.

Flair tries to raise the spirits of those who are still traveling by bus. Ric blurts out, "If Johnny's girl walks by me one more time in that yellow sweater, I'll be gone. ..One week without any!" Our laughter serves to encourage him to continue.

"Let's find a massage parlor across from an Italian restaurant. Massage and spaghetti!" Flair settles down to watch a Steven Segal movie. "Segal's no athlete. Look, he's running with his hands at his side."

The violent videos never seem to stop. Arnold Schwarzenegger's "The Terminator" . . . Stanley Kubrick's "Full Metal Jacket", again . . . Jonathan Demme's "Silence of the Lambs", .again . . . Patrick Swayze's "Breaking Point" . . Finally a break when the bus driver show Penny Marshall's "A League of Their Own".

Crisscrossing Germany night after night meant eating irregularly and sleeping erratically. The result of working overtired and off-kilter caused the loss of one guy after another. Referee Randy Anderson was sent home with torn ligaments in his leg. Ron Simmons (Faarooq) suffered a torn bicep muscle in Munich. Vader suffered a broken eardrum in the tournament final. Frank Anderson was missing in action. And referee Nick Patrick was called home to attend to a family emergency. But the most tragic incident of all was yet to occur.

3-13-94 – Dresden, Germany

Marc Mero perked up as I arrived at the hotel lobby.

"Hey Gar, I heard you've got a new job."

"What now?"

"Referee."

"Referee?"

"Yea. Nick Patrick was sent home. I heard that his father-in-law had a stroke."

The second of two referees is now out of action. Flair teases Alan Sharpe, WCW's public relations representative, about filling in. Didier Gepp arrives from France twenty minutes before show time to referee.

Every time we watch "A League Of Their Own" there's one line that hits close to home. One of the players confesses to Tom Hanks that she is considering quitting the team.

"I'm going home. Baseball is too hard."

Tom Hanks turns to her and says, "It's supposed to be hard. If it wasn't, everyone would do it."

I t happened at the Rudi-Sedlmayer-Halle in Munich before a lackluster crowd. It was a tournament match for the fabricated European Cup. Vader vs. Cactus Jack. Cactus was set to lose this one. But when it was all over, he would lose more than had been planned.

By this point in the tour we were working handicapped. Everyone was glassy eyed from too little sleep, too little space and too little free time. We had watched all of the bus driver's blood and guts videos more than once. We played number games such as Buzz. We matched wits with word games in which sentences are built with words contributed by everyone on the bus. The losers of the games that we played on the long, nightly bus trips downed shots of whiskey. And it all had grown tiresome. One Sportshalle looked like all of the others. The German ring crew was still learning the ropes. Both referees had gone home.

With the loss of Nick Patrick and Pee Wee Anderson, Didier Gepp, a referee imported from France, presided over the bout between Vader and Cactus. In fact, Gepp officiated *all* of the matches on *all* of the remaining shows for the rest of the tour. The workload would have been challenging to an experienced official. It was overwhelming for poor Didier. He was instructed to put on his zebra striped shirt, look official and stay out of the way. The wrestlers were told to work around him.

Despite Didier's incompetence, he had nothing to do with Cactus' loss. It was all the big guy's doing and should have come as no surprise to him.

For years, Cactus orchestrated a spot in his matches

Cactus performed his fateful Hangman maneuver nightly. Cactus is shown supporting his own weight while Eddie Gilbert slams his head with a boot. And that's barbed wire thrown in for the fun of it.

that made his opponent look like Superman. When Cactus gave the signal, his opponent would propel him into the ropes. Using the momentum of the catapult to accelerate his speed, Cactus flew back across to the opposite side of the ring where he inserted his head between the top two ropes as he spun over the top. This move resulted in hanging himself above the arena floor by the ring cables that twisted snugly around his neck - what he called The Hangman.

While this is not a move that I'd recommend to the faint of heart, Cactus' stunt was really harmless. He simply relieved the pressure of the twisted noose by pulling up on the ropes that were wrapped around his neck. The pain that Cactus experienced night after night was not from dangling by his neck. No, the pain came when the referee pulled apart the ropes ever so slightly, allowing him to slip his head through the cables before falling to the floor. Invariably, Cactus would be locked in so tightly that both of his ears would get clipped as his head slipped from between the taut ropes. He invited this abuse on a regular basis.

Every night Cactus performed the same feat. And after every show he cleaned out the self-inflicted wounds behind his ears to avoid infection. And each night the wounds became deeper and lengthier.

His wounds were gruesome even years before the Munich incident. I remember a swing through Florida in the early '90s when Cactus and I decided to visit my mom. Even back then, the oozing, pus-filled wounds behind his ears were so raw that he squealed as my mother swabbed the jagged cuts with alcohol-drenched cotton balls. As be braced himself at her dining room table, my mom did her best to hold him still. And her best was better than most of his opponents. She had him in so much pain, that he didn't dare move.

So by the time we got to Germany, Cactus' ears were in very sad shape. And it didn't help that the steel ring ropes in Munich were stretched around the ring more tightly than usual.

Cactus wasn't as lucky on the night that Didier was unable to pull the top ring ropes apart. I watched as Cactus forced his head through the two strands of steel. He left a clump of hair behind as he crashed to the arena floor. Didier gazed down at the mat and froze. His head jerked from side to side in search of assistance. He nervously glanced across the ring at me. Then he lost all control.

He began to jump up and down as he eyed the mat. His feet were moving but he wasn't going anywhere. His hand went to his heart, then flailed in the air. He looked like Marcel Marceau on speed. He bent over to get a closer look at something that had landed on the canvas. Then he picked it up. In one continuous motion, his fingers, like a pair of trembling tweezers, carefully lifted the object from the mat and then flung it into the air toward the side of the ring where I sat nose to the canvas. It glided above the mat like a frisbee. It soared through the air until it slapped with a thud on the canvas, then skidded across the mat, stopping in front of me. It looked like a piece of uncooked chicken filet with a piece of athletic tape and a few strands of hair stuck on it. Didier had tossed Cactus' ear to me!

It was surreal. It was bizarre. It was grotesque.

I gingerly pinched the ear with two fingers of my left hand and carefully placed it into the palm of my right. Didier was screaming, but I didn't understand what he was saying. He didn't speak English. I didn't understand French. He squealed as he charged full speed in my direction, *"Mon Dieu! Mettez-la ur glace! C'est une urgence! Tragedie! Ambulance!, ambulance!"*

I instantly spun around and headed down the aisle toward the dressing rooms. Security chief Dellinger was snoozing in the metal folding chair that I kicked as I raced by yelling, "Doug . . . we've got an emergency and I've got Cactus' ear. Call an ambulance." I can't blame him for squinting at me like I had lost my mind. I wasn't so sure that I hadn't.

When I reached the back, Flair was waiting for me.

3-16-94 – Munich, Germany

"I've got Cactus' ear, what do I do with it?

Flair: "No it's not. What are you talking about? I just watched the spot."

"Ric, I've got Cactus' ear in my hand. What do I do with it?

"Wait, let me see" . . . Flair studies the ear until he begins to understand what has happened. The boys circle around.

Finally, Flair breaks through the chorus of "ooohs", "aaahs" and groans of disgust. "Bring it to the doctor. Have him put it on ice."

When he gets to the hospital Cactus wants to keep ear, but they wont let him. The doctors try to reattach the ear but it won't take with cartilage. He wants to wrestle to the end the tour, but the WCW suits demand that he returns home immediately.

That night at hotel bar the jokes fly. The boys begin to sing The Beatles' "I Get By With A Little Help From My Friends": *What would you think if I sang out of tune? Would you stand up and walk out on me? Lend me your ears and I'll sing you a song. And I'll try not to sing out of key.* The boys think this is a riot."

We lost valuable time before packing his ear in ice. No one believed me as I raced through the dressing rooms, ear in hand. Everyone had to take a peek for himself. Flair thought I had lost my mind. Sting was mesmerized by the gruesome mound of meat that I carried in my palm. He followed me wherever I went. Harlem Heat Kole couldn't bear to look.

By the time I found the doctor, the match, which had continued as planned, ended with Vader coming out on top. As I retraced my steps through the dressing room area on my way back to the ring, Cactus was wandering toward me. His hand covered the side of his bloody head. His glazed eyes twirled in their sockets as he smiled at me and crowed, "Bang, bang, I lost my ear!" It just doesn't get any more peculiar than this.

The Cactus ear incident reminded me of a match in the late 1950's. Walter Kowalski was wrestling Yukon Erik in Canada. Kowalski climbed to the top corner turnbuckle, propelled himself through the air, and clipped the side of Erik's head with his knee. The force of the blow severed Erik's cauliflowered ear from his head. Kowalski, who from that night forward was known as "Killer", jubilantly boasted on TV interviews that every time Erik walked down the gusty streets of Chicago, the wind entered his one ear, knocking him off balance, causing him to spin around on the sidewalk like a human tornado. A short time later, a depressed and despondent Yukon Erik killed himself.

The only regret that Cactus ever expressed to me was that he was not allowed to take his ear home with him. That may sound strange, but we're talking about a guy who hangs all of the teeth that have been knocked out of his mouth around his neck.

Chapter Sixteen
"The Semi-Final Event"

Nearly all men can stand adversity, but if you want to test a man's character, give him power.

Charles Luckman,
Architect of Madison Square Garden and The Los Angeles Forum

Eric Bischoff's first tenure as World Championship Wrestling's executive vice-president began six months prior to our infamous March 1994 tour of Germany. He was driven like a man possessed, not only to transform WCW into a profitable wrestling company, but to humiliate McMahon in the process. The more fixated he became on replacing Vinnie as wrestling's top dog, the more he distanced himself from those who held no power to help him. With Eric's promotion from announcer to administrator, the friendship that we once shared began to disintegrate.

Throughout WCW's early years, the baffled and dysfunctional Turner family was never able to maintain a singular and focused philosophy. The front office was a revolving door for inept executives, all of whom failed to overcome the dominance that the WWF had maintained for a decade. As I traveled night after night, from city to city across the country, I saw how the ever-changing direction of WCW's wrestling product left the fans confused and frustrated by story lines that ended as abruptly as the careers of the Turner decision makers who were responsible for them.

WCW remained so disorganized that Vinnie even managed to dominate the wrestling industry while facing a steady barrage of negative national publicity on two separate fronts. In addition to accusations of sexual misconduct within his "family-friendly" company, the WWF was nearly brought to its knees when the US Department of Justice indicted McMahon on November 18, 1993 on five drug related charges including possession of steroids with the intent to distribute. But neither the accusations, which forced Vince to defend himself on "The Larry King Show" and "The Phil Donohue Show", nor damaging rumors during the months leading up to his anticipated 1994 trial, were enough to topple McMahon from his throne.

Throughout his corporate crisis, Vinnie played the role of an innocent underdog, maligned by overzealous federal agents and resentful industry insiders. His public face displayed disdain and defiance for the federal prosecutors and media critics who attempted to take the family business owner down. Junior called the charges baseless. He portrayed himself as a common citizen who suffered from the unfair intrusion of a Big Brother government. It was a laughable contention which many in the media were duped into believing. McMahon's self-portrayal as a maligned little guy fighting the trumped up charges of out-of-control bureaucrats was as scripted as a WWF grudge match.

I recognized this side of Junior from my past dealings with him. Not much had changed. He remained as arrogant as the twenty-nine year old TV host I knew when I broke into the business two decades earlier. But as much as I disapproved of Vinnie's ruthless disregard for those who got in his way, I decided to set personal differences aside when I was called by the federal agent assigned to supply evidence of McMahon's guilt.

Tony Valenti, the Justice Department's chief investigator, called me to see if I would offer testimony about the rampant drug use that prosecutors alleged had taken place during my years with the WWF. While I answered all of his specific questions directly and to the point, I refrained from supplying additional, unsolicited information. I felt no animosity toward McMahon. My personal grievances with him had been resolved a long time ago. My dispute over the way he conducted business was settled in a lawsuit of my own. I had proven in a malpractice case against my then lawyer that the WWF had used my past performances on several home videos, as well as on the audio tape for the Hulk Hogan workout set, without properly compensating me. After I won that case there was no reason to look back.

Junior once again beat the odds when on July 22, 1994 the not guilty verdict was announced. And to his credit, although the highly publicized trial tarnished his company's wholesome image, Junior continued to overpower WCW on all fronts. It was WCW's best chance to bring WWF fans over to their side and they blew it.

McMahon's publicly opened wounds were slow to heal, however and Bischoff jumped at the first opportunity to capitalize on Vinnie's weakened state. The combination of WCW's corporate chaos and the bad press that continued to hang over

Junior's head set the stage for the baby face Bischoff to lobby for control of Turner's wrestling company, thus allowing him to step into the spotlight that he had craved for so long.

Eric, who had witnessed how nonstop political game playing had undermined the success of Ted Turner's wrestling product from the beginning, shrewdly arranged a one on one meeting with the well-insulated Turner. By the time they parted company, the smooth talking broadcaster had won Ted's personal seal of approval for the changes that Eric saw as necessary to unseat McMahon. By circumventing Turner's counterproductive layer of middle managers, Bischoff gained permission from the distant CEO to begin using the company's resources that had always been denied the wrestling division. And Eric began spending huge amounts of Turner's money.

I witnessed Eric's aggressive self-promotional style early on. It was only a couple of months after he arrived at the CNN Center for his first WCW job as an announcer. In the green room of our production studios, as we both waited to voice over our weekly programs, Bischoff showed me a storyboard of a kids TV program that he had developed. It was a game show in which WCW's wrestling stars were matched against youngsters in a Nickelodeon style of fun family programming. Eric, of course, would be the host.

That first week he was excited to have arranged an audience with a Turner exec who could give the green light on his project. The next week he returned frustrated at being rejected. The third week he was already pitching his idea to the folks at Disney. The guy never gave up. He always saw wrestling as a springboard to loftier heights. From the beginning, his primary goal was to make a name for himself, that would allow him to hobnob with Hollywood types after his stint with WCW was over.

Predictably, Eric found it distasteful to play the junior announcer to broadcast veterans Jim Ross and Tony Schiavone. But playing second fiddle was only temporary. It would just be a matter of time before he would step over his more experienced, more talented colleagues. They would some day be working for Bischoff. And now that day had finally come.

Some think that power changes a person. I don't think so. Power simply allows one to reveal his true self without fear of reprisal. And with Bischoff, his transformation from toothy grinned telecaster to TBS top brass was radical. As a second string announcer he was a "go along to get along" kind of a guy.

When he moved into the driver's seat, he pushed the pedal to the metal with an "it's my way or the highway" arrogance.

Nevertheless, Eric now had the combination to the company safe. He began to revamp WCW from the ground up. He spent $400,000 to update the sets of WCW's TV shows. He hired former WWF on air talent. He enlisted scriptwriters in an attempt to rival the story line formula of episodic TV that had worked so well for the WWF. He paid big money for Vince's former arena promoter to jump ship. The smooth sales job that convinced Turner to entrust him with control of the company gained Eric the freedom to shape WCW's television product as he saw fit. I naturally wondered what part I would play in Eric's vision. It would not take long to find out the answer.

As Bischoff suited up for his slugfest against Junior, for what would be the biggest wrestling war in the history of the business, Vinnie characteristically scoffed at the notion that anyone could rival his success.

From the first TV taping that Eric produced, his plans for me became clear. Crystal clear. For the preceding five years I had enjoyed a prominent on air role. Jim Cornette had dubbed me "The World's Most Dangerous Announcer". Jesse Ventura playfully referred to me as "Cappetski". Unlike many ring announcers, the production team accepted me as a full member of the broadcast family. The directors were generous with close-ups, name mentions and an occasional interview. But soon after arriving at the Dothan, Alabama Civic Center for his first day as producer of the WCW syndicated television show, Bishcoff began to banish me from the close knit family with little regard to my years of loyalty to the parent company. And as had been the case with McMahon fifteen years earlier, I was appalled at Eric's manner of cleaning house.

"Gary, I just came up with an idea. I want you to try something new starting with these tapings." Eric delivered his message with so much enthusiasm that I was already picturing the Toys R Us! shelves overflowing with the Gary Michael Cappetta Battery Operated Microphone that our head of merchandising had promised me years before.

"Sure, Eric. What is it?"

"I want you to speed up your introductions. You know, make them livelier. Don't change your announcements. They're fine. Just pick up the pace."

"That's not a problem. Whatever ya think would be best."

"Good. So you don't have any objections to changing your style a little?"

When Eric uttered that one crucial question for extra emphasis, I should have suspected that I was being set up. Before long, I learned that he was only telling me a small part of his plan. He failed to mention that he had already instructed our director to avoid capturing me on camera and then told the play by play guys to talk over my muted announcements. In effect, he slyly and subtly eliminated me from the show so that the damage was done without my knowledge. It wasn't until the programs started to air when I realized that this was not a last minute Bischoff brainstorm. Unfortunately, telling me only a portion of the truth became one of Eric's bad habits.

I was further silenced later that same week when word came to me that I would no longer be needed to voice over the commentary for our Spanish language syndicated show as I had done in the past. But it was Eric's third chop to the throat that left me in stunned silence. Not only because it was the blow which stripped me of the lead ring announcer position for our major shows. Not only because he was hiring a boxing announcer, who was unfamiliar with the nuances of wrestling, to work our most prestigious events. No, I was dumbfounded by the hypocrisy that Bischoff demonstrated the day he arranged a meeting to tell me of his plan. Well, at least *part* of his plan.

When I arrived at WCW headquarters, Gary Juster called me into his office where Eric soon joined us. Here is how Bischoff's latest story went.

"Gary, in order to elevate the importance of our next *Clash Of Champions* special, I am going to bring Michael Buffer in to handle the announcements for the main event. Now it will only be for this one show. And I wanted you to hear this directly from me so that you won't misinterpret Buffer's appearance at the *Clash*. I want you to know how much I value your work. Although there are going to be quite a few changes and nobody's position is safe, you should know that you will *not* be affected by the cuts that we are going to make."

Juster took an inner office call, then excused himself from the meeting. As soon as the door shut, Eric lowered his voice, leaned toward me and in hushed tones he continued.

"If there's *anyone* who should be concerned for his job, it's *him*." As Eric sternly gestured toward the closed door with an assertive nod, I sat there in a state of shock. Wasn't he aware that it was through Juster that I got my big break with WCW? Didn't he know that Gary and I had enjoyed a long friendship? Was Eric putting on a show for me or was he really that cold? As I sat facing Bischoff, it was clear that he was not to be trusted.

Either he was setting me up once again, or Eric was demonstrating that he had the compassion of a cleaver-wielding butcher. I began to feel like an animal en route to slaughter. It became clear that I too was being set up for the kill and that's when I decided to seek out legal representation for our upcoming contract negotiations. And that's when an incensed Eric stopped the "I'm your buddy" charade.

I met Chris, my Orlando-based entertainment attorney, while taping a series of WCW shows at the Disney MGM Studios. Until now, I never felt the need to hire an agent. I was comfortable representing myself and was always surprised at the ease with which my past negotiations had gone. I was earning $1,000 per event in addition to being paid extra when I hosted the weekly Spanish language show. Whenever I announced twice a day, the money doubled. All of my travel expenses were paid, thus receiving performer money and corporate perks. I successfully worked my way into a sweet six-figure deal. I had come a long way from the $21.66 that the McMahons paid me for my first TV show.

Chris' job was to protect the deal that I had established since an increased income now seemed out of the question. His challenge had less to do with negotiating a more favorable fee and more to do with insulating me from the obnoxious histrionics of Bischoff.

Eric yearned for Hollywood. But without the limitless cash flow of his new Sugar Daddy Ted, he was nothing more than an ambitious lightweight. After twenty years I had grown impatient with the pretentious air kissing types that Eric exemplified. He needed to understand that his butt was one that I had no interest in kissing. And legal representation was my way of communicating that to him.

By the time I returned from Germany, I learned that Eric had assigned Gary Juster to negotiate on behalf of WCW. I'm not sure whether placing my good friend on the other side of the negotiating table was a touch of irony, or part of Bischoff's strategy. Either way, Gary and I had an unspoken agreement to keep our personal and adversarial roles separate. He remained loyal to the task as evidenced by Chris' message to me when I returned stateside that he was getting nowhere with Gary in his attempt to extend my agreement past the April 30th deadline. From the time that Chris began calling for my contract renewal earlier in the year, Bischoff showed no interest in reaching a resolution. His inattentiveness to my concerns was an indication that our negotiations would go down to the wire.

The contract was to expire two weeks before the next Orlando TV tapings were scheduled to begin. As the May 12th shoot approached, still far from an agreement, Eric asked if I would work the shows for a pro rated fee based on my soon to expire contract. I agreed to continue past the end of my agreement as a sign of good faith provided that Eric would meet with Chris to hammer out an agreement before the end of our week at the Disney-MGM Studios. When he agreed to my request, I accepted the assignment to announce for the three months of shows that would be taped in Orlando.

When I arrived at the Disney back lot, it was clear that Eric had become overwhelmed by the responsibility of running the show. When he wasn't attending to the creative content of the program, he was busy keeping the Turner execs from second-guessing his every move. He spent so much time micro managing every detail, that he paid little attention to the grumbling of the wrestlers that spread through the trailers which served as our dressing rooms.

Vader protested Eric's refusal to allow him to accept an acting role, which did not make the big man happy.

"This is stupid! It could help the company. If I was one of his prima donnas, he'd have no problem with it."

Jesse Ventura whined about being stuck in Orlando for an entire week.

"Two days of voice-overs is understandable. But four days just to do show intros is ridiculous!"

Then Jesse began to coach Vader about contracts.

"They gotta give me at least seven days notice if they want me to work, but they usually don't wait that long. My contract says that if I get called to do a movie, then all I gotta do is inform Eric and I can be gone for twenty-eight days. That time is pro rated and then deducted from my money. That's what caused my split with the WWF. I had an Arnold movie lined up. Vince said, 'No way. Ya can't do it'. I said, 'Like hell I can't! This is a once in a lifetime opportunity.' Leon, ya gotta get yourself a better contract." Jesse was referring to his supporting roles in Arnold Schwarzenegger's *Predator* and *The Running Man*, both of which were released in 1987.

Marc Bagwell's complaint was much more legitimate.

"Hey, Bischoff's bringing a lot of new guys on board for big money and I'm still makin' $65,000 a year. I went down to the office, sat across from Eric and I told him. I said, 'Eric, if you can honestly sit there and look me eye to eye and tell me I'm not worth $100,000, then Eric, I'll walk outta here, no questions asked.' Marc called Bischoff's bluff and rightfully got the raise.

There also was dissatisfaction where you'd least expect it. Even retired wrestler Larry Zbyszko wasn't happy. At the time, he served as a commentator on WCW's secondary program, requiring him to show up for half a day each week. And he already was being paid six figures! Larry worked so little that it was a running joke that his contract was crafted to assure him the best golf game in all of WCW. How did Larry manage to swing such a sweet deal? And why wasn't he happy?

Answering the first question is easy once you know that Larry is married to the daughter of AWA owner Verne Gagne, the man who gave Bischoff his first break in wrestling. The answer to the second question brings us back to the con being a way of life in wrestling.

Larry was ready to battle with his "buddy" Eric

Although Larry's primary role was that of an announcer, he agreed to come out of retirement to wrestle a few TV matches. With Zbysko's story line already airing on the program, he calculated that it was too late for the bookers to cancel his upcoming matches. Not that canceling a feud in the middle of its buildup would be out of the ordinary in WCW.

"Hey, if he thinks I'm gonna do the extra work for nothing, then he's in La La Land. We've already built this thing up on TV. There's no turning back. And I've got two years left on my contract. He can't get rid of me now. Bischoff's got no choice but to pay me more."

With all of the confusion, there was no wonder why I was getting lost in the shuffle. When the week ended I was no closer to sealing a deal. Once again, I felt betrayed by Eric who had never made the time to meet with my agent. By working the week at Disney, he had me on TV for three more months and I was still without a contract.

Amidst the chaos and discord, Arn Anderson took me aside and offered the best advice that anyone could have given. He had been in my shoes more than once. He understood how our hearts could be tugged by the love of wrestling, causing many of us to cave in to the demands of promoters. Arn is also a man who has remained true to his principles and loyal to the sport. He warned me against letting my ego get in the way of what I could realistically expect in a new contract based upon Eric's perception of me and his vision for the future of the company. He urged me to base my decision on what was important to me and not to be influenced by the opinions of others.

"I know how tough it can be. I was making $260,000 a year and they were gonna cut me loose. But I've got a family to think about. I had more to consider than myself. Fair or not, I agreed to stay for half of what I was making."

Arn's words rang true. It was foolish to push for a contract with a company that didn't *understand*, let alone appreciate the work I had done. I was not about to revert to the intimidated kid who had been manipulated by the McMahons many years before. With Arn's help, I was able to look beyond the well-intentioned opinions of advisors and to realize that gaining a new agreement became secondary to retaining my self-respect.

Chapter Seventeen
"A Classic Clash
Career vs. Self-Respect"

. . . the power imbalance and arrogance result in employer - employee relationships that normally are weighted overwhelmingly in favor of the employer, giving rise to the 'shoddy business practices' and 'murky contracts' . . . the average Hollywood contract - perfectly legal terms and conditions - give the studio or the network enormous advantages over the actor, director, writer, or small production company. The powerful and arrogant few tend to take full advantage of every situation, and the lure of working in the industry is so strong that the fearful mass of prospective employees will sign just about anything to do so - often to their later regret.

David McClintick,
"INDECENT EXPOSURE, A True Story of Hollywood and Wall Street"

With an expired contract and all obligations to WCW fulfilled, I returned to my New Jersey home. It was time to assess what would be next for me in a life beyond broadcasting, far from the fantasy world of wrestling. Word had spread that I would soon become a free agent through the wrestling community's rumor mill. News, such as my standoff with Eric, travels from one locker room to the next in a matter of hours. I have always found it interesting that despite the vagabond existence of its participants, the wrestling gossip network is the most efficient of any I've ever seen.

I received offers from smaller wrestling organizations, which I immediately declined. At the time, Extreme Championship Wrestling, among the most successful and cutting edge of the indie promotions, was gaining widespread attention as the bad little brother of the big two. Paul Heyman, the brains behind the organization, had established a faithful following as the first United States promotion to gain widespread popularity for a hard core brand of mat mayhem. It was more violent, more crude and unquestionably more extreme in every way. ECW fans not only expected, but also came to demand blood and guts wrestling. From top to bottom, ECW events were littered with broken bodies and crushed skulls resulting from insane acts of violence and recklessness.

Paul called me on a few occasions to stay abreast of the progress of my negotiations with Eric, and to map out his vision

of my role in ECW. As convincing as Paul can be, my philosophy of wrestling as an art form, in which the merit of your work lies in *simulated* violence as opposed to *actual* acts of self-destruction, were entirely incompatible with his. The only way I would have considered becoming the promotion's pitchman would have been as an announcer to counter the defending voice of ECW mouthpiece, Joey Styles. But Paul had different ideas. He wasn't looking to team me up with Styles. He was looking to replace him due to a dispute that the two were having over Joey's travel schedule. In passing on the opportunity, I did both Paul and myself a big favor. With the talented Joey Styles as his storyteller, Paul has written the textbook that has become required

Paul E. asked me to replace ECW commentator, Joey Styles, which would have been an extreme mistake.

reading for today's successful promotions.

Only three days passed following my return from Disney when I was surprised by a call from Gary Juster.

"Gary, are you okay?" Juster proceeded carefully.

"Sure, everything's fine. But you're the last person I expected to hear from."

"We were wondering what happened to you last night."

I knew exactly what he was referring to, but I decided to have a little fun with him.

"What do you mean? What was last night?"

"You were booked to be in Salisbury, Maryland last night. It was on the calendar that I sent to you, wasn't it?"

"Yeah, I guess it was. But that was when I worked for the company." Damn, I was enjoying this.

"What do you mean?"

"Well, my contract expired at the end of April. This is May 20th. I agreed to work Disney for you with the promise that you and Eric would hammer out a deal with Chris by the end of that week. I held up my end of the agreement and I still don't have anything in writing from you. So as far as I'm concerned, I'm not obligated to do anything more for WCW."

Juster knew me well enough to realize how satisfying this conversation was for me. But to his credit, he remained loyal to his employer throughout.

"I'm sure we can still work something out."

"Then why don't you? Eric knows that I won't back down from my nightly performance fee and perks. I think Chris has told you that more than once. And by the way, shouldn't you be talking to Chris about this? I'm not sure that I should be discussing contracts with you."

"But what about tonight? You're on the calendar for another Maryland show."

"I may be on the calendar, but I'm not on the payroll. So until that happens . . .well, I don't plan on going anywhere."

"And what about the *Slamboree* pay-per-view this Sunday?"

"Like I said, I'm not going anywhere. I've already worked past the end of my contract by agreeing to announce at Disney which puts me on Eric's TV shows for the next twelve weeks and what did I get for it? More of the same bullshit."

"So you want me to tell Eric that you won't be at *Slamboree*?"

"Since I don't work for him any more, I don't think Eric should *expect* me to be there."

Juster paused for a few seconds, considered what I was saying and probably recognized the determined tone of my voice before continuing.

"Alright. I'll tell him. And Gary, I want you to know that I'm not surprised by your answer."

"I realize that. You understand me better than anyone in Atlanta. This is how things started with Turner to begin with. Remember? When you delivered Jim Herd's message that he wanted me to stop working the AWA pay-per-view shows? And I sent word back that unless I was under contract with the Atlanta office that I'd work for whomever I wanted? Remember? You were put in the same bind back then."

"Yeah, I remember. Well, I'll tell Eric and let's see what happens."

Within twenty-four hours, what I thought was a dead issue began to gain new life. Between Friday and Sunday morning, just hours before *Slamboree*, after two days of fax transmissions back and forth between Chris and WCW, my agent called with news that we were able to come to terms on a new one year agreement that were acceptable to everyone. Chris executed a legally binding letter of intent listing the main points upon which we agreed, thus allowing me to arrive just in time to open the pay-per-view show.

We accepted a basic broadcast agreement that would take me off the road except for TV tapings and an occasional tour or promotional event. I would be guaranteed $85,000 for the year, whether WCW called on my services or not. For each appearance past the projected eighty-five dates, WCW would pay an additional $1,000 per event. The corporate travel perks that had been standard in my agreements from the beginning remained unchanged.

At first glance, this agreement seems lopsided in WCW's favor since Eric was able to retain my services for all WCW broadcasts, which was most important to him. At the same time he saved a bundle of money on my air tickets. But the equalizer was my insistence on the terms under which I would agree to give him what he wanted. That's what he had a hard time swallowing. And here's why.

Since eighty-five guaranteed performances accounted for less than one fourth of the calendar year, announcing became a part time job. But even though I would be working only 25% of the year and still earning 80% of my past income, I wanted the freedom to accept projects unrelated to the wrestling business. This was important not only to allow me the opportunity to supplement my WCW income, but also to provide a safe place to land at the end of what I was sure would be my last year with the company. Therefore, additional considerations were raised. Considerations that Vinnie and Eric avoid at all costs.

For instance, promoters expect that their performers will be available at a moment's notice. They are also accustomed to canceling shows at the last minute without paying the talent for a date that can't be rebooked at the eleventh hour. And WCW was also slipping clauses into their contracts, which allowed the company to terminate the agreement every sixty days. They were called "review periods". The performer was obligated for a full year, while the promotion committed for only two months at a time. In short, promoters retained total control of your work schedule with the freedom to change your role with the company at will.

Well, that's all fine and good, except that by taking those liberties, the promoters expect performers to play by the same rules as full time employees. But Vinnie and Eric will tell you that the performers are not employees; they are independent contractors. And the reason for this is simple. As employees, performers would be entitled to company benefits and certain considerations related to their working conditions, two issues that the WWF and WCW stay away from at all costs and more precisely, *because* of the costs.

So I asked Chris to eliminate the "review period" clause and to negotiate limits into my agreement that would ensure my availability to work during the 75% of the time when I wasn't engaged by WCW.

While I held out for several additional modifications to WCW's standard agreement, three key elements were written into my contract. The first made it possible for me to commit to non-WCW work. The second and third guarantied my freedom while on the road. All three are rare accommodations which WCW and the WWF may occasionally afford in their superstar contracts, but are unheard of in their customary performance agreements.

One month advance notice of bookings:
"Announcer shall perform services as and when requested in writing by WCW upon a thirty (30) day notice, however, Announcer shall use his best efforts to accommodate schedule changes by WCW.
Company underwrites travel expenses.
"Any and all travel incurred by Announcer in the performance of services hereunder shall be paid by WCW to GMC pursuant to WCW's (employee) travel policy."
Announcer is free to travel alone.
"It is expressly understood and agreed that Announcer shall not share auto or hotel accommodations."

This abbreviated outline of three contractual clauses that were adopted in my agreement simply balanced the scales of the standard wrestling contracts which have always weighed heavy in favor of the promotions. It does not begin to scratch the surface of considerations for which I would lobby if I represented the wrestlers. Promoters will continue to conduct business as usual, with little regard for the welfare of performers, as long as they can get away with it. It remains my contention, as I mentioned earlier, that The Business of Wrestling 101 should be included in the curriculum of every wrestling school.

For instance, to evaluate the true value of a $75,000 startup contract, rookies should be forewarned that their income will shrink by more than half after deducting the road expenses of car rentals, hotels, food and gym fees that constant travel requires. Add in the huge premiums of health and disability insurance that are not afforded to self-employed contractors. And how much money could possibly be left for life after wrestling? Enough startup capital to invest in a business when the last bell sounds? Enough to provide for his family through his retirement years? We're talking about a guy whose career ends on average twenty years earlier than the typical worker. Without educating the young guys about the finances and more importantly, the working conditions to which they are contractually bound, they are being set up for a rude awakening.

It would take an entire book to adequately address these, and so many more considerations. The title of such a book should be *It's Not What You Deserve, It's What You Can Negotiate.* There is no doubt that such a primer should be required reading to ensure that performers do not sign away their rights in pursuit of the dream.

And by the way, it may not surprise you that although the Turner legal department signed a preliminary list of guarantees before I was on my way to *Slamboree*, the final draft of the contract would take another five months to execute. It was not until October of 1994 when they begrudgingly signed off on it.

When I arrived at the Philadelphia Civic Center for *Slamboree* I was a little nervous. For the two days that I was missing in action, the gossip mill had been churning. Those who were not aware of the circumstances which forced me to take a firm stand were convinced that I was holding up the company on the day of a major pay-per-view program. Anyone who believed that I would pull what I like to call a "Sid Vicious No Show Violation", didn't know me well enough to be worthy of my concern. And they were placing more importance on my role than even I believed it merited.

Larry Zbyszko loved the turmoil that my eleventh hour deal had caused. "Cappetta, you're the only one who can bring them to their knees," he kidded. Unfortunately, Larry must have found a similarity between his Disney shenanigans and my contractual impasse.

Dave Penzer, my ring announce colleague, was pacing backstage for fear that I would not show up. Never having worked a major event he was a nervous wreck. "Gary, thank God you're here!" he repeated over and over.

Ric Flair took me aside to express his relief that I was still on the team. "Eric asked me, and I told him that you are the most professional of all and losing you would be a shame."

The show went on as usual, as I began one more year with WCW.

By the time Eric took over the company, former WWF stars The British Bulldog, Ravishing Rick Rude and announcer Jesse Ventura were already on Turner's payroll due to the notoriety they gained in the WWF. But Bischoff had his sights set on Hulk Hogan. The Hulkster personified the WWF's glory years of the 1980s. Hulk's name was familiar to the general public. Eric was convinced that only with the help of Hulk Hogan would WCW's brand name be elevated to even the playing field in a battle against the World Wrestling Federation.

Another wrestler who gained notoriety with the WWF before being lured by Turner's generous contracts was The British Bulldog, Davey Boy Smith.

In the Summer of 1994 Eric signed Hogan to a six-month contract commanding a two million-dollar guarantee, plus an assortment of lucrative incentives. Compared to the highest paid WCW performers at the time, who earned between $500,000 and $750,000 annually, Hogan's deal was exorbitant. Mid card stars like The Honky Tonk Man and Hacksaw Jim Duggan, also from the WWF's golden years, earned a mere $1,000 a match. But Hogan was in a class by himself. In addition to his sky-high price tag, he gained creative control over his ring persona. Hogan's deal allowed him to pick his opponents and the outcome of his matches.

It was not until 1988, when Turner purchased his wrestling company, that wrestlers received guaranteed contracts. WCW treated their top stars the same as athletes of other Turner owned sports franchises, with secure paychecks whether they performed or not. WWF wrestlers were paid pursuant to the business they drummed up for the McMahon family through ticket sales and merchandise licensing fees. When business was down in the WWF, everyone's income suffered. It didn't take long for other WWF wrestlers to consider hopping aboard the WCW gravy train for the security and profit that the Turner organization offered.

The deal between Bischoff and WWF icon Hogan was unusual. WCW allowed Hogan unprecedented autonomy, including complete control of his role as a performer and the last word on the outcome of his matches. I wondered who worked for whom.

Hogan was everything that Bischoff idolized. He was a household name. He had amassed considerable wealth. And most of all, he was Hollywood. Whenever Hogan arrived on the scene, Bischoff followed him around like an attention-starved puppy dog. Capitalizing on his notoriety in wrestling, The Hulkster had accomplished what Eric dreamed about for himself from the first day he signed on as WCW's newest announcer.

During my final year in wrestling, I continued to appear on all the WCW TV shows. I announced for *WCW Saturday Night* on TBS, for our syndicated shows, for the *Clash of Champions* specials and for all of the pay-per-view events. My infrequent road trips kept me traveling to one nighters throughout the United States.

One weekend tour that took place in mid October of 1994 did brisk business since Hulk Hogan headlined each event.

We began in Salt Lake City, moved to Oakland the next night and wound up in Anaheim for a Sunday matinee. My memories of the weekend linger, since Dr. Tom Bilella is still treating me for the noggin knocking injuries that I suffered at the Oakland Coliseum. But let's start at the beginning.

The Salt Lake show on Friday night was high energy from start to finish. It was the first time we played the Delta Center, so the fans were more energized than usual. Karl "The Mailman" Malone was in Hogan's corner for the main event, turning up the excitement level even one notch higher. Personally satisfying to me was my visit with John Crotty, a former student from the academy where I had taught, who was then signed with the Utah Jazz.

Our Salt Lake stay would have been perfect had it not been for the police being summoned to a local restaurant when some of the wrestlers, after enjoying the food and hospitality of a late night eatery, snuck out without paying the bill. The incident prompted newspaper headlines and more bad press for the promotion.

Nothing had ever gotten in the way of the good times that I enjoyed whenever we played the Bay Area. That is until this, my final performance in Oakland.

The incident was prompted by booker Ric Flair's plan to get us through a potentially difficult situation. He herded those of us who were involved in the evening's semi-final tag team match into the Oakland Coliseum shower to lay out his scheme. Yeah, we met in the shower!

"Okay, this is what we're up against tonight." Flair sounded like an excited Little League coach at the National Championships. "Terry Funk is advertised to be in this six man tag match, but he won't be here. He notified the office a while ago, but you know, the booking committee wasn't told." This was business as usual for WCW.

The Nasty Boys and Dustin Rhodes were scheduled to wrestle Funk, Arn Anderson and Bunkhouse Buck. Always nearby were their manager, Colonel Robert Parker and Meng, a mighty mountain of a man who served as the Colonel's bodyguard.

As we all anxiously awaited Flair's plan of attack in the overcrowded shower, he turned to me. His words echoed off the shiny white ceramic tiles that surrounded us.

"Gary, my plan begins with you . . ."

Ric proceeded to dramatize the detailed vision that had formed in his mind until everyone understood their role in the skit designed to divert the audience's attention away from Terry's absence. Our mission was to direct the crowd's focus to the controversy that we would whip up in center ring. After Ric talked us through his scenario, we filed out of the shower, assuring him that we understood our part in keeping the fans entertained in light of the missing Funk.

According to Flair's dramatization, I called for Colonel Parker's entrance music to signal the beginning of the tag match. As Parker strutted to ringside, flanked by Buck and Meng, the crowd buzzed as to the whereabouts of Terry Funk. Parker and I exchanged a few words in the middle of the ring. When I pantomimed disagreement to what he was saying, The Colonel angrily snatched the mic. He proceeded to incite the crowd with news of Funk's absence and then continued to taunt the fans by declaring the mighty Meng to be Terry's substitute. He smugly looked out at the sea of disapproving fans who shouted their anger at being doublecrossed. Parker and Meng knowingly nodded at each other which cued referee Nick Patrick to race down the aisle to join us.

As Nick pretended to whisper an important message to me, my face slowly brightened. I cast a wary eye on Parker, who was pretending to eavesdrop on what was being said. A few seconds later, my announcement to the Oakland crowd sent the Colonel and Meng into a frenzy.

"Ladies and gentlemen," I waited until the ringsiders settled down.

"Ladies and gentlemen, I have just been informed by referee Nick Patrick that the WCW officials will not allow Meng to substitute for Terry Funk."

When the mighty Meng tossed me head first out of the ring, I thought, "Oh great, I just said "hi" to Dave Meltzer. Now he's going to name me the goof of the week in his Wrestling Observer Newsletter!

The Colonel threw his hands in the air as the taunting fans rejoiced.

"And furthermore," I resumed after a dramatic pause, "Parker's team will have to forfeit the match unless Colonel Robert Parker himself wrestles in Funk's place against The Nasty Boys and Dustin Rhodes!"

That's when all hell broke loose. Parker, Buck and Meng pitched a fit. The people were in an uproar. Arn and Buck ran after the referee, who was lucky enough to scoot back up the aisle. Meng began to stalk me until I was trapped in the corner.

Before I was able to signal for the entrance music, Meng had wrapped his meaty paw around my neck. With one seemingly nonchalant upward movement the powerhouse jerked me off my feet with such force that the momentum propelled me backward over the ring ropes. As I was catapulted through the air, I instinctively wrapped my legs around the top rope, which left me swinging upside down by my knees. The floor, five feet below, moved from side to side as I swayed back and forth.

The crowd roared as the security guards, who thought this was a planned part of the show, looked on in amusement. Even as the blood rushed to my head causing me to feel woozy, I knew that my only hope of being saved from plunging headfirst to the arena floor would be an assist from either Dustin Rhodes or Arn Anderson. I dizzily began to wave my arms in the direction of the clueless sound tech as I shouted over and over, "Play the entrance music! Hit the music!"

Although he was sitting at the ringside table, only a few feet away, he thought I was only pretending to be in trouble. When he didn't respond I became frantic. "Play their damn music!"

The more I flailed my arms from my upside down position, the more I swung, back and forth over the ringsiders, causing my legs around the top rope to slip little by little. Finally, I could hold on no longer. As my legs gave way, I dropped to the ring apron, jamming my head into the top of my spine. With a quick bounce, I landed headfirst at the feet of the first row of fans.

As I looked up at the sound tech from a sprawled position, I quietly seethed: "Would ya please play The fuckin' music!"

As 1994 wound down, Eric began feeling mightier and mightier. After a year and a half as executive vice-president of WCW, he had brought about the cosmetic facelift that prepared the promotion to challenge the dominance that the WWF held over WCW for so long. He had taken full advantage of his leadership position. He now flaunted Hulk Hogan, the biggest media friendly figure to ever set foot in the ring, as his superstar attraction.

The production values of our television shows began to approach the state of the art standards that Vinnie had set for pro wrestling. Our relationship with the Disney MGM Studios benefited WCW by elevating the company's brand name. We were now seen as a more clean-cut, sanitized entertainment form that only a relationship with Disney, the epitome of family-friendly entertainment, could deliver.

By the time we got to Las Vegas in January of 1995 for the National Association of Television Program Executives Convention, (NATPE) where syndicators market their new TV shows to television programmers world-wide, Eric was intent on humiliating Vince, Jr. He confidently scheduled a live *Clash of Champions* broadcast at the Caesars Palace Arena on the Wednesday of convention week to showcase the WCW product and showered convention goers with free tickets to the televised extravaganza.

Bischoff had dreamed about this opportunity to humble the braggadocios McMahon. He was primed to take the swagger out of the step of the king of all wrestling impresarios. And what better place to pick a fight than in full public view on the convention floor of NATPE? The place where multi-million dollar deals are commonly inked with a flick of a pen. The place that sparkles with celebrities who will star in the programs offered for next year's television season. The place where the most powerful media magnates meet to determine the shows that will influence our language, dress and pop culture trends. This was about power. It was about dominance. This was better than anything the two wrestling execs could script for the ring.

At the *Clash* production meeting the night before the broadcast, Flair raced through the lineup in a mere twenty minutes. I sat staring at my watch realizing that his protective, old school mentality had kicked in which forbade us from knowing any more about the show than *TV Guide* offered our viewers. It also occurred to me that he could have faxed the lineup to me, allowing me to spend an extra day at home. I began to feel like this meeting was a waste of time. That is until Bischoff strolled into the room.

He went directly to the wet bar, grabbed a beer by its bottle neck and smirked, "It's only 5:20. Are you guys done already?"

"Running like a Rolex watch," Flair responded.

Eric didn't seem to hear the answer and continued.

"I just came off the convention floor and we are kicking ass! He's (referring to Vinnie) down and bloody and can't get up."

The production crew and announcers stared at Bischoff in silence, as it was obvious that our exhilarated leader had a lot more to say.

"We had a great press conference. I drove a stake into his heart twice and turned it. I wanted to do it again, but time ran out. It was especially fun since he had his spies there and they ran right back to him."

It must have been the stake into the heart comment that left us dumbfounded.

"He had no talent. At one point it was just Vince posing for photos and that went over *real* big. Then he had Doink the wrestling clown. Pretty pitiful to see a clown standing there waiting for someone to ask for an autograph."

As the WCW chief chuckled, then chugged his long neck brew, Flair sarcastically spouted, "Eric, you're showing your sensitive side."

Wiping the dripping beer from his chin, Bischoff ignored Ric's swipe.

"Well, you know the NATPE convention feeds adrenaline through me with huge deals going down all over the floor. That's what I live for. I can't help it. We're writing business, signing up affiliates for our syndicated show. He's the steak and I'm the fork and knife. And we're carving him up!"

I looked across the room at Bobby Heenan and Gene Okerlund, two announcers who had reached their height of celebrity thanks to their work on WWF television. They had been Vince loyalists for many years before being lured by Turner's big money contracts. They slumped in uncharacteristic silence. They seemed embarrassed, perhaps feeling a twinge of guilt upon hearing Bischoff's characterization of their former boss. They sat staring at a pitcher of water, which sat on the otherwise empty banquet table before them.

As I approached the end of my twenty-first and final year in the pro wrestling business, the stage was set for a fight. It would be a battle between Eric Bischoff, with all of the resources of Turner Broadcasting behind him and his opponent, Vince McMahon, Jr., who had proven himself to be the all time preeminent pro wrestling impresario in terms of the revenue generated by the WWF.

In the heat of battle, Vinnie chose to ignore Bischoff. Instead, he threw verbal punches at Ted Turner, even though it was Eric calling all of the shots for WCW. Junior's media assault on Turner was equivalent to shadow boxing with the elusive corporate magnate, as he attempted to elevate himself by making the fight a personal issue with Ted, who actually had little knowledge of the day to day operations of his wrestling company.

It would take Bischoff three years from the start of his reign to overhaul WCW and methodically dismantle Vince's wrestling empire.

Chapter Eighteen
"The Final Bell"

Sports has qualities our daily lives lack. First, it is finite. Most of what we encounter began before yesterday and will not be resolved till past tomorrow. In sports, nearly every game has a winner and a loser - and real heroes, athletes who faced the challenge of the moment and drove on to victory.

"Focusing on these qualities is what popularized the sports sections of newspapers early this century. Other than obituaries, only sports articles guaranteed readers a resolution.
Jerry Gorman & Kirk Calhoun, "THE BUSINESS OF SPORTS"

On May 11, 1995 I taped *WCW Saturday Night* for the last time. I had rejected Eric's final offer, which included working in the production studios at the CNN Center in addition to continuing my announcing on TV, an agreement that required moving from New Jersey to Atlanta. After the free-spirited life that I enjoyed on the road, I had no interest in fighting the political battles that took place on a daily basis in the WCW offices. And I certainly had no desire to move from my home state. So without question, this would be my final telecast. There was nothing more to discuss. This time, there would be no last minute negotiations.

My thoughts drifted back to some of the more memorable moments of my career as I stood before the cameras while waiting for the director's cue to begin the show. The professional side of me attempted to block the mixed feelings that welled up inside. But the many memories that flashed through my mind triggered an emotional tug of war within me.

As I looked out over the crowd, I was split by two very different sentiments. In part, I was relieved that my behind-the-scenes struggle with management was about to end. But another part of me was filled with sadness at leaving behind my many friends, both fans and co-workers alike.

I began to think about all the nonsense that I had endured over two decades. I remembered how as a kid the McMahons exploited my innocence. How the shrewd indie promoters profited from my WWF visibility without paying the price and now how Eric was trying to shake the confidence that took years to develop. After spending my entire adult life exposed to the behind the scenes shenanigans of the spectacle that captured my curiosity as a kid, I wondered how my love of pro wrestling had remained so strong. And yet there is no doubt that I continued to be as captivated by this choreographed combat as the day that Monsoon first asked me to join his team.

I saw a large part of the answer beaming from the faces of the excited crowd which became energized when the TV cameras panned from one end of Center Stage to the other. I realized that both my love of the spectacle and the bond I had formed with the followers of this fun form of athletic theater had filled me with a joy that overshadowed the difficulties that I had faced along the way.

My relationship with the performers who milled around the crowded Center Stage locker rooms and our dedicated core audience in Atlanta was no different from the camaraderie that I shared with the wrestlers and the diehards who made their monthly pilgrimage to the WWWF's tapings at the Philadelphia Arena back in the beginning. For the performers I was a connection to stability. For the fans I was a link to the superstars with whom I interacted for more than twenty years. I had developed many strong bonds of friendship. So while there was a certain relief that my run on Turner's cable network had come to an end, it was difficult letting go.

Although my last night with the company was to be a live pay-per-view broadcast later in the month, this farewell to the fans at our home base was tough. They were my friends who by hamming it up for the cameras every two weeks made my announcements appear more effective than they really were. I had come full circle, back to the people who made the rigors of the road and my skirmishes with management worthwhile.

Since the news had spread that this was my final performance in Atlanta, emotions were running high. The audience members screamed louder than ever when I coached them off camera to make this night of TV more rousing than usual. Toward the end of the evening, when there was a delay in the action, I filled the time by breaking character to address the audience directly.

It was commonplace for personalities to drift in and out of promotions without letting the fans in on what was going on. I wanted this night to be different. I chose to respect the people whose support was so important to me for so long. I decided to be honest by acknowledging that this was my final night at

Center Stage and simply to express my appreciation for their support. And who would have thought that my heartfelt words could cause any apprehension? But remember this is the wrestling business, where everything is looked upon with suspicion.

As I began to thank the fans for their friendship throughout the years, I noticed uneasiness among the crew. David Crockett, the floor director for all of our shows, stopped what he was doing and alerted the production truck as he listened closely. Then, a few of the WCW bosses came out from the dressing rooms and glared at me from the top of the entrance ramp.

I guess they feared that I was about to badmouth the company on my way out. I expect that they were ready to pull the plug on my mic. And I suppose that I should have been insulted by their distrust. But when tears filled the eyes of our more loyal fans, who rose to acknowledge my personal words of thanks, I felt vindicated. Vindicated by the people who from my starry-eyed beginning to this melancholy finale made my long journey a joy.

The paranoia of those in the industry unable to trust anyone remained strong. But it wasn't personal. A more telling moment occurred during my last pay-per-view performance two weeks later.

For more than 2,400 performances there have been only three times when I dreaded traveling to an event. The first trip was to San Antonio, Texas in 1990. It was an Easter Sunday matinee and we were playing one of the most Catholic cities in the country! It was a prime example of mindless booking for a show that offered such a small audience that I easily could have delivered my announcements to each member of the sparse crowd individually. I lamented the second trip because I had to leave my family behind on Christmas morning in 1992 to announce in Jacksonville, Florida. Spinning the radio dial on my drive to the airport, the only songs playing were Yuletide carols, reminding me that this was a morning that I should have been spending at home. But the most dreaded journey of all was to my final appearance at the *Slamboree* pay-per-view broadcast in May of 1995 at The Bayfront Center in St. Petersburg, Florida.

For the first time ever, the WCW travel office booked me on one of the economy airlines. As I waited for the delayed flight to take off, I had the feeling that banishing me to "Free Fall Flights" or "Free For All Air", or whatever it was called, was the last snub that I would endure on my way out. But the situation only got worse when I set foot in St. Pete.

As I entered the hotel banquet room where the *Slamboree* production meeting was already underway, Eric froze in mid sentence as everyone looked in my direction. There was an intense anxiety in the air that I thought was due to my lateness. When I realized that I had interrupted the business at hand, my automatic reaction was to defend myself in light of the fact that my late arrival for this final performance with the company was no fault of my own. So as is my way in a sticky situation like this, my sense of humor kicked in.

"Sorry 'bout barging in, but the jabroni airline that I was booked on delayed all of their flights out of Newark. I promise, this is the last time that I'll be late."

Everyone remained silent. My joke wasn't even met with a chuckle or a snicker or even a grin. I took a *Slamboree* format sheet from the boardroom table and sat on the floor in a corner of the standing room only hall. Eric broke the silence with what I thought was a decent gesture.

"It's not a problem, Gary. I'm glad to see you."

Then Gary Juster rose from the table. He hurried over to where I was sitting. The concern that covered his face suggested that something more was going on to cause the tension that filled the air.

"Don't pay attention to the announcer cues where it says 'Dave Penzer'. Just cross out his name before each of the matches and write yours in instead."

Juster's fidgety stammer would have been appropriate if he were delivering disastrous news. He was as agitated as I had ever seen him. But I didn't understand the reason for his nervousness. Since I was more focused on the urgency of his whispered words than on the meaning of what he was saying, I was confused. It was not until I scanned the program's format sheets that I realized why there was such anxiety when I entered the room. Eric had written me out of the show!

I later learned that when the WCW bosses heard my farewell speech to the Center Stage audience two weeks prior, they assumed that I wouldn't show up for my last performance in St. Pete. Even though I had spoken to the production secretaries during the week leading up to the show and accepted hundreds of dollars worth of air tickets, my absence at the start of the meeting confirmed their suspicions that I was not to be trusted. It was as if they never really knew me.

For the entire time that I was under contract to Turner I had never missed a show. In fact, in all of my years in pro wrestling I only missed two shows! But, once again, this is the wrestling business, a business in which everyone is suspect, a business in which everyone is looked at as self-serving. And if that side of you is not showing now, then it's just a matter of when it will surface. So I guess they really were convinced that even though it took twenty-one years, my dark side had finally emerged. And I think that they felt some sort of sick satisfaction in believing that even "dependable Cappetta" had become bitter about the business.

By this time, I was past caring about what the head honchos thought of me. I suppose they decided that defaulting on my final assignment with the company would have been my way of delivering a spiteful message. They are so steeped in the con that even my simple, straightforward farewell to the fans in Atlanta caused their mistrust. And Eric's disbelief of my final words to him following the pay-per-view event proves my point better than any clever characterization that I can offer.

O nce I realized that the WCW bosses I had worked with for years were so quick to write me off, my goal on this night was to get through the program as best I could and get back to the hotel as soon as possible.

At pay-per-view broadcasts my routine remained the same. I greeted the arena audience fifteen minutes before the live broadcast began in order to get the fans as wound up as possible to ensure an explosive crowd reaction when we went on the air. I handled all of the ring announcements up to the main event and then turned the mic over to Michael Buffer. The *Slamboree '95* lineup was a little different. Buffer was to announce the final two matches, which were considered co-features.

Following the last preliminary match I impatiently waited for Buffer to enter the ring. Without warning, Big Bubba Rogers' music began to play for the first co-feature. I still had the ring mic, so I automatically introduced his match against Sting. I later learned that Buffer refused to introduce the co-feature since his contract called on him to work only main events. This guy, who was being paid $6,000 per night, declined to work a second match! And the director didn't have the courtesy to let me know.

Begin

As soon as I declared Sting the winner, I shot down the aisle, picked up my gear in the dressing room and was back at the hotel before the main event was over. I was scrubbing the show makeup from my face when Chris phoned my room from the lobby. I invited him up, we ordered dinner from room service and discussed a couple of acting opportunities that he was working on for me.

When we finished, Chris asked me to go down to the hotel lounge for a drink. This idea just didn't sound appealing. Not only am I barely a social drinker, but the false good-byes from those who had already excommunicated me from the organization were more than I could stomach.

Even when Chris called from the lounge a half hour later with word that some of the guys wanted to wish me well, I declined the invitation. He finally convinced me that spending an hour with friends who had nothing to do with the shabby treatment that I had received was the right thing to do. As it turned out, I'm glad that his common sense prevailed.

Kansas City was always a great place to visit thanks to the hospitality of former NWA World Champion, Harley Race and his wife, BJ. Their place was a home away from home for barbeques and games of pool. From left to right: Steven Regal, Vader, Bill Dundee, Steve Austin, yours truly, Harley Race and one of Harley's many friends.

When I entered the bar, I was met by well wishers who wanted to swap some of the stories that shaped our WCW experience. We joked about the Halloween Havoc pay-per-view, when the intense heat of the overhead TV lights set the cage decorations on fire during the live broadcast. And how Muta scaled the structure and spit out a mouthful of green mist to save the day. We shared our disbelief about how a few of the guys snuck across the Mexican border when we played El Paso to buy over the counter steroids at a Ciudad Juarez drug store. We reminisced about the great food and hospitality at Harley Race's house whenever we played Kansas City. We marveled at the imaginative promotional schemes of our favorite promoter, CM Christ, who packed an Anderson, South Carolina TV taping with very little top drawing talent by advertising a "Cactus Jack Christmas" and decorating live cactus plants with Christmas lights and garland. And the night that CM promoted Sioux City, Iowa. That was when the country music station's mascot, the KSUX Super Pig, drove the audience wild after I had failed to get the crowd's attention. We relived the horror of the European tour when a couple of the boys drugged the arrogant WCW announcer for our German telecasts and then shaved his head and drew a happy face on his penis.

It was a bittersweet session with some of my best friends. I was having a good time. And that was when I looked across the lounge and saw Eric standing alone at the bar. It was a sad silhouette of the man at the top. At first I ignored him. Then my better sense kicked in. After all, he was the figurehead for a promotion that had treated me well for most of my tenure. In hindsight, I'm glad that I managed to rise above my feelings of disillusionment for the company. In fact, speaking with him on my last night turned out to be a satisfying experience.

I approached Bischoff, who was a little glassy eyed, but still in full control of his senses. Extending my hand, I began our final conversation.

"Eric, I just want to thank you for a good six years with WCW."

"Gary, it has been a pleasure. You have proven yourself to be a true professional."

"Thanks. I appreciate that."

Eric, who still held on to my hand, suddenly pulled me forward. He moved his mouth close to my ear and whispered, "Don't worry. I think we will be working together again in some form in the future."

As I pushed him back to arm's length I recognized right away what I had come to know as "Bischoff babble", which is never to be taken as sincere. This time it was safe to speak from my gut.

"No, Eric, I don't think so. I'm not interested."

He pulled me close one more time.

"No, really, I want you to work with me in the future."

"Eric, you don't seem to understand. I have no desire to ever work for you again, whether you want it or not."

He just peered at me as if he couldn't believe what he was hearing. With that, Flair and Sensational Sherri approached. And while these were my parting words to Eric, it was not the last time that I heard from WCW. I know, I thought that would have been a good ending too. But these guys just never give up!

J ust two weeks passed before I received a message that Gary Juster wanted to talk to me. I couldn't imagine what he wanted. I feared that they found out about the can of mixed nuts that I pilfered from my well stocked mini bar in the St. Petersburg hotel room. Damn! And I thought I had gotten away with the goods!

"Heya Gary, how come you always call when I least expect it?"

"I don't know. Maybe just an occupational hazard."

"Yeah, when ya work for WCW that's just one of many. So what's up?"

"What are you doing on Sunday, June, 21st?"

"Probably going to church. Other than that, nothing I can think of."

"Well, Eric asked me to call to see if you'd be available to announce at our pay-per-view in Dayton, Ohio."

"Why's that? You already hired Dave Penzer to take all of my dates. And by the way Gar, I thought it was pretty shabby the way you guys brought him on. Damn, he deserves the job and you treated him like he was some sort of consolation prize that you are settling for . . . just a runner-up. And Gar, the money. You guys have no heart."

"Don't worry about that. Penzer will be there."

"So why do you need me?"

"Because Buffer can't make it."

"Buffer? But Penzer can out-announce Buffer any day of the week. I still don't understand why you're calling me."

"Because Eric's not sure that Penzer can handle a pay-per-view by himself."

"Damn, that sucks big time! You give the guy the position and then ya show no faith in him."

"Well, do you want to come in for the show?"

"How much are you willing to pay me?"

"Eric has authorized me to offer you $1,500 for the night."

At this point, I realized that Bischoff's ceiling price was $3,000. He always offered half of what he was willing to pay. That's how he worked. But it didn't matter. I wouldn't think of leaving my house for less than what Buffer was making. It was the principle of it all. And it was a principle that cost me $3,000.

"Sorry Gar, that's not enough."

"Not enough? Why not? That's $500.00 more than we were paying you under contract!"

"Because if you're calling me in to replace Buffer, then you should pay me the same $6,000 that you would have paid him."

"$6,000? Are you crazy? Eric will never go along with that."

"Actually Gar, I think Bischoff would be getting a good deal. Buffer announces his tag line and then only what he is told, when he is told. With me, you're getting the best warm up guy in the business. Someone who is familiar with all of the crew and all of the talent. Someone the fans know and trust. And I guess someone you can depend on more than you gave me credit for in St. Pete. So unless you're willing to pay me six grand, then find someone else who can match what you know I can do."

Predictably, Juster called back with a final offer of $3,000, which I turned down. It was the best outcome for Dave Penzer, who went on to Dayton to handle all of the announcing chores single handedly and did a great job. I was proud of him.

A few weeks later, I received one last call, though unofficial, from the Turner organization. A buddy of mine, who still works for WCW and will therefore remain nameless, spoke with the whispered tones that you'd expect from an international spy calling in top secret information to a foreign agent. It was funny because although I recognized his voice instantly, the muffled sound of his message suggested someone trying to disguise his voice. But he wasn't trying to conceal his identity from me. He didn't want to be overheard by anyone in the WCW office. It had been a while since we spoke and I was happy to hear from him.

"Heya, how's it goin' buddy?"

"Things are pretty good. But listen, I can't talk for long."

"How come you're sounding fuzzy?"

"Because I've got some inside info that you might be interested in and I don't want anyone to know that I'm calling you. There are rumors that we're going to start up a new show in the Fall. This is going to be a big deal! It'll be running head to head with the WWF on Monday nights. This would be a great opportunity for you to get back in. They're gonna be paying big money to get this off the ground. Why don't you give Eric a call?"

"Hey man, I appreciate it, but if Eric wants me, he knows where to find me." My answer seemed to surprise him, but he didn't understand the psychology of the negotiation game. Eric would have held the advantage the moment that I expressed interest in returning. And I wasn't about to set myself up for another dose of Eric's arrogance.

The new program that my buddy was talking about was *WCW Nitro*. As it turned out, the show propelled World Championship Wrestling past the WWF for the first time. To his credit, Bischoff refused to be intimidated by McMahon. Under Eric's guidance, *Nitro* succeeded in direct opposition to *WWF Raw* by creating a clique of bully wrestlers called the NWO that was created to run roughshod over the WCW establishment. It was cool to be a fan of the rebellious upstarts that made up the NWO which was led by, you guessed it, Eric Bischoff, in a role in which he finally found a way to feature himself as a star performer.

However, Bischoff was only able to hold the advantage over Vinnie for eighteen months. Junior successfully battled back on the strength of former WCW wrestler, Stone Cold Steve Austin, one of many performers that was held back by the political game playing within Turner's company. In September of 1999, wne the WCW slump persisted, Eric was relieved of his duties as president of WCW. Bischoff has since claimed that after he brought success to WCW, bureaucrats within the Turner organization began meddling in the wrestling division. Eric asserts that he was pressured to rebuild WCW while pleasing the corporate suits who vetoed many of his ideas that would have stopped the WWF resurgence.

Most recently, half way through the year 2000, Eric returned to WCW to square off against McMahon one more time. However, with the popularity of The Rock, Steve Austin, Mick Foley, Triple H, the McMahon Family, and a cast of characters that Vince continues to manufacture and smartly program, it is doubtful that WCW will come close to overtaking the WWF any time soon.

And more ominous for WCW, McMahon has just struck a five year deal with Viacom Inc., one of the world's largest entertainment and media companies, and a leader in the production,

Eric's temporary win over McMahon was cut short by the success of another of his former wrestlers, Steve Austin.

promotion, and distribution of entertainment, news, sports, and music. The partnership agreement includes, among other items, the airing of *Raw Is War*, the No. 1-rated program on cable, as well as *Livewire* and *Superstars* on TNN and *Sunday Night Heat* on MTV; the extension of UPN's broadcast of *WWF SmackDown!*; promotion across all of Viacom's media platforms, including television, radio and billboards; the creation and airing of up to seven annual WWF TV specials and a one-hour drama series; pay-per-view events at Viacom's Famous Players theaters in Canada; events and attractions at Viacom's Paramount Parks; radio programming and more. The deal is huge in terms of the advantage that Vinnie will continue to hold over WCW. Aside from my personal differences with Vince McMahon, he has proven himself, time and again, to be the consummate strategist.

As for me, I have returned to my classroom at the same academy where Jim Crockett, Jr. first called with the Turner offer that launched me into the orbit of WCW. I retain contacts in the entertainment business by managing the career of Michael Vale, a gifted contemporary Christian recording artist. Wrestlers call in from time to time with news of the latest locker room gossip and to ask advice on matters of both personal and professional concern. These are friendships that I will always value.

Fortunately, I was able to resist the many demons of the business that have sucked the breath from so many talented performers who have dreamed of making it in professional wrestling. I admit that I miss the adrenaline rush of holding court in center ring. But I am fortunate to have remained grounded in the real world, so that the fast life and addictive temptations of a touring performer did not consume me.

I have been blessed that my career as a pro wrestling pitchman lasted for so long. Some would say that I've been lucky. But luck is not something that happens by chance. Luck is when opportunity and being prepared for that opportunity are both present in our lives at the same time.

Being prepared is a matter of learning your craft through hard work and dedication. It is not enough to *want* it. You have to *need* it. Whether or not the opportunity presents itself is beyond our control. It is out of human hands. I believe that if it is God's will, then that door of opportunity will swing wide open. It is through His determination that we are allowed to practice those skills that we have worked diligently to perfect.

Before every wrestling event, as the fans stood night after night, in city after city, for the playing of "The Star Spangled Banner", I always escaped the controlled chaos to a private zone, an internal solitude, where I recited a silent prayer: *Lord, thank you for the opportunity to perform here tonight. It is your strength through me that has allowed my work in the profession that I love to continue."* It was a ritual that I maintained through my last night in center ring. It was my way of remembering how *lucky* I was and why.

EPILOGUE

It is seldom that an author can record his thoughts at the dawn of a new millenium. The idea intrigued me so, that I decided to do just that. It was with this intention that I started to write the last chapter of *Bodyslams!* on New Years Eve, 1999.

To my surprise, instead of an even-tempered account of the current state of professional wrestling, I found myself fired up and in the middle of an emotional rant. The result of this experiment follows.

December 31, 1999

Twenty-one years. It just doesn't seem possible. More than two decades smack in the center of the most outrageous traveling burlesque this country has ever known. Pro wrestling is television's longest running soap opera, and it continues to reach new heights in both viewership and excess.

It is inconceivable. What started out as a carnival sideshow now competes for the same ticket revenue, the same television ratings and the same advertising dollars as does all "legitimate" forms of entertainment. And when competing on a level playing field, pro wrestling surpasses the competition more times than not. It is amazing!

From the early forms of the beat the champ scams along carnival midways at county fairs across America, to my discovery of pro wrestling in the 1960's, very little had actually changed other than becoming a show unto itself, as opposed to a sideshow. Pro wrestling, as we have come to know it, originated with European traveling shows, where carnival owners hired "shills", posing as local underdogs to courageously challenge the show's wrestling champ to a match that an audience would pay to witness.

The exhibition eventually moved from midways to arenas and stadiums. In 1948, the attraction became one of the first shows on television and by the time I was first introduced to wrestling in the 1960's, the "shills" no longer pretended to be inexperienced bystanders. The Bruno Sammartinos assumed the exact same roles. Remember how as a kid, Bruno begged me to support him? Remember how he pleaded with me to tune in next week to witness him defend his honor against the heel of the hour? Remember how he asked me to show up the next time he defended the championship in my neighborhood? How he urged me to cheer for him from the ringside section? He needed my help. My support could make the difference between him being humiliated or honored. Remember that? With passion, he tapped the same emotions as the earnest "shills" of yesteryear. But now I didn't have to run down to the county fairground to learn that he needed me in his corner. By the time I discovered wrestling, he had made his way into my living room. It was more personal. He was more of a friend.

However, from the day that I first stepped into the ring, in July of 1974, until my final exit in May of 1995, wrestling had been transformed in appearance and content. The smoke filled arenas, the worn, shadowy platform, the understated wrestling tights, the long minutes of wrestlers laying immobile on the mat, the simplistic themes are of an era that we will never again experience. The only musical sounds, which echoed through those hollow and hallowed wooden buildings of yesteryear, were the thudding clangs of a hammer, striking a ring bell. The only lights to illuminate the wrestlers were four or five light bulbs dangling overhead. The only souvenirs that were available could be bought only at the arenas and consisted of nothing more than black and white, poorly printed, outdated photos of the stars. And those who were lucky enough might get one of the pictured heroes to autograph their glossy treasure at ringside. Security guardrails? They didn't exist. They weren't necessary. Part of the security guard's job was to *help* you to get your autograph without getting hurt.

Political correctness? That was a phrase that had not yet entered into our vocabulary. The villains were enemies of American society. They were the Waldo Von Erichs of World War I, the Mr. Fujis of World War II, the Pak Songs of the Korean War, The Gorgeous Georges and Ricky Starrs who threatened our masculinity and family values. Those that represented a threat to The American Way.

How things have changed during my twenty-one year tenure. We went from pretending that the grunt and groan game was a legitimate contest to admitting that we were an exhibition tagged by McMahon as sports entertainment. From territorial promotions to international corporations. From mom and pop businesses to multi billion dollar conglomerates. From simple and drab presentations, to state of the art productions. It is incredible how things have changed. And tough to believe that I was a part of it all.

Mostly, the changes that have occurred serve to advance the way pro wrestling is viewed. *But the art of the game is too often missing.* The nuances. The slow build. The suspension of belief. What I call *the art of the game* has been lost to an explicitly vulgar product intent on shocking the audience with crudeness, and then once garnering its attention, endorsing the worst of what the human condition offers. And while the game of today may be much more imaginative, it has lost the subtleties upon which the bookers and the performers once prided themselves. *The art of the game.* Simple, yet effective. And still I know that while I mourn the loss of the art form, which thrilled the child in me for thirty-two years, it is a money-driven business. If Vince McMahon, Jr. had not taken the bold steps to give his product a makeover to emulate the rapidly changing entertainment environment of the 1980's, professional wrestling, as a national television attraction, might have faded from our culture's consciousness.

We want to hold on to the way things used to be. Like our Mickey Mantle trading card. Our yellowed and brittle family photo albums. Our kids' first report cards. The things, the objects, the memorabilia that we can still touch and see that conjure up the feelings of years gone by; the good old days. The days that can never return.

Although I do not endorse the risqué themes, vulgar language and sexual content of today's pro wrestling product, I welcome the innovations that have put wrestling on par with competing entertainment forms. While that might sound like a statement of confusing and crossed purposes, I maintain that it is not.

My goal is to preserve *the art of the game* while utilizing the technological advances that exist. I want to see wrestling dig down deep and allow its performers to showcase their extraordinary athletic abilities. Recruit the gifted young workers who are honing their craft in independent clubs from coast to coast.

Jumping from a balcony to the floor far below or stacking table upon table and ramming your opponent's body through them takes the nerve of a daredevil, but little skill and less common sense. Rolling around in barbed wire or broken glass reeks of desperation. I want to see today's wrestling performers hailed for their superior talents, not viewed as a freak show. I want them to be acclaimed for feats that spectators *cannot* achieve, not acts that they *wouldn't* be fool enough to perform. I don't want to see wrestling return to the early time when it was a *side*show. I want to see the entertainment form advance and maintain its status as the *main* show.

To remain a viable entertainment form, pro wrestling must continue to evolve with the times in themes and content. But it does not have to appeal to the lowest common denominator. Entertainment conglomerates like Disney and The Hallmark Company have shown over the years that the public will wholeheartedly support imaginative, well-produced family entertainment. To sink lower in order to catch the attention of an audience is a quick fix, a desperate tactic and a short-term solution. My hope for the continuance and the growth of pro wrestling will only be realized if its foundation remains sound. I want the kids who are fans today to be able to share the majesty of what pro wrestling can be with their kids and their grandchildren. Pandering to the crudest instincts of a select audience through bare breasts, anti-establishment, anti-authority vulgarities and senseless pratfalls and stunts puts pro wrestling at risk. There will be little left after the public's senses are numbed to the point of moving on to the next fashionable and trendy entertainment form.

There are those with regard for the art of the sport who are trying to counter the business as usual trend. They are turning heads. They are gaining respect. Watch Chris Benoit work. See the crispness, the stiffness and the effectiveness of his ring work. Watch how the fans are caught up in the "reality" of his performance. He is a true ring technician. When he gets rolling, it's a thing of beauty.

Take a look at the up and comers who may not yet be household names, but who can fire up an audience with lightning quick moves that are powerful and meaningful and that work. Crowbar, who began wrestling for WCW last year, is a significant talent. If he begins to deliver anything less than impressive work, then you can bet he is being held back due to political considerations of the bookers or by the threatened middle aged superstars or both. If he is permitted to showboat his enormous athletic abilities, then perhaps the tide can continue to turn.

Ever hear of Ace Darling? He is another young lion, who, if anyone is paying attention, should soon get his opportunity to amaze and delight audiences with a mix of solid ring work and high-flying maneuvers.

To watch these young guys perform is to see the future, the healthy future of pro wrestling.

Chris Benoit has earned respect for his solid ring work.

A s this century comes to a close, wrestling is in danger of once again fooling itself. Ratings are soaring, profits have never been higher, and media attention has zoomed. But don't be fooled. Pro wrestling is being used right now. And after the public and the media have been numbed to the current spectacle . . .when the next cool, hip entertainment form catches the public's fancy, this cyclical business that we know as professional wrestling must be left in a healthy state for the future of the game by preserving the solid base that has always been the source of wrestling's resurgence.

Continue to dazzle. Continue to be on the edge. Continue to advance wherever technology may take us. But for the long-term health of the business . . to preserve the vitality of the wrestling . . . the success or failure of its long-term future will always be as healthy as the pureness of *the art of the game.*

APPENDICES

thank you!

*To the many wonderful people who welcomed me to
your hometowns over the past two decades*

*You are the true spirit of this book
Bodyslams! is dedicated to you!*

Aberdeen, Scotland
Albany, GA
Alexandria, LA
Allentown, PA
Altoona, PA
Amarillo, TX
Anaheim, CA
Anderson, SC
Annandale, NJ
Asbury Park, NJ
Asheville, NC
Athens, GA
Atlanta, GA
Atlantic City, NJ
Augusta, GA
Baltimore, MD
Bassett, VA
Baton Rouge, LA
Battle Creek, MI
Bayonne, NJ
Bayreuth, Germany
Bayville, NJ
Beaumont, TX
Beckley, W.VA
Belfast, Northern Ireland
Belleville, NJ
Belton, TX
Bergenfield, NJ
Berkeley Heights, NJ
Biloxi, MS
Birmingham, AL
Birmingham, England
Blackburn, England
Blackwood, NJ

Bluefield, W.VA
Blufton, IN
Boston, MA
Bournemouth, England
Brantford, Ontario
Bricktown, NJ
Bridgewater, NJ
Brooklyn, NY
Browns Mills, NJ
Buffalo, NY
Canton, OH
Carbondale, IL
Cardiff, England
Cartaret, NJ
Cedar Grove, NJ
Cedar Rapids, IA
Charleston, SC
Charleston, W.VA
Charlotte, NC
Charlottesville, VA
Chattanooga, TN
Cherry Hill, NJ
Chicago, IL
Cincinnati, OH
Clark, NJ
Cleveland, OH
Cologne, Germany
Columbia, SC
Columbus, GA
Columbus, MS
Columbus, OH
Corpus Christi, TX
Dallas, TX
Dalton, Ga

Dayton, OH
Daytona Beach, FL
Deptford, NJ
Detroit, MI
Dothan, AL
Dover, DE
Dresden, Germany
Dublin, Ireland
East Brunswick, NJ
East Greenville, PA
East Rutherford, NJ
East St. Louis, MS
Eatontown, NJ
Edison, NJ
Egg Harbor, NJ
El Paso, TX
Elizabeth, NJ
Emmitsburg, MD
Englishtown, NJ
Essen, Germany
Farmland, IN
Fayetteville, NC
Flanders, NJ
Flemington, NJ
Florence, NJ
Forked River, NJ
Fort Bragg, NC
Fort Wayne, IN
Frankfurt, Germany
Fredricton, New Brunswick
Freehold, NJ
Ft. Dix, NJ
Ft. Myers, FL
Ft. Ord, CA

Ft. Pierce, FL
Gadsden, AL
Gainesville, GA
Garfield, NJ
Gessemer, AL
Glen Rock, NJ
Gloucester, NJ
Great Kils, NY
Greensboro, NC
Greenville, MS
Greenville, SC
Greenwood, MS
Greenwood, SC
Hackensack, NJ
Hackettstown, NJ
Halifax, Nova Scotia
Halle, Germany
Hamburg, Germany
Hamburg, PA
Hammond, IN
Hampton, VA
Harrington, DE
Harrison, NJ
Harrisonburg, VA
Hawthorne, NJ
Hazlet, NJ
Highland Park, NJ
Hightstown, NJ
Hillside, NJ
Hof, Germany
Houston, TX
Howell, NJ
Huntsville, AL
Indianapolis, IN
Irvington, NJ
Jackson, TN
Jacksonville, FL
Jacksonville, NC
Jamesburg, NJ
Jekyll Island, GA
Jersey City, NJ

Johnson City, TN
Johnstown, PA
Joplin, MO
Kansas City, KS
Kansas City, MO
Kassel, Germany
Kearny, NJ
Kennilworth, NJ
Key West, FL
Kingsport, TN
Knoxville, TN
Kokomo, IN
Kuschners's , PA
Lacey Township, NJ
Lafayette, LA
Lake Charles, LA
Lakeland, FL
Lakewood, NJ
Landover, MD
Las Vegas, NV
Lawrence Harbor, NJ
Linden, NJ
Little Rock, AR
Little Silver, NJ
Live Oak, FL
London, England
Long Branch, NJ
Los Angeles, CA
Ludwigshafen, Germany
Lynchburg, VA
Macon, GA
Manahawkin, NJ
Manchester, England
Manhattan, KS
Manville, NJ
Marietta, GA
Marlboro, NJ
Marlton, NJ
Mastic Beach, NY
McMinnville, TN
Memphis, TN

Miami, FL
Middlesex, NJ
Middletown, NJ
Milwaukee, WI
Minneapolis, MN
Mobile, AL
Monroe, LA
Montgomery, AL
Montvale, NJ
Morris Plains, NJ
Morristown, NJ
Mount Holly, NJ
Mt. Olive, NJ
Munich, Germany
Murfreesboro, TN
Myrtle Beach, SC
Nashville, TN
Nassau, Bahamas
New Brunswick, NJ
New Haven, CT
New Orleans, LA
New York, NY
Newark, NJ
Newton, NJ
Niagara Falls, Ontario
Norfolk, VA
North Bergen, NJ
North Hagerstown, MD
Oakland, CA
Odessa, TX
Oklahoma City, OK
Old Bridge, NJ
Old Tappan, NJ
Omaha, NE
Orange, NJ
Orlando, FL
Ozark, AL
Panama City, FL
Parsippany, NJ
Passaic, NJ
Paterson, NJ

Paulsboro, NJ
Pensacola, FL
Peoria, IL
Perry, GA
Perth Amboy, NJ
Philadelphia, PA
Phoenix, AZ
Piscataway, NJ
Pittsburgh, PA
Plainfield, NJ
Plymouth Meeting, PA
Point Pleasant Beach, NJ
Portland, IN
Portsmouth, OH
Rainesville, AL
Raleigh, NC
Randolph Township, NJ
Reading, PA
Red Lion, PA
Richmond, VA
Ridgefield, NJ
Roanoke, VA
Rochester, NY
Rock Hill, SC
Rome, GA
Roselle Park, NJ
Rutherford, NJ
Saginaw, MI
Salem, VA
Salisbury, MD
Salt Lake City, UT
San Angelo, TX
San Antonio, TX
San Bernadino, CA
San Diego, CA
San José, CA
Sarasota, FL
Savannah, GA
Sayreville, NJ
Scotch Plains, NJ
Scranton, PA

Sebring, FL
Sheffield, England
Shreveport, LA
Sioux City, IA
Sioux Falls, SD
Sommerville,NJ
South Amboy, NJ
South Orange, NJ
South Plainfield, NJ
South River, NJ
Spotswood, NJ
Springfield, MO
St. John, New Brunswick
St. Joseph, MO
St. Louis, MO
St. Petersburg, FL
Stamford, CT
Staten Island, NY
Sumter, SC
Sunrise, FL
Syracuse, NY
Tallahassee, FL
Terre Haute, IN
Thibodaux, LA
Toledo, OH
Toms River, NJ
Topeka, KS
Toronto, Canada
Totowa, NJ
Trenton, NJ
Troy, NY
Troy, OH
Tulsa, OK
Tupelo, MS
Union, NJ
Uniondale, NY
Valdosta, GA
Vineland, NJ
Waldorf, MD
Waltham, MA
Washington, DC

Washington, NJ
Waterloo, IA
Wayne, NJ
West Long Branch, NJ
West Milford, NJ
West Orange, NJ
West Palm Beach, FL
West Plains, MO
Westfield, NJ
Wheeling, W.VA
Wichita, KS
Wildwood, NJ
Willingboro, NJ
Wilmington, DE
Wilmington, NC
Winston-Salem, NC
Woodbridge, NJ
Woodstown, NJ
Worcester, MA
Wurzburg, Germany
York, PA

photo credits

For permission to reprint pictures in this book, grateful acknowledgement is made to the following sources. Any omission is accidental and will be corrected upon notification in writing to the publisher. Pictures not otherwise credited are courtesy of the author.

Page 58	Rasslin' Wonders Magazine, (Mike Omansky)
Page 100	Gary Michael Cappetta, (Joseph Carrino)
Page 108	Slams and Jams display ad, (USA Today)
Page 136	Newspaper display ad, (Newark Star Ledger)
Page 139	Kamala vs. Rick Martel, (Eddie Gries)
Page 143	Dusty Rhodes and Nikita Koloff, (Eddie Gries)
Page 145	The Barbarian, (Eddie Gries)
Page 148	Jerry Lawler vs. Kerry Von Erich, (Eddie Gries)
Page 153	Ric Flair vs. Lex Luger, {Eddie Gries}
Page 166	Mean Mark Calaway vs. Doug Furnas, (Eddie Gries)
Page 167	The Undertaker, (BlackJack Brown}
Page 170	Mean Mark Calaway and Paul E. Dangerously (Eddie Gries)
Page 176	President Jimmy Carter and Mr. Wrestling II, (Fred Ward), Columbus, Georgia
Page 179	Abdullah The Butcher vs. Bruiser Brody, (Eddie Gries)
Page 180	Abdullah The Butcher vs. Dr. D David Schultz, (Eddie Gries)
Page 182	Killer Cruz, Little Tokyo, Karate Kid and unidentified wrestler in Abdullah's pants, (Eddie Gries)
Page 188	Jim Cornette hitting Dusty Rhodes with racket, (Eddie Gries)
Page 190	Lex Luger vs. Ricky Steamboat, (Eddie Gries)
Page 194	Steve Austin vs. Savio Vega, (BlackJack Brown)
Page 197	Ron Simmons and Gary Michael Cappetta, (Eddie Gries)
Page 199	Marc Bagwell, (BlackJack Brown)
Page 204	The Juicer, (Eddie Gries)
Page 230	Ric Flair drags fan out of arena (Eddie Gries)
Page 240	Eddie Gilbert vs. Cactus Jack, (Eddie Gries)
Page 251	Larry Zbyszko, (Eddie Gries)
Page 254	Paul E. Dangerously, (Eddie Gries)
Page 259	The British Bulldog vs. Rick Martel, (Eddie Gries)
Page 260	Eric Bischoff and Hulk Hogan (BlackJack Brown)
Page 277	Steve Austin and Vince McMahon, Jr. (BlackJack Brown)
Page 283	Chris Benoit, (BlackJack Brown)

For information about the Eddie Gries Collection:
Eddie Gries, PO Box 572, Hackensack, NJ 07602

selected
bibliography

Bruno Sammartino, An Autobiography of Wrestling's Living Legend,
Bruno Sammartino with Bob Michelucci and Paul McCollough,
Imagine, Inc. 1990

Fortune, October 16, 1995

**Hooker, An Authentic Wrestler's Adventures Inside the Bizarre World of
Pro Wrestling**, Lou Thesz with Kit Bauman, 1995

Icon Magazine, August 1997

Indecent Exposure, A True Story of Hollywood and Wall Street,
David McClintick, William Morrow & Company, Inc., 1982

It Ain't As Easy As It Looks, Ted Turner's Amazing Story,
Porter Bibb, Crown Publishers, Inc., 1993

**Mad As Hell, How Sports Got Away from the Fans And How We Get It
Back,** Mike Lupica, G.P. Putnum & Sons, 1996

Necessary Roughness, Mike Trope with Steve Delsohn,
Contemporary Books, 1987

Pro Wrestling Torch, Wrestling's Weekly Journal of News and Opinion,
Wade Keller

Rasslin Wonders 1978-1979 Annual, Mike Omansky

Ring Wrestling Magazine, April 1978

Ring Wrestling Magazine, July 1974

Ring Wrestling Magazine, May 1979

Sports In America, James A. Michener, Random House, 1976

The 1996 Wrestling Almanac and Book of Facts, First Edition,
London Publishing, Inc., 1996

The 2000 Wrestling Almanac and Book of Facts, Fifth Edition,
London Publishing, Inc. 2000

The Business of Sports, Jerry Gorman & Kirk Calhoun,
John Wiley & Sons, Inc., 1994

The Charleston Post and Courier, Mike Mooneyham, April 7, 1994

Under The Big Top, A Season With The Circus, Bruce Feiler,
Charles Scribner, Inc., 1995

Western Boxing & World Wrestling, John F. Gilbey,
North Atlantic Books, 1993

Wrestling Observer Newsletter, Dave Meltzer

Wrestling Revue Magazine, June 1980

index

C

R

S

T

Fall For The Dream

by
Gary Michael Cappetta
A Wrestling-Based Work of Fiction
In Script Format

It is 1982.

Pro wrestling is looking for its first unified internationally recognized titleholder.

Set in a working class district of Chicago, **FALL FOR THE DREAM** tells the stirring story of how star struck wrestler, Dino Corponato, dares to defy the odds when he risks everything to grapple for the gold. Forbidden by his parents . . . censured by his best friend, Sean . . . risking a lifetime with his lover . . . Dino bodyslams his way to the top of the sport, where his biggest battle lies ahead, the fight to retain his self-respect.

What price will the rookie pay on his way to becoming World Heavyweight Champion? Will Dino risk the affection of family, friends and his girlfriend, Angie, for the fame and fortune of the fight game? Can he combat Fred Fitzpatrick, the corrupt kingpin of the squared circle, without selling his soul for the glory of the game?

By 1985, having established himself as the World Heavyweight Champion, Dino finds himself fighting for his life. In **FALL FOR THE DREAM'S** climactic fight scene, the pro wrestling script is set aside and our hero defends the right of us all who dare to dream . . . *because while the sweet smell of success disappears in due time, "dreams can last a lifetime!"*

Order FALL FOR THE DREAM By Phone Or On Line At
WWW.BODYSLAMS.COM